PREHISTORY

and

HISTORY

PREHISTORY

and

HISTORY

Ethnicity, Class and Political
Economy

David W. Tandy, editor

Montréal/New York/London

Black Rose Books No. EE298

Hardcover ISBN: 1-55164-189-5 (bound) Paperback ISBN: 1-55164-188-7 (pbk.)

Canadian Cataloguing in Publication Data
Main entry under title:
Prehistory and history : ethnicity, class and political economy
(Critical perspectives on historic issues ; 10)

Includes bibliographical references and index.
Hardcover ISBN: 1-55164-189-5 (bound) Paperback ISBN: 1-55164-188-7 (pbk.)

1. Economic history–To 500. 2. Mediterranean Region–Commerce–History. 3. Greece–Economic conditions–To 146 B.C. I. Tandy, David W. II. Series.

HC31.P742001   330.938   C00-901403-9

Cover design by Associés libres, Montréal

BLACK ROSE BOOKS

C.P. 1258	2250 Military Road	99 Wallis Road
Succ. Place du Parc	Tonawanda, NY	London, E9 5LN
Montréal, H2W 2R3	14150	England
Canada	USA	UK

To order books in North America:
(phone) 1-800-565-9523 (fax) 1-800-221-9985
In Europe: (phone) London 44 (0)20 8986-4854 (fax) 44 (0)20 8533-5821

Our Web Site address: http://www.web.net/blackrosebooks

A publication of the Institute of Policy Alternatives of Montréal (IPAM)

Printed in Canada

CONTENTS

NOTES ON THE CONTRIBUTORS

Darel Tai Engen is an Assistant Professor of History at Gonzaga University in Spokane, Washington. He earned his Ph.D. from UCLA in 1996 and is currently working on a monograph tentatively entitled, *Honor and Profit: Athenian Trade Policy, 415-307 B.C.E.*

Jeremy McInerney is Associate Professor of Classical Studies at the University of Pennsylvania, and is currently chair of the Graduate Group in the Art and Archaeology of the Mediterranean World. His Ph.D. from the University of California, Berkeley, he has excavated in Israel, at Corinth and on Crete. His research interests include topography, epigraphy and historiography. In addition to articles in major journals, he has also written *The Folds of Parnassos: Land and Ethnicity in Ancient Phokis* (University of Texas Press, 1999), a study of state formation and ethnic identity in the Archaic and Classical periods.

Astrid Möller (Ph.D. Berlin) is affiliated with Freiburg University where she is undertaking research on ancient Greek chronography. She was fellow at the Center for Hellenic Studies in 1998–99 and held a Feodor-Lynen scholarship from the Humboldt Foundation at the Dipartimento di Scienze Storiche dell'Antichità at Perugia in 1999–2000. She is author of *Naukratis: Trade in Archaic Greece* (Oxford University Press, 2000).

Ruth Palmer, Associate Professor of Classics at Ohio University, has been investigating aspects of the Mycenaean agricultural economy as recorded in the Linear B texts since the late 1980s. In addition to *Wine in the Mycenaean Palace Economy* (Université de Liège, 1994), she has also published articles on figs, grains, and garden crops as seen in the palace records, and is currently working on deer in the Linear B tablets, and the history of Linear B research on agricultural products.

David W. Rupp is Professor of Classics at Brock University in St Catharines, Ontario. He has excavated extensively in Greece and Cyprus, and is the author of many articles on Bronze Age and Dark Age Greece, Cyprus, and Crete.

David W. Tandy is Professor of Classics at the University of Tennessee. His interests are in early Greek economic and social history, social evolutionary theory, and epic poetry. He is editor, with Colin Duncan, of *From Political Economy to Anthropology: Situating Economic Life in Past Societies*, and author of *Warriors into Traders: The Power of the Market in Early Greece* (University of California Press, 1997), which focuses on the role of the market and poetry on the shaping of early Greek society.

Thomas F. Tartaron is Assistant Professor in the Department of Anthropology at Yale University. Among his research interests are landscape archaeology, scientific applications in fieldwork and artifact analysis, and the dynamics of Mycenaean/native interactions around the Mediterranean. He has participated in excavations and surveys in many parts of Greece, as well as in Iraq and the United States. He holds a Ph.D. in Archaeology from Boston University, awarded in 1996.

INTRODUCTION

David W. Tandy

If Karl Polanyi were still alive he would have encouraged the editor to be as perfunctory as possible in this introduction. He always felt that introductory material was regularly "peripheric," to use one of his favorite adjectives. So let me get right to the papers.

These seven papers grew from the Sixth International Karl Polanyi Conference, which took place at Concordia University, Montreal, in November 1996. In addition to three papers delivered there (Möller, Rupp, Tandy), there are several from the joint meeting, in December 1996, of the American Philological Association and the American Institute of Archaeology (Engen, McInerney, Palmer) and one from the December 1997 meeting (Tartaron). What the papers have most prominently in common is the understanding that Karl Polanyi's approach to historical economies and their managements is still of great value. One specific, remarkable aspect of this volume is that several of the contributors independently took up and explained the formalist/substantivist debate that Polanyi himself inspired, probably especially by his *Great Transformation* (Polanyi 1944), but also by his *Trade and Market* (Polanyi, Arensberg, and Pearson 1957). This is remarkable not so much because it is testimony that the debate is still with us, but rather because it illustrates how differently the debate can be presented by the several practitioners. The debate is new and different each time it arises.

The papers are arranged according to their chronological focus, stretching from the Mycenaean Greeks of the second millennium to the Athenians of the fourth century B.C.E. This was precisely the range of Polanyi's interest in ancient Greece, whether he was writing about accounting in the citadels of the Mycenaeans (Polanyi 1960) or about the movement and pricing of grain in the Aegean in the fourth century (Polanyi 1977, 240-51).

Polanyi's concept of the port of trade takes center stage in three of the papers. Thomas Tartaron's paper focuses on Epirus in northwestern Greece, and the institutions that we can reconstruct for the exploitation of the area by Mycenaean Greeks from the south. David Rupp's paper on Iron Age Cyprus and Astrid Möller's on Naukratis on the Nile Delta also illustrate how richly instructive Polanyi's concept of the port of trade continues to be.

Group identity, whether we treat it terms of status, class, or ethnicity, is the main focus of Jeremy McInerney's paper on the nineteenth-century treatment of early Greek "tribal" developments; it is a secondary focus of at least two other papers (Möller, Tandy).

Allocation of resources was of great interest to Polanyi, as well as to Darel Engen on fourth-century B.C.E. Athens, Rupp, and David Tandy on Hesiod's economic realities and his region's prospects for economic development; agricultural production and allocation are the focus of Ruth Palmer's paper on the continuity of agriculture from the Mycenaean period to the time of Hesiod.

All these contributors are concerned, as Polanyi was, with how communities generated and managed their resources; how they acquired and how they allocated; and, in the cases of the chronologically later papers, how they talked about these activities and thereby integrated these activities into their everyday lives. This is nowhere more clear than in Darel Engen's paper, one of the clearest demonstrations of the embeddedness of the economy that the editor has ever read. Karl Polanyi would have been very satisfied and grateful that his ideas have endured so long and so persistently. How is this not pertinent to the very questions that are being asked today in many quarters about where we are going as the new millennium engages us? It is an additional, optimistic sign that the seven contributors to this volume include only two senior scholars; the remaining five have earned their doctorates in the last dozen years. This demographic fact is a terrific sign of the vitality of Polanyi's approach to preindustrial economies and societies, especially in the Mediterranean. This is important for the past and also for the future.

The editor wishes to thank each of the contributors to this volume, especially those who entered into the project very early on and were forced thereafter to exhibit monumental sums of patience while the rest of the crew got on board. But to all of the authors: sincerest gratitude for the privilege of working with each of you. New friendships and political alliances have developed. Thanks go to Bonnie Watson, Principal Secretary for the Department of Classics at the University of Tennessee, for her assistance in the not infrequent formatting adventures. As always, thanks to Marguerite Mendell of the Karl Polanyi Institute of Political Economy in Montreal for inviting me to put together this volume, and to her assistant Ana Gomez, who steadfastly holds the Institute together and does such a wonderful job of putting on the biennial international conferences. In the final stages, Linda Barton was a great help at Black Rose Books. Finally, special thanks to Dimitri Roussopoulos at Black Rose Books for sponsoring this series for the Polanyi Institute.

BIBLIOGRAPHY

Polanyi, Karl. 1944. *The great transformation: The political and economic origins of our time*. New York: Holt Rinehart.
———. 1960. On the comparative treatment of economic institutions in antiquity with illustrations from Athens, Mycenae and Alalakh. In *City invincible*, Carl H. Kraeling and Robert M. Adams, 329-50. Chicago: University of Chicago Press.
———. 1977. *The livelihood of man*. Edited by Harry W. Pearson. New York: Academic Press.
Polanyi, Karl, Conrad M. Arensberg, and Harry W. Pearson, eds. 1957. *Trade and market in the early empires*. Glencoe, Ill.: Free Press.

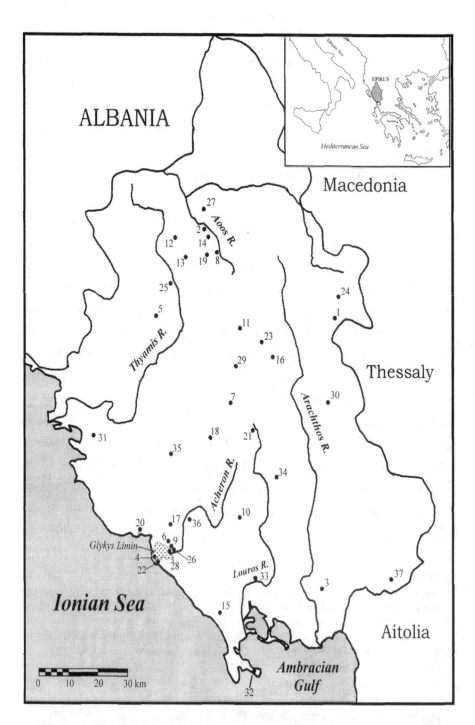

Figure 1: Map of Epirus showing the locations of known sites with Mycenaean remains.

Chapter One

GLYKYS LIMIN: A MYCENAEAN PORT OF TRADE IN SOUTHERN EPIRUS?

Thomas F. Tartaron

Introduction

The archaeological record of coastal southern Epirus (Figure 1) preserves unambiguous evidence that local communities came into contact with bearers of Mycenaean material culture in the years corresponding to ceramic phases LH IIIA–LH IIIC.

Table 1. *Chronology of the Mycenaean Palatial Period. (After Shelmerdine 1997: table 1)*

Ceramic phase	Approximate calendar dates B.C.E.
Late Helladic (LH) IIIA1	1400–1370
Late Helladic IIIA2	1370–1310/1300
Late Helladic IIIB	1310/1300–1190/1180
Late Helladic IIIC (postpalatial)	1190/1180–1065

For decades, we have known of a tholos tomb, a fortified acropolis, and imported pottery and bronze objects of Aegean type. These finds have been interpreted as markers of a time when the Epirote coast was part of a maritime trading route to southern Italy and the Balkans. Research has not progressed beyond broad inferences however, because the region has never been explored systematically, and thus the Mycenaean finds, while provocative, lack environmental, social, and economic context.[1] If we wish to admit the case into wider discussions of Mycenaean activity around the Mediterranean, we must consider not only the political and economic agendas of Mycenaeans, but also the participation of native groups in social and economic transactions, and the mechanisms by which such interactions took place.

The strongest evidence for Mycenaean presence in Epirus is found in the coastal zone of the lower Acheron River, which in antiquity emptied into a bay on the Ionian coast known from ancient sources as *Glykys Limin* (Figure 2-A).[2] From 1992 to 1995, surface survey and geomorphological analysis were applied to the region as part of the Nikopolis Project's broader program of landscape archaeology in southern Epirus.[3] A principal objective of this research was to reconstruct the Bronze Age natural environment and patterns of human activity upon the landscape, thus to create an environmental, social, and economic context within which Mycenaean engagement might be addressed by more sophisticated models than were possible previously.

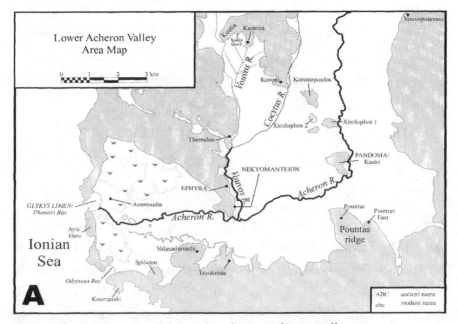

Figure 2-A: Area map of the modern lower Acheron Valley.

Karl Polanyi's concept of the port of trade provides one such model with the potential to illuminate the interactions between natives and Mycenaeans. The port of trade model seeks to identify and describe the common arrangements by which cross-cultural trade is carried out among precapitalist economies. Its specific focus on problems inherent to cross-cultural contact is especially germane to the case of Mycenaean expansion into peripheral locations on the Mediterranean littoral. Accordingly, I pursue two principal aims in this paper: first, to present the evidence for Mycenaean presence in the vicinity of Glykys Limin, and second, to evaluate the utility of the port of trade model in explaining the nature of that presence. The full implications of the port of trade concept can only be understood in the context of Polanyi's wider paradigm of the ancient economy, to which I now turn.

Polanyi and the Economy

In his landmark article, "The Economy as Instituted Process" (1957b), Karl Polanyi presented the essential elements of what would become his paradigm describing the institutional arrangements of "premarket" or "nonmarket" economies, by which he meant those economies in which a modern price-making market is not the primary means of economic integration and transaction.[4] In practice, this refers to all those predating the capitalist economies of the last two centuries in Europe and North America, as well as some peripheral modern examples. His main purpose was to refute the prevailing formal approach to economic analysis, urging instead the adoption of a substantive view of economic behavior.[5] Polanyi maintained that formal economic theory, which focused on the universality of the concepts of maximizing, economizing, scarcity, and supply-and-demand as rational faculties of human behavior and thus applicable to all economies, was appropriate only for nineteenth- and twentieth-century capitalism. In nineteenth-century Europe, industrial capitalism with its attendant proliferation of international price-making markets had "disembedded" the economy, freeing the economic sphere from social control and allowing economic activity to operate according to its own rational laws. Before that era, however, economic relations were still "embedded" in the social system, and therefore the provisioning of material needs was determined by non-material relationships managed by nonmarket institutions. If this was so, the conceptual vocabulary of microeconomic price theory was not suitable to describe nonmarket economies of past and present.[6] In opposing the formal definition of the economy, Polanyi did not deny the logical consistency of microeconomic analysis, or the universality of economic rationality as an aspect of human behavior; rather, he asserted that this body of theory was incapable of providing the organizing principles of nonmarket economies, or of describing their economic transactions (Pearson 1977, xxx).

To develop an alternative theoretical framework for earlier economies, Polanyi contrasted the formal and substantive meanings of the term *economy*. If the formal definition implies a universal logic of economically rational action, the substantive is concerned solely with the empirical means through which material needs are satisfied. Since all societies at all times must concern themselves with finding the material means for survival, the substantive definition provided a common point of departure for the study of any economy. Beginning from material goods and their movements, one may observe the operational patterns and institutional arrangements that drive the economy, and from these construct comparative economic models. Polanyi suggested three "forms of integration"[7] by which economies were organized: *reciprocity*, denoting transactions between correlative points of symmetrical groupings; *redistribution*, designating appropriational movements toward a center and out of it again; and *exchange*, referring to the transactions in a price-making market system.[8] He also identified three institutions, or mechanisms, through which transactions were effected: money, markets, and external trade. Polanyi was eager to demonstrate that these institutions were just as much a part of nonmarket economies as of modern market systems, though each had a function very different from its modern counterpart (Polanyi 1957b, 256-69). Trade is of particular concern here. For Polanyi, all trade was external in the sense that the purpose of trade was to acquire goods not available locally. This institutional definition parts company with the market definition of trade in certain significant ways (Polanyi 1975; Dalton 1975, 104). Rather than reflecting cost differentials, aboriginal trade focused on the acquisition of needed products from a distance; the emphasis was thus on imports, and production for export was not an important impetus for trade. Trading expeditions were sporadic rather than continuous, and lacked a monetary standard linking different economies. Polanyi enumerated the ways in which goods may be acquired from a distance, including raiding, tribute, taxation, gift exchange, market trade, and politically administered trade (Dalton 1975, 104-109). The port of trade is the main institution of politically administered *foreign* trade (Polanyi 1975, 152).

Polanyi and the Port of Trade

The port of trade emerged as one of many fruitful concepts from Polanyi's economic paradigm. Polanyi's programmatic statement, "Ports of Trade in Early Societies," appeared in 1963 in *The Journal of Economic History*, and has since been amplified and clarified.[9] The port of trade was conceived to describe foreign or cross-cultural exchange in the context of politically administered, nonmarket economies, and naturally to contrast such activity with modern market trade. It was envisioned as nothing less than "a universal institution of overseas trade preceding the establishment of international markets" (Polanyi 1963, 31).

Polanyi and his colleagues believed that ports of trade emerged as mechanisms for the safe transfer of goods from one system to another, typically involving two societies with differently patterned economic institutions, as for instance a nonmarket society encountering professional traders exhibiting market behavior. These ports arose most often at coastal or riverine sites with extensive inlets or lagoons and easy overland connections, i.e., at nodal points articulating seaborne traders with producers and products of the hinterland, although inland sites at zones of ecological change (e.g., ancient Petra) could be considered quasi-ports of trade (Polanyi

1963, 31). The physical features of the port of trade included facilities for anchorage, debarkation, and storage and transshipment of goods.

Because of the security concerns and risks involved in trade under early state conditions, ports of trade may have developed as neutral sites, perhaps derived from the type of "silent" trade encountered in Herodotus[10] and in many historical accounts (Smith 1987, 145-48). The neutrality of the port of trade preserved the military security of the native communities, while also ensuring civil protection for foreign traders. The port of trade thus became a political and economic buffer zone between the foreign trader and the desired products of the hinterland (Humphreys 1978, 54). Because disputes may arise in any event, some form of judicial recourse was available on a permanent or ad hoc basis.

In accordance with Polanyi's substantive paradigm, economic transactions at the port of trade were an extension of the administered economy, involving redistributive arrangements that structured and controlled the interactions of natives and foreigners. The political authority that administered the port determined the terms of trade by means of treaties that established set prices or ratios at which goods were to be exchanged, and through other administrative (i.e., nonmarket) measures. Trade was strictly controlled and confined to official channels, with the result that local market exchange and long-distance trade remained completely separate. In such a system, competition was eschewed as a mode of transaction; as Polanyi maintains, competition was "relegated to the background or was merely lurking on the periphery."[11]

The port of trade was clearly conceived as a flexible institution meant to embrace a broad range of variability (Polanyi 1963, 31; Dalton 1978, 102-103). Polanyi and others described examples from several parts of the world, including Africa, Asia, the Near East, Indonesia, the Mediterranean, and Mesoamerica (Arnold 1957; Chapman 1957; Revere 1957; Polanyi 1966; Austin and Vidal-Naquet 1977, 233-35; Leeds 1961; Geertz 1980). Polanyi made an initial attempt to classify ports of trade based on the locus of administrative control; according to this classification, ports could be organs of independent small states (Sidon, Tyre); possessions of hinterland empires (Whydah after 1727); neutralized by consensus of hinterland empires (Ugarit, Al Mina), or by consensus of foreign trading powers (Whydah before 1727); or independent as a result of their own naval strength (Tyre) (Polanyi 1963, 33-38). Richard Hodges (1978) proposed a four-fold classification of ports of trade for early medieval Europe, to which Torrence (1978) suggested further refinements. In the Mediterranean world, the most explicit application of the port of trade concept has been that of Michel Austin and Pierre Vidal-Naquet to the Greek trading settlement at Naukratis and to the Phokaian colony of Emporion in Catalonia.[12] But Polanyi's broader paradigm of the economy has had wide influence among archaeologists and historians of ancient Greece, notably through the work of Moses Finley.[13]

Merits and Criticisms of the Model

The concept of the port of trade holds natural appeal for archaeologists and historians, because it offers a single, broad framework in which to evaluate data drawn from diverse examples of interregional and cross-cultural exchange. That is, within the single theoretical framework defined by Polanyi's substantivist economics (and the specific characteristics of the port of trade derived from it),[14] the port of trade model accommodates a wide variety of individual occurrences, from prehistory to modern times, reflecting diverse local conditions. Torrence notes that Polanyi's model "incorporates data from a range of specific situations in such a way that the general economic relationships between traders, goods, administration and settlement location can be recognized" (Torrence 1978, 108). She continues by advocating a deductive approach in which models of entire trading systems are constructed, and the archaeological correlates of each class of port of trade within the system are predicted and tested against the data from excavated sites.[15]

    In spite of this apparent promise, scholars of ancient Greece have been generally reluctant to adopt the port of trade model in their analyses of trading settlements, a fact for which there are several plausible explanations.

It may first be noted that the port of trade, like many other components of Polanyi's economic theory, remained an unfinished concept at the time of his death, with the result that ambiguity and a lack of clarity characterize Polanyi's own writings on the subject (Dalton 1975, 74; Dalton and Köcke 1983, 22-23; Hodges 1978, 100). Several individuals, particularly George Dalton, have extended and clarified Polanyi's thought (Dalton 1971; 1975; 1978; Dalton and Bohannon 1962; Bohannon 1959; 1960; Neale 1971; Sahlins 1965; 1972; Humphreys 1978; Cartledge 1983), though it is fair to ask who are the legitimate arbiters of the port of trade concept. Sally Humphreys doubts, for example, that neutrality was essential to the economic functioning of the port of trade (Humphreys 1978, 55); others have taken liberties with the concept in ways that violate Polanyi's general theoretical formulations (Gledhill and Larsen 1982, 199; Figueira 1984). The ambiguity inherent in Polanyi's original model may have resulted in an inability to make meaningful distinctions among dissimilarly constituted trade centers, compelling Hodges and others to create new classification schemes.

Polanyi's credibility among scholars of Mediterranean and Near Eastern history has also suffered on account of his many factual errors and questionable interpretations of textual and archaeological evidence. Apart from obvious blunders, such as translating the Greek *chrysos* (gold) as silver (Polanyi 1960, 342), Polanyi has been widely criticized for his impressionistic and misapprehending treatment of a wide range of phenomena (Gledhill and Larsen 1982; Figueira 1984; Sherratt and Sherratt 1991, 353). To cite one example here, Near Eastern scholars have taken a dim view of Polanyi's assessment of the ancient Mesopotamian economy.[16] A great many of Polanyi's claims, such as the pervasiveness of a Sumerian "temple economy," the absence of money and price-making markets, and his static picture of economic institutions essentially unchanged for three millennia, appear to be cast in doubt if not flatly contradicted by the preponderance of the textual and archaeological evidence. These lapses are symptomatic, according to Humphreys, of "those who cover a wide range of materials in comparative studies," but they are not easily forgiven, even if "the problems he raises are not trivial" (Humphreys 1978, 57). Nor has it helped that Polanyi's narrative tone can be didactic and unqualified, appearing to exclude alternative interpretations (Tandy and Neale 1994, 10-14).

Many researchers are further disinclined to accept the substantivist paradigm from which the port of trade is drawn. The specific model can scarcely be separated from the paradigm; whatever the merits of a universal mechanism for cross-cultural trade, the port of trade has been rejected, ignored, or relegated to irrelevance precisely because of its association with one or more of Polanyi's strictures on markets, money, prices, and so forth (Figueira 1984; Sherratt and Sherratt 1991, 376).

The analytical power of the port of trade model is perhaps most limited, however, by its *static* (or *descriptive*) nature, an attribute acknowledged by Polanyi's apologists: "neither formal economics (price theory) nor Polanyi's substantive economics provides a theory of change under aboriginal conditions. Both are concerned exclusively with static structure and performance...at specific...dates" (Dalton 1975, 75). This is a serious limitation, because a most crucial aspect of any cross-cultural contact scenario is dynamic development over time, which may involve conflict, adjustment, and accommodation affecting all social and cultural subsystems. From the archaeologist's point of view, theories of change are essential means of finding explanations for changes observed in the archaeological record. Changes in artifact assemblages and spatial patterning may denote population shifts, adjustments in subsistence and land use, redefined economic roles, the emergence of elites, or a host of other transformations potentially associated with the interactions taking place at a port of trade. Discontinuity and dynamic process characterize economic institutions and forms of economic integration over time, and for that reason it is easy to understand the doubt expressed by many observers that the Polanyian model can provide useful explanations of economic phenomena in the medium and long term.

In summary, the port of trade has an important utility as a universal model of the locational, physical, and institutional arrangements of cross-cultural trade among nonmarket societies. If we wish to investigate the diachronic processes of interaction and their consequences, however, the substantivist paradigm is insufficient and we must seek theories of change and dynamic models to complement it.

Ports of Trade and the Mycenaean Economy

In spite of the these limitations, there is reason for optimism that the phenomenon of Mycenaean overseas trade may find enlightenment in Polanyi's paradigm. Working from the recent decipherment of Linear B by Michael Ventris, Polanyi noted patterns in the accounting system that suggested to him a moneyless, marketless Mycenaean economy (Polanyi 1960, 340-46; cf. Ventris and Chadwick 1973 [1956], 290ff., 302-303). Later, in an important analysis of the Mycenaean economy through the Linear B records, Killen detected close similarities with the Near Eastern "Asiatic" economies, and concluded that the key role in the movement of goods and the employment of labor was played not by a market or money, but by the central redistributive agency of the palaces:

> All our evidence strongly suggests that there was neither a market nor money in the Mycenaean world; and there is little question that in the absence of these means of exchange the palaces themselves played a major entrepreneurial role in the economy, and had a deep involvement both in the movement of goods and in the employment of labour in the kingdoms.[17]

The archaeological and textual evidence supports an interpretation of the palaces as redistributive centers, though there is no universal agreement on the circumstances of their origin and development.[18] The tablets document palatial control of substantial tracts of land and their productive capacity,[19] and each stage of the redistributive process—the collection of goods, storage at the palaces, the allocation of resources to dependent workers, and the distribution of commodities—is represented in the Linear B records (Shelmerdine 1997, 567). The results of archaeological investigation at the palaces confirm this general picture: extensive workshops, archives, and storage facilities are regular features (e.g., Shelmerdine and Palaima 1984), and a system of roads radiating from the palace at Mycenae has been traced (Hope Simpson 1981, 11-17; Wells, Runnels, and Zangger 1990, 223-27; Lavery 1995; Jansen 1997).

Yet it remains extraordinary that within the entire Linear B corpus, few records imply the existence of external relations, and none refers to merchants of any kind. The exceptions include lists of slave women from the coast of Asia Minor at Pylos, the names of exotic products such as sesame and ivory, and a tablet at Mycenae that mentions a transaction with Thebes (Cline 1994, 128-31; Killen 1985, 268; Chadwick 1976, 80-81). Nevertheless, the implication that one might draw from the Linear B archives that interregional exchange was an insignificant sector of the Mycenaean economy does not square well with the emerging archaeological record from around the Mediterranean. Durable Mycenaean imports, chiefly fine pottery and bronze weapons and implements, continue to be found in the eastern and central Mediterranean. Mycenaean architecture, including tholos tombs and walls of Cyclopean masonry, is found in many peripheral locations, and Mycenaean colonies, trade missions, or enclaves are proposed for the Aegean and Ionian islands, Asia Minor, and even Italy and Sardinia (e.g., Mee 1982, 81-92; Hope Simpson 1981, 155-59; Jones and Vagnetti 1991, 141). We must wonder if the distribution of extant objects betokens a much broader trade in goods that do not survive in the archaeological record, particularly as many researchers have taken the view that pottery was transported primarily as spacefiller, and not as a main item of trade (Gill 1991; 1994). A partial answer comes from Bronze Age shipwrecks excavated by Bass and his colleagues on Turkey's Aegean coast at Cape Gelidonya and Ulu Burun, which provide a glimpse of the breadth of material being transported around the Mediterranean.[20] The Ulu Burun ship contained hundreds of ingots of copper, tin, and glass, along with pottery from Egypt, Cyprus, the Aegean, and Syro-Palestine, and numerous other objects that suggest elite gift exchange. The Gelidonya wreck contained mainly metal ingots and implements of a clearly less elite character. With the notable exception of the pottery, many of the items on the two shipwrecks would qualify as rare or unique finds in a terrestrial archaeological context: most ingots have long since been melted down or otherwise rendered unrecognizable, and among the rarities from the Ulu Burun wreck are ostrich eggshells, ivory, ebony, terebinth resin, and other organic remains (Knapp 1991; Haldane 1993).

The apparent contradiction between the textual and archaeological evidence has engendered a divergence of opinion regarding the scale of Late Bronze Age trade in the Mediterranean, with opposing camps that may be labeled "minimalist" and "maximalist," corresponding to the primitivist and modernist points of view, respectively. The former group draws from the Polanyian tradition, through Finley, but is also influenced by the sentiment of Max Weber and Johannes Hasebroek that early societies were agrarian in orientation, and thus interregional trade was of little importance. This position has been outlined recently by Keith Hopkins, who emphasizes regional, agrarian self-sufficiency in the ancient world (Hopkins 1983). Anthony Snodgrass specifically doubts that *commercial* trade was consequential to the Bronze Age economy, but also maintains that a redistributive center would only send its ships abroad "when it needs resources from overseas, and this may be very infrequently" (Snodgrass 1991, 18). John Chadwick finds it difficult to imagine private individuals trading independently in the Mycenaean system (Chadwick 1976, 156-58). For the minimalists, the archaeological record is best explained in terms of infrequent, directional elite gift exchange that has nothing to do with money, markets, or private enterprise.

The maximalist or modernist school tends to view Bronze Age trade as extensive, driven by market forces, and involving a substantial contribution from private merchants. George Bass argues that the shipwreck evidence supports a large, but archaeologically invisible, trade in raw materials, which may help to solve the conundrum of the lack of Near Eastern objects in

Aegean archaeological contexts.[21] He interprets the Gelidonya ship as a private Levantine merchant venture, and the commander of the Ulu Burun ship as either a wealthy private merchant or a royal emissary (Bass 1991, 75). The most thoroughly modernist position is advanced by Eric Cline, who portrays Mediterranean Bronze Age trade as primarily commercial, with gift exchange playing a comparatively small role. Further, he suggests that the scale of trade encompassing Egypt, the Near East, Italy, and the Aegean in the Late Bronze Age rivals that of today (Cline 1994, 106). Andrew Sherratt and Susan Sherratt conclude that the Bronze Age economy was a market economy in the formal sense (Sherratt and Sherratt 1991, 376).

A compromise presents itself if the volume of trade is distinguished from its significance. Sherratt and Sherratt suggest that although the quantities of goods transported over long distances were small relative to total production, their importance should not be underestimated, for they represent the efforts of a minority to acquire goods possessing tremendous social significance (Sherratt and Sherratt 1991, 354). Mycenaean centers sought raw materials from which prestige items could be fashioned, either from established markets in the Eastern Mediterranean or from peripheral areas at lower levels of economic organization. This demand on the part of elites for goods to further their social agendas forms an integral part of the Sherratts' conspicuous consumption model, to which I will return in some detail below.

The Mycenaean Presence in Southwestern Epirus

Taking into account the discoveries of the Nikopolis Project, remains of Mycenaean provenience or inspiration are known at just fewer than 40 sites in Epirus (Figure 1). Although these sites are distributed widely throughout the province, the coastal region surrounding the lower Acheron River valley in southwestern Epirus is unique for the quantity and quality of the indicators of Mycenaean presence. It is only here that architectural remains of Mycenaean type, implying a level of involvement beyond simple exchange or sporadic contact, have thus far been discovered. By contrast, the portable objects found at inland sites appear to trace the movement of goods from coastal points of entry, and do not imply the presence of individuals from Mycenaean Greece.

Mycenaean elements in the lower Acheron region (Figure 2-B)

Important evidence of Mycenaean presence in the lower Acheron region has long been recognized. At Kiperi, on the Ionian coast some fifteen kilometers north of the Acheron mouth, a small but skillfully constructed tholos tomb was discovered in the 1930s (Dakaris 1960). The architectural features of the tholos, as well as the fabric of some sherds found therein, find close parallels in the Ayios Ilias tholoi in Aitolia (Wardle 1972, 198; Papadopoulos 1981a, 12, 22-23). The tomb, plundered in antiquity, produced some 50 sherds, more than 30 from imported Mycenaean vessels. Among the Mycenaean vessel forms are alabastra dating primarily to LH IIIA1, stirrup jars of LH IIIA–B, and kylikes belonging to LH IIIA.[22] Some wall segments beside the tomb that employ the canonical Cyclopean construction technique, as well as foundations spread over a relatively level terrace nearby, may belong to an associated settlement, though there is at present no conclusive proof (Dakaris 1960, 125; Tartaron 1996, 74, 76, 181-84).

Near the modern mouth of the Acheron, approximately four kilometers from the Ionian coast, lies the fortified hill of Xylokastro, known by its probable ancient name Ephyra (Thucydides 1.46; cf. Homer, *Odyssey* 1.259, 2.328). The hill rises to over eighty meters above sea level, sloping steeply on the north and east, and more gently on the south and west. From this acropolis-like settlement comes the strongest evidence for Mycenaean presence in Epirus. A circuit wall employing Cyclopean masonry, much of which can still be traced, enclosed the Late Bronze Age settlement.[23] Of particular interest is the South Gate, the main entrance into the settlement. Although in a ruined state today, enough of it remains intact to indicate the plan of the gate and the huge, rectangular blocks from which it was constructed. The South Gate is flanked by bastions, with the unusual feature that the eastern bastion projects forward asymmetrically relative to the western bastion; the closest parallel for this configuration is the South Gate at Gla in central Greece (Iakovidis 1989, 59–61, plan 5, plate 26).

Thirteen seasons of excavation at Ephyra uncovered three burial tumuli containing cist graves, and yielded massive amounts of local and imported pottery in burial contexts and settlement debris (Dakaris 1958; Dakaris and Papadopoulos 1976; Papadopoulos 1978; 1979; 1980; 1981b; 1982; 1983; 1986; 1987a). A remarkable result is that the percentage of Mycenaean fineware may reach 10–15% of the total Bronze Age pottery assemblage, the balance comprised of local handmade ware of general Bronze Age type.[24] Among the Mycenaean forms represented are kylikes, alabastra, stirrup jars, and cups. The dates of these imports range from LH IIIA to LH IIIC, with apparent peaks of frequency in LH IIIA2 and LH IIIB. Unfortunately, the stratigraphy at Ephyra is very poor, with the result that little has been learned about the spatial and functional organization of the settlement in the Bronze Age.[25]

Isolated finds of bronze weapons and scatters of pottery of Mycenaean type have been reported from other locations in the lower Acheron region (Andreou 1994, 242, figs. 27, 28; Dakaris 1963; Soueref 1986, 58-68), but even with those additions, little was known about settlement and other uses of the landscape in the Late Bronze Age. Large tracts of the region had never been explored systematically; in particular, almost no information existed on native settlements or subsistence activities, making it difficult to place the Mycenaean evidence in any meaningful framework for studying trade and other interactive processes.

Intensive surface survey and geomorphological study in the lower Acheron region by the Nikopolis Project contributed substantially to filling these lacunae. The survey produced 21 new Bronze Age loci, of which at least ten preserve evidence of use in the late Bronze Age. At five of these locations, remains of Mycenaean provenience or inspiration were found: two examples of walls of Mycenaean type were recognized, and four sites yielded sherds from Mycenaean fineware vessels.

One objective of geomorphological research was to estimate the extent of Glykys Limin in the Bronze Age. Whereas the bay has now completely disappeared, ancient sources inform us that sizable fleets were once moored in it: Thucydides (1.46) reports that the Corinthians anchored 150 ships there before the Battle of Sybota in 433 B.C.E.; from Cassius Dio (50.12.2) we learn that Octavian brought his fleet of 250 ships to port in the bay before the decisive battle off Actium in 31 B.C.E.; and still in C.E. 1084 a large fleet under the command of Robert Guiscard of Normandy was able to find anchorage there (Anna Comnena, *Alexiad* 4.33). A program of geological coring traced changes in the configuration of the shoreline over time, furnishing for the first time an accurate measure of its position in the Bronze Age.[26] On the basis of a series of radiocarbon dates, the Bronze Age shoreline should be placed at least six kilometers from the modern Ionian coast.

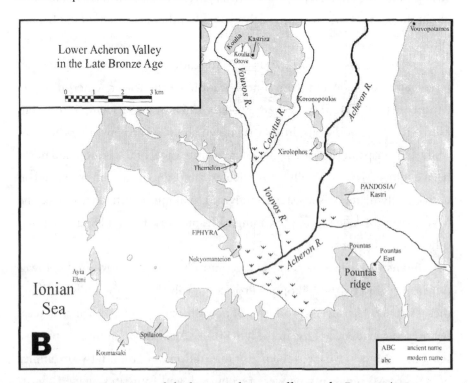

Figure 2-B: Area map of the lower Acheron valley in the Bronze Age, showing Late Bronze Age site locations and the approximate extent of the bay of Glykys Limin. (Base map courtesy Mark Besonen)

Other geomorphological findings furnish further details about environmental conditions in the Bronze Age. The profile of bedrock within the bay suggests that the gentle southern shore, particularly at Koumasaki and Spilaion, would have been ideal for pulling Bronze Age boats onto the beach from about three to four meters of water. The island of Ayia Eleni served as a natural breakwater, protecting the bay from waves and making it an ideal haven from storms and rough seas. The location of the settlement of Ephyra on the Xylokastro hill makes perfect sense in light of the fact that it lay less than 500 meters from the shore, rather than several kilometers as is the case today. Other environmental data, moreover, establish the likelihood that the lower Acheron region was characterized by mild temperatures, high rainfall, perennial water courses, and copious springs in the late Bronze Age.[27] This information leads to two important conclusions: 1) Glykys Limin was ideally suited to maritime activity; and 2) the lower Acheron region was a favorable location for human habitation and subsistence.

The most important new indications of Mycenaean material culture produced by the archaeological survey are two sites with walls of Cyclopean masonry. At Ayia Eleni, two parallel walls were detected near the base of the hill, the lower of which could be traced for approximately 150 meters. Their construction typifies the Cyclopean technique: large boulders, hammer dressed and stacked in irregular courses, with smaller stones inserted into the interstices for stability. These walls may have formed part of a system of agricultural terraces, or were meant to support a series of built structures. Late Bronze Age activity on Ayia Eleni may be connected either with an expansion into more marginal locations in times of economic prosperity,[28] or with the use of the island to monitor traffic entering and exiting the bay.

Of similar interest is a walled settlement at Kastriza, a small hill just over five hectares (twelve-thirteen acres) in area, tucked away in the valley of the Vouvos River, a tributary of the Acheron. The walls and a gate at Kastriza show a similar use of Cyclopean techniques, but on a more impressive scale and with a clearly defensive function. In this case, the wall consists of outer and inner faces of large boulders, in places skillfully dressed, and a thick rubble core. The construction technique conforms closely with Loader's (1998, 23-38) definition of Cyclopean fortifications. The total thickness of the wall is approximately three meters, a figure that compares favorably with many examples of defensive wall construction at small sites elsewhere in the Mycenaean world (Hope Simpson 1981; Loader 1998, appendix 2). A few sherds from Mycenaean fineware vessels were found at the site among copious fragments of local pottery. Kastriza is intriguing for its powerful fortification and for its location. We may wonder if it was inhabited by Mycenaeans, or perhaps by a local group with connections to Mycenaeans living on the coast. The location of Kastriza, midway between Ephyra and Kiperi on a plausible inland route between the two sites, may also be significant. Was this overland route used in times of danger at sea? Or was Kastriza a node serving as an intermediary between Mycenaeans on the coast and inland sources of supply?

Twenty-seven sherds from Mycenaean vessels were collected from the surface of the lower Acheron valley. Though the sherds are in a fragmentary condition, it appears that the assemblage conforms in chronological and formal terms to Mycenaean pottery already known from Epirus. The kylix is the most commonly identifiable shape, with fewer sherds belonging to stirrup jars, kraters, cups, and other shapes. The chronological range is also approximately the same as in the rest of Epirus: LH IIIA 1 or 2 to the end of the Bronze Age. The imported Mycenaean ware is of provincial manufacture, the most likely points of origin being Aitoloakarnania and the Ionian islands (Soueref 1986, 145-50).

Just as important as the Mycenaean evidence is the information acquired concerning patterns of native settlement, which presented a more difficult task. In the lower Acheron region, 21 new loci and almost 2,000 locally produced pottery sherds of Bronze Age date were discovered, but local artifacts are not particularly helpful in revealing chronology or change over time. At least until the Shaft Grave era, Epirus was intensely isolated from developments taking place elsewhere, primarily by the Pindos mountains to the east, and by the Ionian Sea to the west. One effect of this long isolation was extreme conservatism in material culture, making it difficult or impossible to develop relative chronologies based on stylistic or technological criteria. An example may be found in the Epirote Bronze Age pottery, whose forming, firing, and decoration changed little if at all during the entirety of the Bronze Age, including the years of Mycenaean contact (Wardle 1977, 181-87; Tartaron 1996, 191-223).

Chronological development

The Mycenaean artifacts and their spatial distribution do permit certain chronological developments to be discerned (Soueref 1986; Papadopoulos 1987b). There is little physical evidence for contact with the Mycenaean world before the first half of the fourteenth century B.C.E. The earliest well-dated context is the tholos tomb at Kiperi, from which the Mycenaean pottery ranges from LH IIIA1 to LH IIIA2–B, indicating a use life covering approximately the entire fourteenth century. If indeed the Ayios Ilias tholoi in Aitoloakarnania served as models for the Kiperi tomb, a construction date in LH IIIA1 accords well with the prominence of Ayios Ilias as a Mycenaean center in LH IIB–LH IIIA1.

The earliest Mycenaean pottery at Ephyra dates to LH IIIA, perhaps LH IIIA1, but because the ceramic material from Ephyra remains unpublished, it is not possible to discuss phasing and ubiquity in detail. The preliminary reports suggest, however, that LH IIIA pottery was by no means rare at Ephyra (Papadopoulos 1980; 1983; 1984). It was apparently in LH IIIA2 (the second half of the fourteenth century) that Mycenaean objects began to appear at inland settlements such as Dodona, and to the end of LH IIIA or the first years of LH IIIB we may assign the earliest use, at Mazaraki in the interior of northern Epirus, of Aegean pottery and bronze objects as burial goods in cist graves (Wardle 1977, 177, fig. 10 nos. 476, 477; Vokotopoulou 1969, 191-203).

In LH IIIB (ca. 1310-1190), Mycenaean material culture spread widely throughout coastal and inland Epirus; in this period Mycenaean engagement in Epirus was strongest, both quantitatively and qualitatively. Though the

Kiperi tholos may have gone out of use early in LH IIIB, the Cyclopean wall
found there, as well as those at Ephyra, Kastriza, and Ayia Eleni, cannot have
been built before (and probably not after) LH IIIB. Major fortification walls
were constructed at a few of the largest sites of the Mycenaean core area (e.g.,
Mycenae, Tiryns, Thebes, Gla) in LH IIIA1 and IIIA2, but most of the other
Mycenaean fortifications belong to LH IIIB (Loader 1998, 160-61). There is
no reason to imagine that these constructions in Epirus would have been
among the first, although construction dates in the first half of LH IIIB are
not unlikely. The settlement of Ephyra prospered in LH IIIB, and Mycenaean
pottery and bronzes continued to be imported there into LH IIIC. Other cist
grave cemeteries of the interior now join the list with pottery, bronze swords
and spear points, and other small finds of LH IIIB date; most continued to be
used into LH IIIC. It seems that a very active phase of contact encompassed
the latter half of LH IIIB and early LH IIIC, probably reflecting influences
from the Ionian islands of Ithaka and Kephallenia.

Tangible changes arrived in Epirus in LH IIIC (ca. 1190-1065),
following the collapse of the Mycenaean palace system. As Mycenaean
influence waned, northern influence is seen in novel pottery and bronze
types, and in the burial tumuli that sometimes still contain Aegean artifacts of
LH IIIC and Submycenaean date, or local imitations inspired by them. The
three tumuli excavated at Ephyra may have been used before LH IIIC
(Papadopoulos 1990, 364), though this is unlikely, and the mixed deposits
associated with them will not decide the question. Mycenaean influence is
apparent in many of the vessels and bronze weapons that are found in cist and
tumulus burials from the beginning of the twelfth century to the end of the
second millennium (Andreou 1983; 1984; Douzougli n.d.; Wardle 1993),
but most of these pieces are either imitations or reflect a mixing of northern
and southern traditions.

Discussion

With these new data, it is possible to address essential but still unanswered
questions. For example: What was the nature of Mycenaean interest in the

lower Acheron valley, what forms did it take, and what sorts of interactions took place, where, and among whom? There is also an opportunity to evaluate the explanatory power of Polanyi's port of trade and other models. Some preliminary comments on the archaeological evidence will highlight several significant issues.

The discovery of Glykys Limin was surely occasioned by the expansion of Mycenaean activity to the north and northwest in the seventh through the fifteenth centuries, fueled by the demand for raw materials among an emerging elite. The broad bay would have been identified quickly as one of few good landfalls on the rugged Epirote coast. The incipient visits must have been to find shelter and fresh supplies of food and water, and probably left few, if any, tangible remains. Once maritime routes became more systematic in the fourteenth and thirteenth centuries, Glykys Limin offered an attractive node at which resupply and exchange could take place. In addition to a superb harbor, the lower Acheron region possessed an agreeable climate, in which water was abundant and crops familiar in the Mycenaean world could be grown. It was likely this combination of a favorable natural environment and obvious advantages for trade that enticed a community from the south to establish a small settlement on the coast—indeed, there can be little doubt that Mycenaeans were in residence in the lower Acheron region. The most compelling argument for this claim is the striking contrast between traditional Epirote material culture and the novel Mycenaean forms, particularly in the area of monumental architecture. There existed in Epirus no prior tradition of large-scale stone architecture, nor even any sign of significant cooperative building efforts (Papadopoulos 1990). One could argue for simple emulation on the basis of portable goods, such as fine pottery and metal objects, but it is difficult to sustain the notion that local chiefs had fortresses, terrace walls, and tholos tombs, with all that they imply in terms of engineering expertise and social organization, built for them without the slightest evidence of comparable traditions or even functional equivalents.

The surface survey results make it clear that the Mycenaeans did not encounter an empty landscape upon arriving in the lower Acheron region, however. An important revelation of the survey was that Bronze Age sites tend to be buried at a depth of a meter or less. Many artifact scatters owe their detection to road building and bulldozing, and the implication that other shallowly buried sites of similar age await discovery is clear. Study of settlement data from the lower Acheron valley has led me to propose a Late Bronze Age site hierarchy with four tiers: *major settlement*; *village*; *farmstead or small rural residential compound*; and *non-residential special purpose site* (Tartaron 1996, 406-27). The survey evidence, supported by previous excavation data from settlements and burials, indicates a genuine population increase in LH IIIB, the time of greatest Mycenaean presence. At that time the highest, and probably the two highest, tiers of the settlement hierarchy were added, with the apparent complicity of Mycenaean interests.

The archaeological record from the shores of Glykys Limin is plausibly interpreted to indicate concentrated economic activity. In addition to the primary center at Ephyra, two other sites (Koumasaki and Spilaion) are among the largest surface scatters discovered by the survey, in terms of both artifact quantity and spatial extent. These sites are located on hills that slope gently to the southern shore of the bay, and each produced interesting artifact patterns that may shed light on the types of activities that took place there in the Late Bronze Age. At Spilaion, the pottery assemblage is weighted heavily toward medium to heavy storage vessels, raising the possibility of some sort of storage or warehousing operation. At Koumasaki, many thousands of flint flakes and abundant debitage, far in excess of the amount encountered on other surface sites, presumably belong to a Bronze Age flaked stone industry (Tartaron, Runnels, and Karimali, 1999). The sheer volume of material suggests some occupation on an industrial scale. A credible explanation is the processing of plants (a few sickle elements with silica gloss were found) for food or for construction material. But an alternative hypothesis is intriguing: the artifactual and environmental data may point to an industry for scraping and processing animal, probably cattle, hides. Bones of domesticated cattle are found in excavated contexts in Epirus from late Neolithic times (Douzougli and Zachos 1994, 17); Ephyra and the adjacent Nekyomanteion site have produced them alongside those of domesticated sheep and goat (Dakaris 1963; Papadopoulos 1982; 1986). Epirus was renowned in ancient literature for the size and quality of its cattle (Hesiod, fr. 349; Pindar, *Nem.* 4.52-54; Aristotle, *Historia Animalium* 3.2.1). The flat, swampy terrain that surrounded Glykys Limin in the Bronze Age would have provided ideal grazing for large-bodied animals with prodigious water requirements.

Examples from the ethnographic record may illuminate the operation of such an industry. Richard Dana's account of two years aboard a merchant ship working the California coast in the 1830s provides a unique glimpse at the trade in cattle hides with Native Americans (Dana 1964).[29] In several widely scattered passages, Dana describes the process by which the exchanges were effected: the Native Americans transported the hides, which had first been stretched and dried, by mule or cart to beaches where the merchant ships dropped anchor (Dana 1964, 92-93). On some occasions, the merchants' agent visited local Spanish missions to negotiate the purchase of large quantities of hides, which the Native Americans brought to the waiting ships (Dana 1964, 100).

Because the hides were received in a rough, uncured state unsuitable for long voyages, the merchant crew was compelled to cure the hides by soaking, pickling, scraping, and cleaning them (Dana 1964, 153-54). Though Dana describes this process in some detail, he says little about the specific tools the curers used. We may turn, however, to ethnoarchaeological approaches to suggest the elements of a toolkit that may survive in the material record. A recent study of modern hide processing in Ethiopia assesses the archaeological implications of the manufacture, use, and discard of stone tools used in the curing process (Gallagher 1977). It is possible, therefore, to construct a model of a putative hide processing industry that takes into account spatial and artifactual attributes, and which can be tested against the archaeological record. The lithic assemblage from Koumasaki shares certain functional similarities with the various categories of material remains described by Gallagher, but further artifact study will be required to substantiate or reject this hypothesis. If such an industry did exist at Koumasaki, the scale of the remains implies craft specialization and surplus production for trade.

The question of interactions between Mycenaeans and natives might best be framed in terms of each group's priorities. A primary consideration for any group attempting to establish a foothold in foreign territory is security. The Mycenaean party was small in number and facing a variety of known and unknown dangers. Similarly, for the natives it must have been intimidating to encounter a group with superior weaponry and technical skills. It is possible that some accommodation was reached before the settlers arrived (cf. Graham 1990). Evidence that there was a need, at least perceived, for defensive measures may be seen in the strong walls at Ephyra and Kastriza. Once security was addressed, the Mycenaeans presumably sought alliances to ensure a continuous flow of necessary goods and services: staple goods, including foodstuffs and pottery; a supply of labor for building projects, crafts, and industries; and access to existing exchange networks articulating the coast to the interior. Such alliances held advantages for natives as well. Far-reaching social and political opportunities attended the acquisition of superior technology and prestige items. The acquisition of metal weapons and implements and monumental architecture may have been particularly important, because they conferred not only prestige, but a competitive advantage in war and in subsistence productivity.

The initial social and economic transactions by which natives obtained exotic goods may have been gift exchanges intended to mobilize and cement these alliances. The relationships also provided scope for the emergence of elites from a probably tribal social organization. But what evidence is there for emergence of an elite and what effects did such a process have on social and economic organization? These questions may now be approached by placing the archaeological evidence within the theoretical framework of the port of trade.

Glykys Limin as a Port of Trade

Many of the arrangements by which cross-cultural trade was accomplished in the lower Acheron region are admirably described by the port of trade model. In taking several components of the model in turn, I hope to demonstrate that something quite like a port of trade did exist around Glykys Limin in the Late Bronze Age.

A mechanism of cross-cultural trade

Archaeological study of the inhabitants of Bronze Age Epirus leaves no doubt that the Mycenaeans encountered local communities with differently patterned social and economic institutions (Tartaron 1996). These differences are reflected in aspects of material culture ranging from architecture to pottery, and in varied attributes of settlement pattern and land use. There is no evidence that the Epirotes had anything resembling a price-making market economy, though Mycenaean traders may have exhibited rational market behavior in their dealings with the local inhabitants. The encounter of these societies may be seen as part of a broader pattern in which growing economies send out trading missions to exploit the resources of surrounding areas at lower levels of economic organization (Sherratt and Sherratt 1991, 356).

Locational imperatives

As would be considered typical at a port of trade, Ephyra is situated at a suitable coastal landing point with easy access to the hinterland. The bay of Glykys Limin lay on a maritime route from western Greece to Italy and the Balkans that makes archaeological and navigational sense (Hodge 1983). It was an optimal spot to seek shelter from rough seas, drop anchor, and find fresh water and food. The Acheron River system and the surrounding low-lying land extending inward from the coast permitted relatively easy access to the interior of the country.

The locations of settlements and other focal points of activity are also consistent with the port of trade model. Ephyra was founded on an easily defended hill a mere 500 meters from the shore of Glykys Limin. Koumasaki and Spilaion, if they indeed operated in concert with a Mycenaean trade mission, were situated directly on the shores of the bay, and signal the existence of functional specialization at certain sites, and craft specialists removed at least seasonally from subsistence pursuits. The fortified settlement at Kastriza, located in the floodplain of the Vouvos River valley just more than five kilometers from Ephyra, may have been a node articulating the coastal port to the products of the hinterland. Ports of trade, once established, often build their own subsidiary networks of supply and communication nodes (Curtin 1984, 6-11).

Role as a buffering and segregating entity

The physical separation of the two societies is most clearly manifest in the defensive walls that enclosed Ephyra, Kastriza, and possibly the settlement associated with the Kiperi tholos tomb. The risks perceived by both parties may be expressed in this monumental architecture, although we may speculate that crews of local laborers actually built the walls under the supervision of Mycenaean masons. Moreover, the circumscription of the Mycenaean community may be inferred from the limited coastal distribution of nonportable (i.e., architectural) elements of Mycenaean material culture. Ephyra in particular, and perhaps Glykys Limin as a whole, may be regarded as a buffer zone between the outward-focused activity in which Mycenaeans were engaged on the coast, and the native communities residing in the hinterland. It is difficult to know whether Glykys Limin was administered as a neutral zone, though the preponderance of local material suggests it may have been, or whether arrangements for judicial recourse were in place.

Administrative control

Outside of Ephyra, exotic or luxury items of Mycenaean type—imported pottery and bronze weapons and utilitarian objects—were deposited primarily in graves and hoards throughout Epirus, suggesting the circulation of such goods in a prestige sphere over which some measure of control was exercised. Obviously, luxury items lose their prestige if they are widely disseminated, and the restricted quantities and depositional contexts may reflect a deliberate strategy on the part of Mycenaean merchants and emerging local elites to maintain alliances through which the priorities discussed above might be pursued. The provisioning of everyday needs may have been effected in a parallel subsistence sphere; if both spheres did exist, local and foreign trade may have been kept largely separate.

In the port area, a certain level of control, or at least supervision, must be imputed to the Mycenaean community, notably in the mobilization of labor for commodity production and construction projects. In aboriginal subsistence economies, there is typically no labor available for the commodity market, with the result that colonizers must create this need (Gregory 1982, 118-29). One important aspect of the relationship between Mycenaean merchants and local elites may have involved arrangements for the release of persons to serve as craft specialists or laborers. The construction of the walls at Ephyra, Kastriza, and Ayia Eleni, and the tomb and wall at Kiperi, required the recruitment, by whatever means, of sizable crews of laborers under the direction of Mycenaean engineers and masons. Similarly, craftspersons for commodity production and personnel for the port facilities would have to be enlisted and supported.

Dynamic Processes and the Role of Conspicuous Consumption

In spite of the insights it offers, the static port of trade model fails to explain the process by which Glykys Limin was transformed over time from a seafarer's refuge to a maritime trading center. The development of the port of trade at Glykys Limin depended on the interaction of a multiplicity of external and internal forces, among which might be mentioned demand on the part of local elites and their counterparts in Mycenaean Greece, the elaboration of trade relations with other areas of the central Mediterranean, navigational conditions, piracy, and the interactive processes of conflict, adjustment, and accommodation between foreigners and natives. A dynamic model is required, and one that is especially suitable to the conditions of Bronze Age Mediterranean trade is that of conspicuous consumption, recently elucidated by Sherratt and Sherratt (1991). The Sherratts' model is informed principally by Sombart's (1967) notion of conspicuous consumption as an explanation for the origins of capitalism, as well as a body of archaeological theory and fieldwork that examines the role of emulation in the emergence of complex societies under exogenous influence (Flannery 1968; Tourtellot and Sabloff 1972; Renfrew 1975, 33).

According to this model, conspicuous consumption on the part of emerging local elites may cause a transformation of local society by what the Sherratts call a "contagious process." In the first instance, foreign traders effect gift exchanges with local leaders in order to mobilize desired products and the relationships necessary to ensure their uninterrupted flow. These leaders are recruited primarily to mobilize *commodity* production in what may be characterized as a non-commodity economy;[30] the gifts they receive bestow both prestige and practical advantage, placing them in an improved position to enlist the necessary labor and resources. Along with luxury items, the nascent elites acquire some of the values, and emulate some of the practices, of the foreign society. What begin as gifts may be transformed into commodities as demand and competition among emerging elites increase. But this demand may precede, or be "out of step" with, the local production of commodities for exchange. Elites face a double predicament: they are charged with furnishing goods and labor to fulfill obligations for gifts received, and simultaneously wish to satisfy their desire for practical and symbolic markers of personal power.

This dilemma may bring about a restructuring of the local economy to increase production of commodities (including labor power as a commodity: Gregory 1982, 116-62, esp. 118 ff.) that elites may exchange. The Sherratts envision a three-stage process (Sherratt and Sherratt 1991, 358): 1) initial provision of a few high-value, low-bulk manufactured goods (luxuries) to local leaders in exchange for high-value, low bulk raw materials (e.g., metals); 2) some transfer of lifestyle and technology to local elites, together with their participation in the form of high-value, low-bulk manufactured goods (e.g., leather goods); and 3) full linkage, involving the restructuring of agrarian production to provide bulk materials for local manufacturing processes, and full participation in complex bulk exchanges. The transition from the first to the second phase may involve a concentration of craft specialists without the mobilization of large rural surpluses. But the third phase can only be achieved through the restructuring of the economy to provide bulk raw materials for local manufacture, on a large scale, of commodities for exchange.

There is some evidence, though it is hardly conclusive, that such a transformation may have taken place in the lower Acheron region. The archaeological record from excavation and survey shows clearly that a suite of novel activities emerged in the latter stages of the Bronze Age from an essentially egalitarian subsistence-based society.

Taking first the evidence for Epirus as a whole, the deposition of luxury metals (bronze weapons, implements, and ornaments), ceramics, and other materials of Aegean type in hoards and burials indicates that consumption was limited to a minority that we may identify as elites. Epirus possesses a large quantity of bronze weapons relative to other regions on the periphery of the Mycenaean world, a remarkable fact that suggests that a high level of demand existed for these products. These observations point to the fulfillment of phases 1 and 2 of the Sherratts' scheme, though we can only guess at the high-value, low-bulk raw materials or manufactured products that Epirote leaders offered in exchange.[31]

The surface survey and landscape data are uniquely suited to address the attainment of the third phase, a restructuring of the economy for commodity production. The Cyclopean walls noted at several sites and the tholos tomb at Kiperi indicate unambiguously the reallocation of workers away from subsistence pursuits to corvée labor on a large scale. From the survey data, I have proposed a concentration of population and industrial activity around the shores of Glykys Limin, as well as expansion into previously marginal zones throughout the lower Acheron region. The voluminous remains of flint flakes and debitage at Koumasaki may represent large-scale production of a commodity such as cattle hides, and the sherd assemblage at Spilaion may mark the location of a storage or warehousing facility. Expansion into marginal zones may signal a effort to increase agricultural and pastoral production to supply food and raw material to the port of trade. If such interpretations are broadly valid (if not in every detail), they supply examples of a local transformation from a subsistence-based economy to one geared to commodity production, articulated directly to the Mycenaean trading settlement.

The conspicuous consumption model explains these changes in the archaeological record as correlates of an interactive sequence by which Epirotes and Mycenaeans accommodated one another, and ultimately, in a very limited coastal zone, achieved some measure of economic integration. An emphasis is placed upon the incentives of participants to engage in trade, and notably, on the social significance of trade. In the context of Mediterranean Bronze Age trade, exotic goods and technologies were desired for their ability to impart symbolic prestige or practical advantage, and were manipulated, hoarded, displayed, or dispatched to serve the desires of those who possessed them to constrain or mobilize social action. In the case of Mycenaean engagement in coastal Epirus, such exotic gifts may have set into motion a social and economic transformation, though this phenomenon did not long outlive the presence of Mycenaean merchants in the region.

Conclusions

In response to the rather unsophisticated treatment that Mycenaean engagement on the coast of southern Epirus has received, I have portrayed the region of Glykys Limin as a Mycenaean "trading colony" or "trading mission."[32] Making use of recently acquired archaeological and environmental data, I have applied two models, Polanyi's port of trade model and Sherratt and Sherratt's conspicuous consumption model, which I view as complementary rather than incompatible. Independently, neither is able to provide a complete picture, nor to make full use of the archaeological record. The static port of trade model elucidates spatial and structural attributes, while the dynamic conspicuous consumption model highlights the interactive and processual. Together, they provide a broad framework against which the archaeological evidence may be tested.

The interpretations offered here should be viewed with appropriate caution. The chronology of many of the surface sites, and for that matter most sites in Epirus, remains problematic. Until well-stratified Bronze Age sites are identified, excavated, and published, many of our interpretations must remain provisional. Nevertheless, I have attempted to show that by integrating static models such as the port of trade with dynamic ones such as that of conspicuous consumption, which emphasizes the social and economic implications of an interactive process, we move toward a framework in which the phenomenon of Mycenaean engagement among peripheral societies may be fruitfully studied. The application of such a framework to territories on the periphery of the Mycenaean world that are better documented than Epirus may produce especially interesting results.

NOTES

I would like to express my gratitude to Curtis Runnels, Jeremy B. Rutter, and David Tandy, all of whom read an earlier draft of this paper and provided numerous comments and suggestions. Their good advice has improved the final product greatly; yet the deficiencies that remain are solely my own. I am particularly grateful to the co-directors of the Nikopolis Project, James R. Wiseman, Angelika Douzougli, and Konstantinos Zachos, for their long-term support and encouragement. An early version of this paper was delivered at the 99th Annual Meeting of the Archaeological Institute of America in December 1997 in Chicago, Illinois.

1. The most important interpretive writings on this topic are by Kostas Soueref; see Soueref 1986, 157-82, and especially Soueref 1994.

2. 1.46.1-5; Strabo 7.7.5; Cassius Dio 50.12.2. In this paper I refer to the putative port of trade as Glykys Limin ("Fresh[water] Harbor") rather than by the name of Ephyra, the primary settlement, because the archaeological evidence suggests that the economic entity comprised several locations encircling the bay.

3. 1992; 1993; 1994. The Nikopolis Project was a collaboration of the 12th Ephoreia of Prehistoric and Classical Antiquities, the 8th Ephoreia of Byzantine Antiquities, and Boston University, and was sponsored by the American School of Classical Studies at Athens.

4. Polanyi further distinguished "primitive" from "archaic" nonmarket economies, the former typical of nonliterate societies organized mainly along kinship lines, the latter characterized by literacy and plow agriculture, but lacking the use of money as a usual means of commercial market exchange (Polanyi Mimeo no. 1, 11,

quoted by Dalton [1975, 81]). Dalton (1975, 71) uses the term "aboriginal" for economies in which price-making markets are not dominant.

5. For a brief overview of the development of Polanyi's opposition to formalist economics, see Pearson 1977. Although the "formalist-substantivist debate" is often characterized by strident rhetoric (e.g., LeClair 1962; Dalton 1975, 80-81), others see the disagreement as one of emphasis, and note the potential of applying the two approaches in combination (Humphreys 1978, 58 n. 108).

6. Polanyi had already developed this argument in *The Great Transformation* (1944); see Dalton and Köcke 1983, 24-26.

7. Dalton (1975, 92) prefers the term "modes of transaction."

8. These concepts have of course attained great currency among anthropologists and archaeologists, especially as modified by Sahlins (1965) and appropriated for evolutionary schemes (Sahlins and Service 1960; Earle 1977), in spite of Polanyi's (1957b, 256) insistence that forms of integration do not represent stages of development.

9. Polanyi had earlier discussed the port of trade in 1957b, 262-63. See also Polanyi 1957a; 1966; 1975, 151-53; Humphreys 1978, 53-56; Dalton 1978; Möller this volume.

10. Herodotus 4.196. Polanyi (1963, 33-35) also discusses at some length putative low-walled *emporia*—extramural meeting spots for traders usually sited on the coasts of rivers, lakes, or seas—in the prehistoric Mediterranean, for which the evidence is tenuous at best.

11. Polanyi 1963, 30. For a recent application of this idea, see Morris's (1994) contention that profits and competition were marginalized in classical Athens. It is worthy of note, as this comment demonstrates, that Polanyi does not deny that competition and profit-making behavior existed in archaic economies; rather, he maintains that economic activity was managed predominantly by administrative action.

12. Austin and Vidal-Naquet 1977, 66-68, 233-35; cf. Figueira 1984, 23-30, who argues that the application of the term to these sites is inconsistent and a distortion of Polanyi's theoretical position. But see Möller in this volume.

13. Among Finley's influential writings, see 1957a; 1957b; 1970; 1973; 1975; 1978. Tandy and Neale (1994) discuss in particular the application of Polanyi's ideas to ancient Greece by Finley, Tandy (1988), Donlan (1982; 1985; 1989), Redfield (1986), and Morris (1986a; 1986b), and point out (1994, 23) that Polanyi's contribution resides not in his own work on Greece, but in framing the debate between primitivists and modernists, and thus encouraging new analytical and interpretive perspectives on ancient economies.

14. Polanyi (1963) shows clearly the relationship between the port of trade and Polanyi's wider paradigm.

15. Torrence 1978, 109-11. In this, she acknowledges the value of Polanyi's concept, while at the same time aligning herself with the deductive approach that is closely associated with economic theory (see Cook 1966) and with the concern among processual archaeologists for comparison and generalization.

16. Curtin 1984, 63-70; Gledhill and Larsen 1982, 200-13. It should be noted that much of the scholarly work that transformed our perception of these economies was accomplished after Polanyi's death.

17. 1985, 252. Killen was influenced by Polanyi's thought through the work of Finley. Note that Killen (1984, 49 and n. 1) accepted the notion of a "non-market, non-money 'Asiatic' economy," a position at odds with that of many historians and archaeologists of the Near East; see above n. 16.

18. Halstead (1988) traces the development of ideas on the nature of the redistributive function of the palaces. Earle (1977, 215-18) identifies as many as four types of "redistributive" economic institutions.

19. The palace at Knossos controlled as many as 100,000 sheep in central Crete: Killen 1984, 49-51.

20. Bass 1991, with references to earlier bibliography on the shipwrecks. See also Knapp 1991.

21. Bass 1997. An important exception is the port of Kommos in southern Crete, which preserves a large quantity of objects imported from the Eastern Mediterranean in the fourteenth and thirteenth centuries B.C.E. (Cline 1994, 276-77, table 70; Knapp and Cherry 1994, 138-41; Rutter n.d.). I am grateful to Jeremy Rutter for this reminder.

22. Papadopoulos 1981a. These are three of the more common Mycenaean shapes. The alabastron is a low vessel with a restricted orifice, often with three small handles on the upper shoulder, which was designed to hold oil or perfume. The kylix is a stemmed drinking goblet, found primarily in domestic (though also ritual) contexts, which gained wide popularity particularly in palatial times. The stirrup jar is closed vessel with a true spout and a false spout supporting two handles, which was widely utilized to transport perfumed oil and other valued commodities around the Mediterranean.

23. Loader (1998, 38) does not recognize Ephyra's wall as a genuine example of Mycenaean Cyclopean masonry. But her definition is perhaps too restrictive to allow for provincial variation in construction techniques that may respond in part to local circumstances. Moreover, although the masonry of the circuit wall clearly does not fall into one of Loader's canonical categories, the construction of the South Gate at Ephyra is strongly Mycenaean in character, and it is difficult to propose an alternative source of inspiration for it.

24. Kilian 1986, 284 n 28 suggested the figure of 15%. Because the pottery from Ephyra has never been analyzed in a systematic way, this figure is nothing more than an educated guess. My own similarly unsystematic inspection of 43 excavation contexts produced an estimate of 8–13%.

25. This problem is a pervasive one: no Bronze Age site exists in Epirus with stratigraphic phasing.

26. Besonen 1997. Dakaris (1958, 110) had earlier offered, as proof of a wider ancient bay, a deep boring made near the site of Ephyra, in which a layer of sand and marine shells was discovered at 17.5–18.0 m below the modern surface. Since that layer was not dated, however, no timing for the marine transgression to that point, and thus no association with any particular archaeological phase, could be proposed.

27. These data are summarized and discussed in Tartaron 1996, 309-44.

28. For an example of the exploitation of offshore islands in the past, see Kardulias, Gregory, and Sawmiller 1995.

29. Many thanks to Curtis Runnels for calling my attention to Dana's work.

30. Gregory (1982) would call this an "indigenous" or "gift" economy.
31. Soueref 1994, 404-407 provides a list of resources that merchants may have sought in Epirus. Apart from hides as suggested here, there is now the evidence of a Middle–Late Bronze Age amber-processing workshop in Pogoni in northern Epirus (Andreou and Andreou 1996). This exciting discovery may confirm a long-suspected amber route that passed through northwestern Greece from central Europe.
32. Placing Glykys Limin in a typology of Mycenaean contacts around the Mediterranean is beyond the scope of the present paper, but see Kilian 1990 on the varied manifestations of Mycenaean presence.

BIBLIOGRAPHY

Andreou, Ilias. 1983. Tumbos kato Meropes. *Archaiologikon Deltion* 38:229-30.

———. 1984. Merope Pogoniou. *Archaiologikon Deltion* 39:177-78.

———. 1994. Nees proistorikes Theseis sten Epeiro. In Tzouvara-Souli, Vlachopoulou-Oikonomou, and Gravani-Katsiki 1994, 233-46.

Andreou, Ilias, and Ioanna Andreou. 1996. Un atelier de travail de l'ambre à Pogoni (Valée du Gormos, Épire). Paper presented at the 6th International Aegean Conference, Philadelphia, 18-21 April 1996.

Arnold, Rosemary. 1957. A port of trade: Whydah on the Guinea coast. In Polanyi, Arensberg, and Pearson 1957, 154-76.

Austin, M.M., and P. Vidal-Naquet.1977. *Economic and social history of ancient Greece: An introduction.* Berkeley: University of California Press.

Bass, George F. 1991. Evidence of trade from Bronze Age shipwrecks. In Gale 1991, 69-82.

———. 1997. Prolegomena to a study of maritime traffic in raw materials to the Aegean during the fourteenth and thirteenth centuries B.C. In *TEXNH: Craftsmen, craftswomen and craftsmanship in the Bronze Age Aegean,* edited by Robert Laffineur and Philip P. Betancourt, 153-70. *Aegaeum* 16. Liège: Université de Liège.

Besonen, Mark R. 1997. *The middle and late Holocene geology and landscape evolution of the lower Acheron River valley, Epirus, Greece.* M.A. Thesis, University of Minnesota, Duluth.

Bohannan, Paul. 1959. The impact of money on an African subsistence economy. *Journal of Economic History* 19:491-503.

———. 1960. Africa's land. *Centennial Review* 4: 439-49.

Cartledge, Paul. 1983. "Trade and politics" revisited: archaic Greece. In Garnsey, Hopkins, and Whittaker 1983, 1-15. Berkeley: University of California Press.

Chadwick, John. 1976. *The Mycenaean world.* Cambridge: Cambridge University Press.

Chapman, Anne C. 1957. Port of trade enclaves in Aztec and Maya civilizations. In Polanyi, Arensberg, and Pearson 1957, 114-153.

Cline, Eric H. 1994. *Sailing the wine-dark sea: International trade and the late Bronze Age Aegean.* BAR International Series 591. Oxford: B.A.R.

Cook, C. Scott. 1966. The obsolete 'anti-market' mentality: A critique of the substantivist approach to economic anthropology. *American Anthropologist* 68:323-45.

Curtin, Philip D. 1984. *Cross-cultural trade in world history*. Cambridge: Cambridge University Press.

Dakaris, Sotirios I. 1958. Anaskaphai Ereunai eis ten Omeriken Ephyran kai to Nekyomanteion tes archaias Thesprotias. *Praktika*:107-13.

———. 1960. Anaskaphe tou Nekyomanteiou tou Acherontos kai tholotou taphou plesion tes Pargas. *Praktika*:114-27.

———. 1963. Anaskaphe eis to Nekyomanteion tou Acherontos. *Praktika*:89-92.

Dakaris, Sotirios, and Athanasios Papadopoulos. 1976. Anaskaphe sten akropole tes Ephyras. *Praktika*:149-52.

Dalton, George. 1975. Karl Polanyi's analysis of long-distance trade and his wider paradigm." In *Ancient Civilization and Trade*, edited by Jeremy A. Sabloff and C.C. Lamberg-Karlovsky, 63-132. Albuquerque: University of New Mexico Press.

———. 1978. Comments on ports of trade in early medieval Europe. *Norwegian Archaeological Review* 11: 102-108.

———, ed. 1971. *Studies in economic anthropology*. Washington, D.C.: American Anthropological Association.

Dalton, George, and Paul Bohannan, eds. 1962. *Markets in Africa*. Evanston, Ill: Northwestern University Press.

Dalton, George, and Jasper Köcke. 1983. The work of the Polanyi group: Past, present and future." In *Economic anthropology: Topics and theories*, edited by Sutti Ortiz, 21-50. Lanham, Md.: University Press of America.

Dana, Richard Henry, Jr. 1964. *Two years before the mast*. Los Angeles: The Ward Ritchie Press.

Descoeudres Jean-Paul, ed. 1991. *Greek colonists and native populations*. Oxford: Clarendon Press.

Donlan, Walter. 1982. Reciprocities in Homer. *Classical World* 75:137-75.

———. 1985. The social groups of Dark Age Greece. *Classical Philology* 80:293-308.

———. 1989. The unequal exchange between Glaucus and Diomedes in light of the Homeric gift-economy. *Phoenix* 43.1:1–15.

Douzougli, Angelika. n.d. Koilada Aoou: Archailogikes marturies gia ten anthropine drasterioteta apo tous proistorikous chronous os ten ustere archaioteta. Paper presented at "He eparchia Konitsas sto choro kai sto chrono," Konitsa 12-14 May 1995.

Douzougli, Angelika, and Konstantinos Zachos. 1994. Archaiologikes ereunes sten Epeiro kai te Leukada: 1989-1990. *Epeirotika Chronika* 31:11-50.

Duncan, Colin A.M., and David W. Tandy, eds. *From political economy to anthropology: Situating economic life is past societies*. Montreal: Black Rose Books.

Earle, Timothy K. 1977. *How chiefs come to power: The political economy in prehistory*. Stanford, Cal.: Stanford University Press.

Figueira, Thomas J. 1984. Karl Polanyi and ancient Greek trade: The port of trade. *The Ancient World* 10:15-30.

Finley, Moses I. 1957a. The Mycenaean tablets and economic history. *Economic History Review* (series 2) 10:128-41.

———. 1957b. Homer and Mycenae: Property and tenure. *Historia* 6:133-59.

———. 1970. Aristotle and economic analysis. *Past and Present* 7:3-25.

———. 1973. *The ancient economy*. London: Chatto and Windus.

———. 1975. *The use and abuse of history*. New York: Viking.

———. 1978. *The world of Odysseus*. 2d rev. ed. New York: Penguin.

Flannery, Kent V. 1968. The Olmec and the valley of Oaxaca: A model for interregional interaction in formative times. In *Dumbarton Oaks conference on the Olmec*, edited by Elizabeth P. Benton, 79-110. Washington, D.C.: Dumbarton Oaks.

Gale, N.H., ed. 1991. *Bronze Age trade in the Mediterranean*. Jonsered: Paul Åströms Förlag.

Gallagher, James P. 1977. Contemporary stone tools in Ethiopia: Implications for archaeology. *Journal of Field Archaeology* 4:407-14.

Garnsey, Peter, Keith Hopkins, and C.R. Whittaker, eds. 1983, *Trade in the Ancient Economy*. Berkeley: University of California Press.

Geertz, Clifford. 1980. Ports of trade in nineteenth-century Bali. *Research in Economic Anthropology* 3:109-22.

Gill, David W.J. 1991. Pots and trade: Spacefillers or objets d'art? *Journal of Hellenic Studies* 111:29-47.

———. 1994. Positivism, pots and long-distance trade. In *Classical Greece: Ancient histories and modern archaeologies*, edited by Ian Morris, 99-107. Cambridge: Cambridge University Press.

Gledhill, John, and Mogens Larsen. 1982. The Polanyi paradigm and a dynamic analysis of archaic states. In *Theory and explanation in archaeology: The Southampton conference*, edited by Colin Renfrew, Michael J. Rowlands, and Barbara Abbott Segraves, 197-229. New York: Academic Press.

Graham, A.J. 1990. Pre-colonial contacts: Questions and problems. In Descoeudres 1990, 45-60.

Gregory, C.A.. 1982. *Gifts and commodities*. London: Academic Press.

Haldane, Cheryl. 1993. Direct evidence for organic cargoes in the late Bronze Age. *World Archaeology* 24:348-60.

Halstead, Paul. 1988. On redistribution and the origin of Minoan-Mycenaean palatial economies. In *Problems in Greek prehistory*, edited by E.B. French and K.A. Wardle, 519-30. Bristol: Bristol Classical Press.

Hodge, A. Trevor. 1983. Massalia, meteorology, and navigation. *Ancient World* 7(3–4):67-88.

Hodges, Richard. 1978. Ports of trade in early medieval Europe. *Norwegian Archaeological Review* 11:97-101.

Hope Simpson, Richard. 1981. *Mycenaean Greece*. Park Ridge, N.J.: Noyes Press.

Hopkins, Keith. 1983. Introduction. In Garnsey, Hopkins, and Whittaker 1983, ix–xxv.

Humphreys, S.C. 1978. *Anthropology and the Greeks*. London: Routledge and Kegan Paul.

Iakovidis, Spyros. 1989. *Gla: H anaskaphe 1955-1961*. Vivliotheke tes en Athenais Archaiologikes Hetaireias 107. Athens: He en Athenais Archaiologike Hetaireia.

Jansen, Anton. 1997. Bronze Age highways at Mycenae. *Echos du Monde Classique* 41 (n.s. 16):1-16.

Jones, R.E., and L. Vagnetti. 1991. Traders and craftsmen in the central Mediterranean: Archaeological evidence and archaeometric research. In Gale 1991, 127-47.

Kardulias, P. Nick, Timothy E. Gregory, and Jed Sawmiller. 1995. Bronze Age and late antique exploitation of an islet in the Saronic Gulf, Greece. *Journal of Field Archaeology* 22:3-21.

Kilian, Klaus. 1986. Il confine settentrionale della civiltà Micenea nella tardo Età del Bronzo. In *Traffici Micenei nel Mediteraneo: Problemi storici e documentazione archeologica: Atti del convegno di Palermo 1984*, edited by M. Marrazi, S. Tusa, and L. Vagnetti, 283-301. Taranto: Istituto per la storia e l'archeologia della Magna Graecia.

———. 1990. Mycenaean colonization: Norm and variety. In Descoeudres 1990, 445-67.

Killen, J.T. 1984. The textile industries at Pylos and Knossos. In *Pylos comes alive: Industry and administration in a Mycenaean palace*, edited by Cynthia Shelmerdine and Thomas G. Palaima, 49-63. New York: Archaeological Institute of America.

———. 1985. The Linear B Tablets and the Mycenaean Economy. In *Linear B: A 1984 survey*, edited by Anna Morpurgo-Davies and Yves Duhoux, 241-305. Louvain-la-Neuve: Cabay.

Knapp, A. Bernard. 1991. *Spice, drugs, grain and grog: Organic goods in Bronze Age east Mediterranean trade*. In Gale 1991, 21-68.

Knapp, A. Bernard, and John F. Cherry. 1994. *Provenience studies and Bronze Age Cyprus: Production, exchange and politico-economic change*. Madison, Wisc.: Prehistory Press.

Lavery, John. 1995. Some "new" Mycenaean roads at Mycenae. *Bulletin of the Institute of Classical Studies* 40:264-67.

LeClair, Edward E., Jr. 1962. Economic theory and economic anthropology. *American Anthropologist* 64:1179-1203.

Leeds, A. 1961. The port-of-trade in pre-European India as an ecological and evolutionary type. In *Proceedings of the 1961 annual Spring meeting of the American Ethnological Society*, 26-48. Seattle: American Ethnological Society.

Loader, N. Claire. 1998. *Building in Cyclopean masonry*. Studies in Mediterranean Archaeology and Literature PB-148. Jonsered: Paul Åströms Förlag.

Mee, Christopher. 1982. *Rhodes in the Bronze Age*. Warminster: Aris and Phillips.

Morris, Ian. 1986a. Gift and commodity in archaic Greece. *Man* 21:1-17.

———. 1986b. The use and abuse of Homer. *Classical Antiquity* 5:81-138.

———. 1994. The community against the market in classical Athens. In Duncan and Tandy 1994, 52-79.

Neale, Walter C. 1971. Monetization, commercialization, market orientation, and market dependence. In *Studies in economic anthropology*, edited by George Dalton, 25-29. Washington, D.C.: American Anthropological Association.

Papadopoulos, Thanasis. 1978. Anaskaphe Ephyras. *Praktika* 107.

———. 1979. Anaskaphe Ephyras. *Praktika* 119-20.

———. 1980. Anaskaphe Ephyras. *Praktika* 44.

———. 1981a. Das Mykenische Kuppelgrab von Kipari bei Parga (Epirus). *Mitteilungen des Deutschen Archäologischen Instituts, Athenische Abteilung* 96:7-24.

———. 1981b. Anaskaphe Ephyras. *Praktika* 78.

———. 1982. Anaskaphe Ephyras. *Praktika* 89-90.

———. 1983. Anaskaphe Ephyras. *Praktika* 81-82.

———. 1984. Ephyra. *Ergon* 45-46.

———. 1986. Anaskaphe Ephyras. *Praktika* 101-102.

———. 1987a. Anaskaphe Ephyras. *Praktika* 125.

———. 1987b. To problema ton exoterikon scheseon tes proistorikes Epeirou ste 2e chilietia p. Chr. *Dodone* 16(I):159-64.

———. 1990. Settlement types in prehistoric Epirus. In *L'habitat Égéen préhistorique*, edited by Pascal Darcque and René Treuil, 359-67. Athens: École Française d'Athènes.

Pearson, Harry W. 1977. Editor's introduction. In Karl Polanyi, *The livelihood of man*, edited by Harry W. Pearson, xxv-xxxvi. New York: Academic Press.

Polanyi, Karl, 1944. *The great transformation*. New York: Holt Rinehart.

———. 1957a. Marketless trading in Hammurabi's time. In Polanyi, Arensberg, and Pearson 1957, 12-26.

———. 1957b. The economy as instituted process. In Polanyi, Arensberg, and Pearson 1957, 243-70.

———. 1960. On the comparative treatment of economic institutions in antiquity, with illustrations from Athens, Mycenae, and Alalakh. In *City invincible: A symposium on urbanization and cultural development in the ancient Near East*, edited by Carl H. Kraeling and Robert M. Adams, 329-50. Chicago: University of Chicago Press.

———. 1963. Ports of trade in early societies. *Journal of Economic History* 23:30-45.

———. 1966. *Dahomey and the slave trade: An analysis of an archaic economy*. Seattle: University of Washington Press.

———. 1975. Traders and trade. In Sabloff and Lamberg-Karlovsky 1975, 133-54.

Polanyi, Karl, Conrad M. Arensberg, and Harry W. Pearson, eds. 1957. *Trade and market in the early empires: Economies in history and theory*. Glencoe, Ill: Free Press.

Redfield, James M. 1986. The development of the market in archaic Greece. In *The market in history*, edited by B.L. Anderson and A.J.H. Latham, 29–58. London: Croom Helm.

Renfrew, Colin, 1975. Trade as action at a distance: Questions of integration and communication. In Sabloff and Lamberg-Karlovsky 1975, 3–59.

Revere, Robert B. 1957. "No man's coast": Ports of trade in the eastern Mediterranean. In Polanyi, Arensberg, and Pearson 1957, 38–63.

Rutter, Jeremy B. n.d. Cretan external relations during LM IIIA2–B (ca. 1370-1200 B.C.): A view from the Mesara.

Sabloff, Jeremy A., and C.C. Lamberg-Karlovsky, eds. 1975. *Ancient civilization and trade.* Albuquerque: University of New Mexico Press.

Sahlins, Marshall D. 1965. On the sociology of primitive exchange. In *The relevance of models for social anthropology,* edited by Max Gluckman and Fred Eggan, 139–236. London: Tavistock.

———.1972. *Stone age economics.* Chicago: Aldine-Atherton.

Sahlins, Marshall D., and Elman R. Service. 1960. *Evolution and culture.* Ann Arbor: University of Michigan Press.

Shelmerdine, Cynthia W. 1997. The palatial Bronze Age of the southern and central Greek mainland. *American Journal of Archaeology* 101:537-85.

Shennan, Stephen. 1993. Commodities, transactions, and growth in the central-European early Bronze Age. *Journal of European Archaeology* 1.2:59-71.

Sherratt, Andrew, and Susan Sherratt. 1991. From luxuries to commodities: The nature of Mediterranean Bronze Age trading systems. In Gale 1991, 351-86.

Smith, Thyrza R. 1987. *Mycenaean trade and interaction in the west central Mediterranean 1600-1000 B.C.* BAR International Series 371. Oxford: B.A.R.

Snodgrass, A.M. 1991. Bronze Age exchange: A minimalist position. In Gale 1991, 15-20.

Sombart, Werner. 1967. *Luxury and capitalism.* Ann Arbor: University of Michigan Press.

Soueref, Kostas I., 1986. *Mykenaikes marturies apo ten Epeiro.* Ph.D. diss., University of Thessaloniki.

———. 1994. Eisagoge sten protoistoria tes N. Adriatikes kai tou B. Ioniou. In Tzouvara-Souli, Vlachopoulou-Oikonomou, and Gravani-Katsiki 1994, 221-31.

Tandy, David W. 1988. *"Never any good": Changing forms of economic integration in Hesiod's world.* Occasional paper of the Karl Polanyi Institute of Political Economy. Montreal: Karl Polanyi Institute.

Tandy, David W., and Walter C. Neale. 1994. "Karl Polanyi's distinctive approach to social analysis and the case of ancient Greece: Ideas, criticisms, consequences. In Duncan and Tandy 1994, 9-33.

Tartaron, Thomas F. 1996. *Bronze Age settlement and subsistence in southwestern Epirus, Greece.* Ph.D. diss., Boston University.

Tartaron, Thomas F., Curtis Runnels, and Evangelia Karimali, 1999. Prolegomena to the study of Bronze Age flaked stone in southern Epirus. In *Meletemata: Studies presented to Malcolm H. Wiener,* edited by Philip Betancourt, Vassos Karageorghis, Robert Laffineur, and Wolf-Dietrich Niemeier, 819-24. *Aegaeum* 20. Liège: Université de Liège.

Torrence, Robin, 1978. Comments on ports of trade in early medieval Europe. *Norwegian Archaeological Review* 11:108-11.

Tourtellot, Gair, and Jeremy A. Sabloff. 1972. Exchange systems among the ancient Maya. *American Antiquity* 37:126-35.

Tzouvara-Souli, Chryseis, A. Vlachopoulou-Oikounomou, and K. Gravani-Katsiki, eds. 1994. *Phegos: Timatikos tomos gia ton kathegete Sotere Dakare.* Ioannina: University of Ioannina.

Ventris, Michael, and John Chadwick. 1973 [1956]. *Documents in Mycenaean Greek.* 2d ed. Cambridge: Cambridge University Press.

Vokotopoulou, Ioulia. 1969. Neoi kivotioschemoi taphoi tes YE IIIB-G periodou ex' Epeirou. *Archaiologike Ephemeris* 179-207.

Wardle, Kenneth A., 1972. *The Greek Bronze Age west of the Pindus.* Ph.D. diss., University of London.

———. 1977. Cultural groups of the late Bronze Age and early Iron Ages in north-west Greece. *Godisnjak* 15:153-99.

———. 1993. Mycenaean trade and influence in northern Greece. In *Wace and Blegen: Proceedings of the international conference "Pottery as evidence of trade in the Aegean Bronze Age, 1939-1989,"* edited by Carol Zerner, Peter Zerner, and John Winder, 117-41. Amsterdam: J.C. Gieben.

Wells, Berit, Curtis Runnels, and Eberhard Zangger. 1990. The Berbati-Limnes archaeological survey: The 1988 season. *Opuscula Atheniensia* 18.15:207-38.

Wiseman, James R. 1992. Archaeology and remote sensing in the region of Nikopolis, Greece. *Context* 9(3–4):1-6.

———. 1993. Harbors, towns, and prehistory: Survey and field school in Greece. *Context* 11(1–2):1-4.

———. 1994. *Nikopolis newsletter no. 4.* Boston: Center for Archaeological Studies, Boston University.

Chapter Two

BRIDGING THE GAP: THE CONTINUITY OF GREEK AGRICULTURE FROM THE MYCENAEAN TO THE HISTORICAL PERIOD

Ruth Palmer

Introduction

The period between 1400 and 700 B.C.E. in Greece is considered the time of the most extreme changes in social organization, economy and population size. It begins with Mycenaean palace control over territories and their resources, and then the destruction of the palaces and their redistributive system ca. 1200; it continues with slow impoverishment, loss of population and simpler social structure in the Dark Age, and ends by 700 with population growth, development of a market economy, the emergence of the *polis* and the spread of the Greek alphabet. The differences in social structure and economy between the beginning and end of this period seem extreme because of the lack of information about the Dark Age. Changes in population are inextricably linked with changes in agricultural strategies,[1] and here again, the control held by the Mycenaean palaces over agricultural products in the redistributive system is contrasted with the citizen farmers of the *polis*, raising crops for market exchange. The reconstruction of ancient agriculture at all levels of society is difficult, even when there is a good body of information from textual and archaeological sources. It is necessary to look at the range of strategies available to individual farming households for scheduling, producing and circulating crops and livestock within society. However, most of the information about agricultural strategies comes from texts that focus on elite production and consumption, not about the small farmers that made up the bulk of the population at all periods.

The most widely accepted view at present of the changes in the agricultural economy between the Mycenaean and the historical period emphasizes the differences between the two periods, and does not consider what elements continued. According to this view, Mycenaean palaces were rich because of their manipulation of different aspects of the economy, in particular specialized grain and wool production. When the palaces were destroyed, the economic and social disruption and severe depopulation were so great that the survivors were forced to develop pastoralism as a new subsistence strategy (Snodgrass 1980, 21-36; 1987, 193-208). Consequently small sites and pastoralism characterize the Dark Ages, and meat makes up the main portion of the diet, as depicted in Homer's epics. Population growth and Hesiod's *Works and Days* mark the (re)development of grain agriculture. Recent works accept with few questions the pastoralism model, and its implied contrast to Mycenaean agriculture.[2] But the discontinuity between Mycenaean agriculture and Dark Age pastoralism does not take into account the nature of the Mediterranean mixed farming tradition which began in Greece in the Early Neolithic. The staple crops and animals have remained the same until the modern period, with the introduction of additional crops from the New World.

How did this model of the change from arable farming to pastoralism to arable farming develop? It is formulated from a number of hypotheses derived from different traditions of scholarship, and has been developing for nearly fifty years, in response to the decipherment of the Linear B script in 1952, and the first formal presentation of the information in the tablets in 1953 (Ventris and Chadwick 1953). In particular, the view illustrates the great divide between the study of the Bronze Age material, and the Classical material. In this paper, I shall present briefly the works from the 1950s to the 1990s which have dealt with aspects of the Bronze and/or Dark Age agricultural economy, and point out the factors emphasized in each work. I shall pay particular attention to how Karl Polanyi's theories of redistribution, reciprocity and market exchange have been incorporated into the view. It is also illustrative to see how Polanyi himself handled the problem of interpreting the Linear B evidence to reveal some sort of economic construct, since the approach he took was not that of the theoretical archaeologists. Then I will present my view of Mycenaean agriculture as interpreted from the Linear B texts, and address the place of pastoralism in the context of the Greek agricultural system, and the nature of the evidence used to support the dominance of pastoralism in the Dark Age.

History of the Model

Since the 1950s, the approaches taken to study Late Bronze Age Greece, and the close parallels of the Linear B economic records with Near Eastern palace records, rather than Homeric or Classical economy and society, have accentuated the differences between Mycenaean and Classical Greece. Bronze Age and Classical scholars differed greatly over approaches to their subjects; while Bronze Age scholars were quick to apply the system theories devised by the New Archaeology, Classical scholars still used a positivist, text-based approach. Moreover, the similarities between Mycenaean and Near Eastern monarchies made the Mycenaeans seem not truly Greek. In the eyes of scholars, the Dark Age then marked a fresh start for the Greeks, enabling them to reject Eastern despotism, and create the *polis*.

Before 1952, the Mycenaean culture had been synonymous with the Homeric picture of society in the epics, as is shown by works such as Hilda Lorimer's *Homer and the Monuments*. In his initial excavation report for Pylos, Carl Blegen confidently identified the newly excavated palace as belonging to the legendary King Nestor (Blegen 1939, 576), and entitled his later preliminary excavation reports, and final publication, *The Palace of Nestor*, thus firmly tying Homeric legend to Mycenaean culture. In their initial 1953 article demonstrating the language of Linear B as Greek, and then in their 1956 book, *Documents in Mycenaean Greek*, Michael Ventris and John Chadwick showed the close connections of Linear B words to Homeric vocabulary, and cited many passages from the epics to illustrate the possible economic contexts of classes of tablets. But in many cases, the closest parallels to the information in the tablets were drawn from Near Eastern and Egyptian administrative texts. In *Documents*, Ventris and Chadwick did not aim to present a synthesis of the economic system. However, Moses Finley, in his 1957 review of *Documents*, labeled the economy shown by the tablets as "Asiatic," based on redistribution of goods, and implied that the palace owned or somehow controlled all the resources listed. He then contrasted it with gift exchange (reciprocity) as practiced in the Homeric poems, and the "market-oriented" world of the Archaic poleis, where citizen farmers who owned their own land formed the core of the *polis* (Finley 1957, 205-206, 211; 1954, 63-71). Thus Finley was the first to call the Mycenaean economy "redistributive."

Finley did not specifically address the issue of agricultural production. But Thalia Howe's 1958 article, entitled "Linear B and Hesiod's Breadwinners," compared Mycenaean agriculture as she reconstructed it from the tablets discussed in *Documents* and the archaeological evidence collected by Kenton Vickery (1936) with Hesiod's instructions about grain agriculture. According to her view, Mycenaean diet involved mainly meat with herbed sauces, vegetables and olive oil; and grains were not staple foods. This meat-intensive diet was also the diet of the Dorians, "flock-breeding nomads" (Howe 1958, 55). The focus of her argument was upon the didactic nature of Hesiod's *Works and Days*, and by contrasting the Mycenaean range of foods with Hesiod's emphasis on grain farming, she sought to prove that intensive grain farming was new to Geometric Greece.

Finley had drawn the term "redistributive" from the work of his colleague Polanyi. Polanyi himself wrote about the Mycenaean economy only once, in his 1960 article, "On the Comparative Treatment of Economic Institutions in Antiquity with Illustrations from Athens, Mycenae and

Alalakh" (Polanyi 1960 [=1968, 306-34]). In the first four pages, he introduced the theoretical framework of reciprocity, redistribution and exchange, and their embeddedness in political and religious institutions. He also mentions a fourth pattern, "householding," i.e., how a peasant economy or manorial estate is run, "though formally this is actually redistribution on a smaller scale" (1960, 330; 1968, 307-308). This indicates that when Polanyi uses the terms reciprocity, redistribution or exchange, he is referring to the application of these systems to the highest levels of society (1957, 253-54 [=1968, 153-54]). "Householding," however, refers to *oikonomia*, or self-sufficiency at the level of the *oikos* (Polanyi 1944, 53-54), and describes the strategies of production and consumption for all households, from the smallest small farmer or tenant, to the royal estate. In the remainder of the 1960 article, he investigated the ways in which Mycenaean palaces could operate without money or equivalencies of exchange, through staple finance (1960, 340-46; 1968, 321-28), but did not try to demonstrate the relationships of the various items collected to agricultural production as a whole.

Meanwhile, archaeological investigations had uncovered much more material dating to the Mycenaean period, and the Dark Age. In the 1960s, extensive site surveys showed that in the thirteenth century B.C.E., the number of settlements was exceptionally high, but from the twelfth century until the ninth, there was a great drop in the population (Hope Simpson 1965, McDonald and Hope Simpson 1972). Then Anthony Snodgrass in his ground-breaking 1971 book *The Dark Age of Greece* proved that the disruption of Mycenaean culture at the end of the thirteenth century was not due to invaders such as the Dorians (as had been the accepted interpretation) because the material culture showed essential continuity from the Mycenaean period through the Dark Age. He discussed how, from the twelfth through the eighth centuries, each region of Greece developed differently, some keeping in contact with Cyprus and the East longer than others, so there was no uniform response to depopulation and lack of resources. He linked the depopulation with the destruction of the palaces and disruption of trade, as a symptom of economic disaster; initial depopulation would lead to lower standards of agriculture, and consequently decreased production, even though natural resources were still available (Snodgrass 1971, 365-67). In *The Dark Age of Greece*, Snodgrass characterized Mycenaean agriculture as predominantly pastoral, based on the evidence of the stockbreeding tablets from Knossos, the bone material, and Howe's reconstruction of Mycenaean agriculture; he postulated that stockbreeding continued to be the focus of agriculture from the Mycenaean period through the Dark Age until the time of Hesiod, when population pressure forced a change to arable farming and grains as staple foods (Snodgrass 1971, 378-79). Thus in his initial presentation of the changes between the Mycenaean period and the Dark Age, he thought that the agricultural system continued unchanged into the Dark Age.

In 1972, Colin Renfrew published *The Emergence of Civilisation*, a major work which systematically investigated the evidence for the development of complex society in the Aegean, in terms of interlocking models based in part on Polanyi's models of redistribution, reciprocity and exchange (Renfrew 1972, 296-97, 461-62). Renfrew was a major proponent of New Archaeology, introducing anthropological models to test how cultures worked as systems. He looked specifically at the interconnection of subsistence agriculture in Greece, from the Neolithic to the Late Bronze Age, with the growing complexity of society culminating in the redistribution practiced by the Mycenaean palaces. He showed that the crops and animals traditionally raised by farmers since the Early Bronze Age have remained the same up to the present, and that diversity was the hallmark of Mediterranean mixed farming (298-302). Grains were always the main source of nutrition in the Mycenaean diet while livestock played a minor role as food; rather they were sources of wool, milk and traction. The main change from the Neolithic to the Bronze Age was in the organization of specialized production according to micro-ecosystems. In such a system, the elite in each territory would oversee the distribution of specialized crops from the various micro-ecosystems through collection and redistribution (462, 482); he implied that the elite would also dictate what crops would be produced in which area, and ultimately control both land and labor.

Renfrew used the consensus view of the Mycenaean palaces as controlling the redistribution of all resources within a territory, as a starting point to explain the development of this complex society from the beginning of the Bronze Age. But except for a few specific references, he did not employ the Linear B tablets in his reconstruction of the Mycenaean economy. He did not discuss land-tenure or the work force, beyond a mention of "semi-free" workers who do not receive meat as rations (303). Nor is there any mention of the economic disruption after the destruction of the palaces, or what agricultural practices took place in the Dark Age, because the book ends with the Mycenaean period. The strength of *Emergence of Civilisation* lies in its incorporation of a wide variety of material evidence into models of development that emphasize interconnection between systems. Renfrew succeeded in demonstrating how redistribution *might* have developed from the Early Bronze Age, based upon control of agricultural resources on a local level. Most importantly, he showed the interconnection between crops produced in the traditional subsistence system, and their movement in the redistribution system. One effect of his work was to identify firmly that the Mycenaean economy was palace directed, and so completely different from the Classical *polis* with its market economy.

The lack of a synthetic overview showing how the classes of Linear B tablets illustrate different aspects of the palatial administrative system was remedied by J.T. Killen's article "The Linear B Tablets and the Mycenaean Economy." Killen followed Finley in calling Mycenaean economy "Asiatic" and in emphasizing the importance of the palace to the whole economy (Killen 1985, 241, 258-59), with the implication that the palace dictated the type of produce to be raised on certain plots of land (246-48). Thus Killen supported Renfrew's view that the Mycenaean agricultural economy was primarily redistributive, and directed from above.

Meanwhile, in his 1980 and 1987 books, *Archaic Greece: The Age of Experiment*, and *An Archaeology of Greece*, Snodgrass had been refining his view of a pastoral Dark Age economy. Discounting Howe's hypothesis that the Mycenaean diet was primarily meat based, Dark Age reliance on pastoralism now signified another major break with the Mycenaean period: "the Mycenaean economy at any rate was a mixed one, in which cultivation played an important part. The pastoral phase, if real, would have to be seen as an interlude that began in the post-Mycenaean age." (1987, 198). And so pastoralism and its accompanying pattern of land use, tribal social organization, and strong regional diversity are all seen as reactions against the previous Mycenaean pattern of palatial control of agriculture, and a uniform culture at the elite level (1980, 27, 35). Nor did the early *polis* develop directly from the Mycenaean town, "which is hardly surprising since the process which had begun in the Neolithic age and reached its final stage in the Mycenaean town had suffered a total interruption." (1980, 29-31). The high rate of depopulation left plenty of good land for the survivors, and pastoralism provided a way to maintain a claim to and use of a territory. Also, Homer speaks of stockrearing as a major form of wealth, and a staple of the diet (1980, 35). Snodgrass sought to explain certain aspects of Dark Age archaeological material, such as short-lived settlements, the memory of place-names for no-longer occupied sites, and the control of large territories as signs of a primarily pastoral economy; animal figurines from Olympia and other sanctuaries, fodder crops in Thessaly and cattle bones at Nichoria all suggest emphasis on animal husbandry (1980, 26-27, 35; 1987, 193-207). If pastoralism characterizes a period of low population, then the increase in population shown in the cemeteries and the appearance of "granary" models in graves from the ninth century on, and instructions in Hesiod's *Works and Days* on how to build a plow, and plant grain, must mark a return to intensive grain agriculture, and the rise of the citizen-farmer. Snodgrass's view was accepted by Classical scholars because it incorporated both the textual and the archaeological evidence into a tripartite system—Mycenaean (Linear B), Dark Age (Homer), and Archaic Greece (Hesiod), and postulated changes from grain farming (controlled by the palaces) to herding (controlled by by primitive tribal chiefs) to grain farming (controlled by the citizen-farmer) for all Greece.

Snodgrass's model of Dark Age economy and society has become widely accepted and incorporated into the basic handbooks (although probably not for the reasons he intended[3]) because it is essentially text-based, and so acceptable to Classicists and historians in general, and has the advantage of incorporating the archaeological material in a plausible manner. It also carries the same ideological overtones as the theory of the primitive, nomadic (i.e., pastoral) Dorians causing the overthrow of the highly civilized Mycenaean kingdoms; pastoralists are seen as uncivilized and bad while sedentary grain farmers are the bulwark of civilized life, and so good (Cherry 1988, 29-30; cf. the portrait of Polyphemos the monster-shepherd in *Odyssey* 9). Even though Dorians are discounted and replaced by post-Mycenaean pastoralists (however blameless of the destruction of Mycenaean civilization the pastoralists may be) the sequence of civilized to uncivilized to civilized continues as valid. The greatest flaw in Snodgrass's model is that there is never any attempt to illustrate the connection between crop cultivation and stockraising in Greek agriculture, beyond stating that most forms of animal husbandry are only effective in a context of the wider mixed farming tradition (Snodgrass 1987, 193). The widespread acceptance of this model of pastoral economy also accentuates the great divide between prehistorians, who have adopted Polanyi's tripartite modes of economy and regularly use analogies from other cultures to explain cultural processes, and Classicists who are firmly set in a descriptive text-based tradition. This is ironic because Polanyi's models are best applied to cultures with a large corpus of historical and/or economic texts, such as Mesopotamia or Classical Greece, rather than Mycenaean Greece.

Because of the widespread acceptance of Snodgrass's view of discontinuity between Mycenaean and Archaic agricultural practices, most studies on Classical agriculture and land use, even those which use anthropological parallels, ignore Polanyi, and consider agriculture in the Mycenaean period as irrelevant to their subject (e.g. Burford 1993, 11-12;

Osborne 1987, 57). Mycenaean society was seen as too hierarchical, the economy based on redistribution and dictated by the palaces, the destructions too complete and the methods of analysis too different, to be included in analyses of Classical agricultural systems, even if a degree of continuity from the Mycenaean period might be postulated (Isager and Skydsgaard 1992, 19-20). In fact, the redistribution system as practiced by the Mycenaean palaces is seen as alien to the Classical ethos of the citizen-farmer. Victor Hanson, in his discussion of farming traditions, compares the Mycenaean administration of agriculture to collectivized farming in modern authoritarian regimes (1995, 29-30). Instead, the study of agriculture in the historical period has used primarily literary and epigraphic sources rather than bone and plant analysis, or site survey, and has been tied to questions about the development of the *polis*, and relationships between different classes of citizens (Isager and Skydsgaard 1992; Burford 1993). To some extent, the apparent discontinuity between Mycenaean and *polis* agriculture is due to the reluctance of Classical scholars to deal with Bronze Age evidence, and the tendency of Bronze Age scholars to consider only the elite administrators rather than the actual producers of agricultural goods. It is time to look at the evidence for Mycenaean agriculture and Dark Age pastoralism as different aspects of traditional Greek mixed farming, in terms of self-sufficiency, availability of land and labor, and social status.

Development of the Mixed Farming System

Of the scholars discussed above who contributed to the consensus views of Mycenaean and Dark Age agriculture, only Renfrew really discussed the Mediterranean farming tradition, and its aim of self-sufficiency through diversification. In his view, an emerging elite oversaw specialized production of various crops and animals in suitable ecological niches, and coordinated redistribution of the products. In the 1970s and 1980s, several scholars interested in reconstructing ancient subsistence agriculture from material remains and ethnoarchaeological parallels, were particularly interested in analyzing farming in terms of risk management through diversity of crops and animals raised. The types and amounts of crops and animals raised depend upon the availability of land and labor. Paul Halstead in particular has focused upon how the Minoan and Mycenaean palace economy could have developed from the mixed farming tradition, and how the palace administration interacted with traditional subsistence farmers (see especially Halstead 1989, 1992a, 1992b).

The mixed farming tradition which developed first in the early Neolithic involves a range of crops—wheat, barley and legumes, perennial tree crops (such as fig and olive trees and vines, first domesticated in the Early Bronze Age), and herd animals (sheep, goats, cattle, and pigs by the Late Neolithic, and horses and donkeys by the Early Bronze Age), as well as wild resources. Barley and wheat always formed the largest component in the diet. Barley was more common than wheat because it could grow on poorer land, and was hardier; but wheat was considered more valuable than barley, although liable to greater crop failure. Legumes and pulses needed more weeding than grains, but replenished the soil with nitrogen, and could be a major source of protein and carbohydrates for humans and animals. Animal husbandry complements arable farming, because through livestock, humans can exploit not only uncultivated land, but also otherwise useless agricultural residue, such as weeds on fallow land, stubble from harvested fields, prunings from trees and vines, vineyards after harvest, and the residue from oil pressing (Forbes 1995, 329). Their manure could fertilize the fields, and they would provide meat, milk, hides or wool, and in the case of cattle and horses, transport and traction (Halstead 1981, 314-15, 319). In Neolithic Greece, when land was plentiful, labor was the deciding factor in crop and animal husbandry. Subsistence farmers would look for land where they could raise a variety of both crops and animals in the same area with the lowest possible labor input. Land suited to crops is ideal for pasturing animals too. When population density grew, then the amount of labor needed to grow sufficient food from the same land also increased. Only then would herding be restricted on arable land, and relegated to areas not suited to cultivation (Fotiadis 1985, 72-86).

Therefore, from the Early Neolithic, small scale animal husbandry for meat and hides complemented plant cultivation. The Late Neolithic is characterized by population growth, exploitation of sheep and goats for wool and milk, and cattle for traction. With the development of the ox-drawn plow, a greater area of land could be cultivated by one household, creating grazing for herds when fallow, and fodder if planted in pulses. But cattle require large quantities of fodder and water, so only those households with access to good grazing or land to spare for fodder crops could afford cattle. Stephen Hodkinson suggests that in the Classical period, a household needed to possess at least five hectares (12-13 acres) of land for there to be enough return to offset the maintenance cost of oxen. Farmers with smaller plots might cultivate them with a hoe, and not leave half the land in fallow (1988, 39). Such farmers with little land had to put proportionally more of their effort into growing staple grains, while households with more land could invest more labor and land in animal husbandry, and from the Early Bronze Age, orchard husbandry. The surplus generated by the larger household could be given to other households in need, as a form of reciprocity which Halstead calls social storage, thereby incurring the obligation to repay with future produce, or labor. This could lead to an imbalance in exchanges of resources, culminating in a hierarchical society with a network of obligations (Halstead 1989, 77-78), which would be expressed in a patron-client or landlord-tenant relationship, where redistribution of goods is governed by status. In periods of low population density, enough land would be available for all households, resulting in non-intensive use of arable land, and equal access to non-cultivated land. To accommodate a growing population, more land would be brought under cultivation, and farmed intensively, where the amount of labor per unit of land increases (see Halstead 1992a, 109 for overlapping definitions of "intensification" in agriculture). Intensive cultivation allows a holder to produce more per unit of land, but the increased yield never matches the extra labor, and can exhaust the land. With greater competition for land, some of the poorer households would become increasingly obligated to the wealthier households, and would lose both land

and labor to them (Bintliff 1982, 107-108 and n. 5). A few wealthier households would then control a disproportionate amount of the cultivated land, and have the labor to exploit the uncultivated periphery more extensively with large flocks. The majority of the farming households would aim for self-sufficiency through mixed farming, but due to the lack of land, and to labor owed to their patrons, they would be unable to achieve it fully. The Archaic and Classical *polis* system was based upon citizen farmers practicing exactly this kind of mixed farming, where the large flocks were owned by those richest in land (Hodkinson 1988, 46-47; Skydsgaard 1988, 81). Yet the question of the transmission of this farming system through the Dark Age has been ignored by scholars or discussed only in terms of literary evidence such as *Works and Days*.

Interpretation of the Linear B Texts

The Linear B tablets are extremely important to the reconstruction of the Mycenaean economy because they deal with ways of manipulating archaeologically invisible resources, grain, flax, wool, livestock, spices, even people, which never could have been discovered through excavation alone. But because the Linear B tablets are temporary records, covering a period of less than a year, they simply do not provide enough data (compared to equivalent Near Eastern or Classical Greek texts) to reconstruct fully the workings of the palatial economic system. Data from excavations, and most importantly from ethnoarchaeology, can provide some ideas about aspects of the Mycenaean economy which are not overtly mentioned in the Linear B texts. The palaces practiced a form of redistribution called mobilization, where the goods collected by the palace were not usually redistributed to the towns and villages, but used by palace personnel (Morris 1986, 29-31; Tandy 1997, 104-105). However the population providing the goods would feel satisfied that the palaces would provide suitable intercession with the gods through public rituals, protection from attack, and disaster relief.

The information on the clay tablets is very one-sided, since they only record assessment, collection and distribution of resources of interest to the palace. In a few rare instances, such as the Pylos landholding tablets which mention the *da-mo* (*demos* in later Greek), the tablets show social and economic organization on a local level. Intensive site survey has begun to reveal the settlement pattern of Mycenaean Greece, but the tendency is to identify the places listed on the tablets with the sites found. Furthermore, when information from palace records is used in conjunction with archaeological material such as carbonized plants or animal bone, it tends to overwhelm any alternative economic interpretations which might focus on the archaeological data alone. The reconstruction of patterns of production and consumption in the Mycenaean period is so dependent upon the interpretation of the Linear B tablets, that we speak of a Mycenaean palace economy, rather than a Mycenaean economy seen from the point of view of the palaces. It has become obvious that we must study which aspects of the economic system the texts do not cover, and try to determine whether these aspects are under the *de facto* control of the palaces, or are part of an extra-palatial system running parallel to the palatial system. This approach has become more common, and has even made it into at least one handbook (Dickinson 1998, 42).

Because of lack of extensive written records from private as well as institutional archives, few scholars try to analyze Mycenaean and Dark Age economy fully in terms of Polanyi's systems. Holly Morris (1986) first investigated the background and implicit assumptions in the various interpretations of the economy of Mycenaean Pylos. Then she set up and tested a model based on Polanyi's modes of exchange, especially redistribution and market exchange, within palatial, regional and local production systems. Morris was especially interested in identifying modes of exchange in the archaeological record as well as in Linear B texts, but did not concentrate on any one class of information, such as agriculture. David Tandy (1997) has presented an exhaustive interpretation of Dark Age economy, combining Polanyi's modes with demographics and Snodgrass's interpretation of the archaeological material, to show a pastoralist Dark Age society with a rudimentary redistributive system, gradually forced to change by rising population to a grain-based agricultural economy competing to produce goods for markets.

The consensus view that Mycenaean agriculture was dictated from above by the palaces has been based upon interpretation of the Linear B records from Knossos, Pylos and, to a lesser extent, Mycenae. We assume that the administrators who produced these texts only recorded resources in which the palaces had an interest. There are two ways to interpret this interest—either the palaces directly owned the resources, or had control through a system of obligations, without direct ownership. Even if the palaces did directly own the land and the crops and animals listed in the tablets, the majority of the population, and their land, would be outside of direct palace control except for taxation, and would continue in the mixed farming tradition. To make the analysis of the tablets more complicated, although the texts from Knossos, Pylos and Mycenae show that all three centers used similar assessment and collection techniques, the actual resources owned and managed by each palace would differ according to the way each center gained dominance over its territory (cf. Bennet 1995 on the development of the Pylian state).

Mesopotamian archives from palaces and temples also record different degrees of palace involvement in agricultural production similar to the information in the Mycenaean texts. The land controlled directly by the ruler or the temple can be divided into three categories: 1) land given to subordinates as payment for official duties (some of the produce might be paid as rent or tax); 2) land rented to tenants in return for labor service and a portion of the crop; and 3) royal or temple estate, considered as the private property of the king or the god, and divided into specialized areas for monocropping. The overseers and workers on royal estates were considered part of the household of the ruler or god, while the tenants of rented land or the palace officials holding plots were not, because they were heads of their own households. The payment of staples as rent from tenants meant that the ruler could afford to devote more of his estate to specialized crops. The wealthier subordinates who received larger amounts of land would themselves sublet some to tenants, and use the rest to diversify (Postgate 1992, 187-90). The rulers would also draw upon revenue in the form of goods and manpower from subject cities, but this would be considered tax or tribute, not rent, or services in return for land

The Mesopotamian pattern of palace estate versus royal land rented or granted to others can provide a good parallel for the information about land and crops in the Linear B tablets. The more detailed the information about production or assessment of certain commodities in the tablets, the more likely is direct palace ownership of those resources. Both Knossos and Pylos have unusually detailed records about sheep and clothmaking, which implies that the centers provided access to land, animals, and clothworkers to selected collectors/holders, collected a specified amount of cloth, and allowed the holder to keep the surplus. It is unclear whether the collector/holder might be considered then to belong to the palace household.[4] On the other end of the scale, the tablets of the Pylos Ma series show that the palace collected the same basic commodities in proportional amounts from all the districts of the kingdom; these would be items such as oxhides, or simple garments widely available throughout the kingdom as part of traditional household production. The towns and villages providing these goods then would not be considered palace land. However, it is difficult to determine how much palace control over production occurs in the Pylos Na series, which list flax owed to the palace by groups who hold land, or the Pylos E- landholding series, which record in great detail the amount of land held, and the status of landholders and their tenants. The palace may or may not be the ultimate owner of the lands listed, but the fact that they are held in the name of individuals, or corporate groups such as smiths or priestesses, implies that these holders are free to use the land as they wish, once they have fulfilled the obligation which was tied to the land, to provide flax, or grain, or other farm produce (Halstead 1992b; Killen 1998; Palmer 1999, 481-82).

Halstead's work analyzes ways in which the palace draws upon the non-palatial economy. He starts with the assumption that all land and staple crops such as grains and olives are owned by the palaces. In his view, the palace at Knossos directly controlled the majority of land in central Crete as palace estates, worked by palace oxen, where they specialized in producing wheat for rations and sheep for the palace cloth industry. However, other basic commodities used as food and raw materials for palace dependent workers would have been obtained by taxing traditional farmers (Halstead 1992a, 108-109; 1992b, 65-68). The palaces relied on a specialized agricultural regime and supported large numbers of non-agricultural personnel through redistribution. This interpretation is based primarily upon the grain harvest records and the sheep tablets from Knossos; it implies that the farmers on palace land were told by the palaces what to grow.

KN E 668				E: ethnic
.1 ru-ki-ti-jo (E)	GRA 246 T7			T: title
.2 tu-ri-si-jo (E)	GRA 261	ra-ti-jo (E)	GRA 30 T 5	MN: man's name
KN E 669				WN: woman's name
.1]ti-jo (E)	GRA 195	OLIV+A 43	OLIV+TI 45	GN: group name
.2]I-jo (E) GRA 143		da-*22-ti-jo (E)	GRA 70 OLIV 45	PN: place name

These two harvest tablets, KN E 668 and 669, record large quantities of grain and olives from several groups of men in regions that Halstead assumes are palace estates; the GRA ideogram has been interpreted as wheat, which would suggest that these communities specialized in wheat and olives. One dry unit is presumed to have the value of 96 liters (*Docs*[2], 394). In KN E 669, line 2, the men of *da-*22-to* have produced a total of 70 units of grain, and 45 of olives. KN Dn 1093 shows that 1370 sheep are pastured at *da-*22-to*.

KN Dn 1093	
.1 da-*22-to (PN)	OVIS^m 1370
.2 *56-ko-we-I (PN)	OVIS^m 2003

KN De 1151

.A		we-we-si-jo (MN)	OVIS^m 264	OVIS^f 22
.B	su-di-ni-ko (MN)	, / da-*22-to (PN),	o OVIS^m 14	

KN Dn 1093 is a totaling tablet which records sheep in the thousands from two areas in southern Crete; the numbers are irregular, implying that this is the actual count. KN De 1151 on the other hand shows a flock in one of these areas, *da-*22-to*, with the optimal strength of 300. The entries in De 1151 itemize how many sheep are currently in the flock, of what sex, and how many (14) are missing (*opheilon*, abbreviated as o). All but 22 of the sheep are males; castrated males were most commonly used for wool production. Such large flocks imply movement of flocks long distances, first grazing on fallow land, and then in summer, moving to uncultivated upland. Grazing on fallow in cultivated land may actually require more labor than grazing in uncultivated marginal land, because more supervision is required to keep the herds out of the crops. A single herder can look after several hundred sheep or goats by himself on pasture away from cultivated land (Halstead 1996, 24). Halstead postulates that the palace ran such large herds in areas such as *da-*22-to* under cultivation, because the palace also held the grain land as part of royal estate, and therefore had the right to graze the wool herds on the fallow (Halstead 1992a, 115). However, Killen has found in several Knossos harvest tablets references to the *da-mo*, or names of individuals, in one case, the name of a collector/owner. This implies that the land is not part of royal estate, but held by individuals who owe service or crops (Killen 1998).

Similarly, the Knossos sheep tablets highlight the power and responsibility of the collector/owners. In KN De 1151, there are two names, *we-we-si-jo* and *su-di-ni-ko*; the other sheep tablets show that *we-we-si-jo*'s name appears in connection with 23 other flocks and a textile workshop (Bennet 1992, 89), while *su-di-ni-ko*'s name occurs only once. *We-we-si-jo* therefore has control of this flock and many others, but the actual shepherd is *su-di-ni-ko*. *We-we-si-jo*'s exact status in the palace hierarchy is unclear (see note 4), but he surely wielded great economic and political control in his region. The existence of such large individual flocks implies that *we-we-si-jo* and the other flock managers had secure access to grazing, which would then limit the grazing available to those without palace connections (Chang 1994, 358; Halstead 1996, 35). The flocks were organized primarily to produce wool, but would also be a source of meat (although not the tenderest meat) as sheep got too old to produce good wool. Halstead estimates that the female sheep listed in special breeding flocks in the Knossos records could not produce enough lambs per year to replace old wool sheep, so the palaces must have relied upon landholders in the traditional farming system to provide new sheep for palace herds (Halstead 1990/91, 360-61; 1996, 32-33). Since non-palace herds would not be able to compete with palace herds for grazing rights, this may have been a way for farmers to dispose profitably of animals they could not feed.

Halstead's model of specialized palace agriculture on a large scale versus local households practicing mixed farming on a small scale closely follows the model of the Mesopotamian royal or temple estate, where a large portion of the land is used for specialized monoculture. This view of Mycenaean agriculture emphasizes the large gulf between palace-organized crops, herds and workers, and traditional small-scale mixed farmers. However, there is an important difference between Mesopotamian and Greek agriculture because the Mesopotamian irrigation system could make agriculture on large estates much more dependable, but large scale irrigation did not exist in Greece (Foxhall 1995, 240). Palatial control of agricultural resources is a natural development from the traditional patterns of exploitation and unequal access to land that appeared first in the Late Neolithic (Bintliff 1982, Halstead 1989), so we would expect to see more middle level landholders, engaging in moderate diversification, which is what we find in Pylos tablets Un 718 and Er 880 (see below). Furthermore, we must remember that the administrative systems represented by the latest Linear B tablets from each site probably were in place no more than three generations during a period of high population density and intensive agriculture (cf. Donlan and Thomas 1993, 63), whereas the mixed farming tradition based on grain as the staple food, supplemented by tree crops and livestock, had been practiced for over 1500 years. We need to look more closely at the economy from the bottom up, in terms of communities and individual landholders, rather than from the top down.

The model of Mycenaean agriculture as palace-directed does not explain the common values connected with landholding, labor and agricultural crops, found in the Linear B tablets, the Homeric epics and the Classical *polis*. The large landholders, including the palaces, must have seen the link between their own holdings and the traditional small farmers, in the ethos of self-sufficiency through diversity. The palaces were able to diversify on the largest scale because they could draw upon staples produced by other farmers, as rent or taxes (Foxhall 1995, 242-43). Each landholder needed enough land to fulfill basic subsistence needs. Farmers would use extra land and labor not to produce even more staples, but to raise more animals and higher status crops such as vines. The ability to produce wine and livestock for conspicuous consumption was the mark of an aristocrat in all periods, since it implied that basic subsistence needs had already been met. This ethos developed early in the Bronze Age and can be traced through the Dark Age into the Classical period.

If we look for evidence of communities and individual landholders, we find that Mycenaean agriculture was not as specialized as the standard reconstructions suggest. I have argued that the main grain represented by the Linear B GRA ideogram was not wheat, but barley (Palmer 1992), so the farmers providing grain were not forced to specialize in wheat, a crop with a higher risk of failure than barley. Furthermore the focus on single crops seen in the Linear B tablets does not necessarily indicate crop monoculture but rather administrative bureaus which handle only one or two types of commodities. The palaces may have relied heavily upon non-palatial supplies of certain commodities such as flax[5] or olives, normally raised by landholders in the kingdoms, rather than specialize in these crops themselves. The records for animals however do point to specialized production of wool for the palace textile industries but responsibility for the herds and for cloth production was delegated to the "collectors," who either may be members of the palace household, or may be considered as separate "owners," operating a wool franchise. These "collector/owners" also had to have access to grain rations, to feed the workers cheaply. Regardless of the exact status of the "collector," the large numbers of sheep recorded at Knossos must have had a great impact on land use at the community level.

Another form of interaction between the palaces and the traditional farming communities lay in preferential access to land. In the kingdom of Pylos, rather than giving out food rations, the palace distributed land to upper level craft specialists and religious officials so that they could support themselves by farming; landholding was apparently a mark of status, in part because of the ethos of self-sufficiency. This parallels the Mesopotamian practice of allotting land to high and mid-level officials, in return for services. One effect of such land distribution would be to weaken community self-interest, and to focus more on ties between the community and the palace. This could be done in two ways: by arranging for palace personnel to hold land in a community, and by including local elites in the palace hierarchy. Consequently the towns and their territories were not fully self-contained units. The Pylos land tenure tablets in the E- series for *Pa-ki-ja-na* show a sense of community and a developed local hierarchy of landlords and tenants, similar to that found in Archaic poleis.

PY En 609

.1	pa-ki-ja-ni-ja (PN) , to-sa , da-ma-te , DA 40
.2	to-so-de , te-re-ta , e-ne-e-si VIR 14
.3	wa-na-ta-jo-jo (MN in gen.) ko-to-na ki-ti-me-na to-so-de pe-mo GRA 2 V 1
.4	o-da-a₂ , o-na-te-re (T) , e-ko-si , wa-na-ta-jo-jo (MN in gen.), ko-to-na
.5	a-tu-ko(MN) e-te-do-mo (T) wa-na-ka-te-ro o-na-to e-ke pe-mo GRA V 1
.6	i-ni-ja (WN) te-o-jo do-e-ra (T) o-na-to e-ke to-so-de pe-mo GRA T 2 V 4
.7	e-*65-to (MN) te-o-jo do-e-ro (T) o-na-to e-ke to-so-de pe-mo GRA T 2
.8	si-ma (WN) te-o-jo do-e-ra (T) o-na-to e-ke to-so-de pe-mo GRA T 1
.9	*vacat*

.10 a-ma-ru-ta-o (MN in gen.) ko-to-na ki-ti-me-na to-so-de pe-mo   GRA2 T 3

.11 o-da-a₂e-ko-si a-ma-ru-ta-o (MN in gen.) ko-to-na o-na-te-re (T)

.12 so-u-ro (MN) te-o-jo do-e-ro (T) o-na-to e-ke to-so-de pe-mo   GRA V 3

.13 e-do-mo-ne-u (MN) te-o-jo do-e-ro (T) o-na-to e-ke to-so-de pe-mo   GRA T 1

.14 e-sa-ro (MN) te-o-jo do-e-ro (T) o-na-to e-ke to-so-de pe-mo   GRA V 3

.15 wa-na-ta-jo (MN) te-re-ta (T) o-na-to e-ke to-so-de pe-mo   GRA T 1

.16 e-ra-ta-ra (WN) i-je-re-ja do-e-ra (T) o-na-to e-ke to-so-de pe-mo   GRA T 1

.17 po-so-re-ja (WN) te-o-jo do-e-ra (T) o-na-to e-ke to-so-de pe-mo   GRA T 1 V 3

.18 i-je-re-ja (T) pa-ki-ja-na (PN) o-na-to e-ke to-so-de pe-mo   GRA T 3

PY En 609 lists major landholders and their tenants (*o-na-te-re*) on private land, *ko-to-na ki-ti-me-na*; the first landholder has 4 tenants, and the second has 7, including the first landholder, *wa-na-ta-jo* (l. 15). However there is a sharp division in status and amount of land held between the major landholders and the tenants holding *o-na-to*, rented plots, who were mostly religious personnel or officials with ties to the palace. The major landholders tended to have several plots of land, perhaps in different ecosystems; this would fit the pattern of diversified holdings in traditional agriculture. The area of land is given in terms of grain; we have no idea what these landholders or their tenants actually cultivated. But traditionally tenant farmers were allowed to raise what they wanted, so long as they gave a portion to the landlord, and did not degrade the land or damage the fruit trees (Burford 1993, 179- 81; Isager and Skydsgaard 1992, 24).

What was produced on the land? Pylos tablet Un 718 lists important individuals and groups (underlined below) who contributed agricultural produce including sacrificial animals and wine for a festival for Poseidon (Palmer 1994, 103-105), and Er 880 records a double estate of the important figure *e-ke-rya-wo* (*Enkhelyawon*) who appears on Un 718.

PY Un 718

.1   sa-ra-pe-da (PN) po-se-da-o-ni do-so-mo

.2   o-wi-de-ta-I (verb?) do-so-mo to-so <u>e-ke-rya-wo</u> (MN)

.3   do-se (verb) GRA 4 VIN 3 BOS^m 1

.4   tu-ro$_2$ TURO$_2$ 10 ko-wo *153 1

.5   me-ri-to , V 3

.6   *vacat*

.7   o-da-a$_2$, <u>da-mo</u> (GN) , GRA 2 VIN 2

.8   OVIS^m 2 TURO$_2$ 5 a-re-ro , AREPA V 2 *153 1

.9   to-so-de <u>ra-wa-ke-ta</u> (T) do-se (verb)

.10   OVIS^m 2 me-re-u-ro FAR T 6

.11a   -ma
        VIN S 2 o-da-a$_2$ <u>wo-ro-ki-jo-ne-jo</u> (MN) , <u>ka</u> (GN)

.12   GRA T 6 VIN S 1 TURO$_2$ 5 me-ri[

.13   *vacat* [   ]1 V 1

In Un 718, *e-ke-rya-wo* gives barley, wine, cheese probably from sheep or
goats, honey, an oxhide and a bull. The other donors, the *da-mo*, or *demos*,
the *ra-wa-ke-ta*, *lawagetas*, an important palace official, second to the king,
and the *ka-ma* land of *Wroikion* (Killen 1998, 21) contribute sheep, cheese
and wine also. *E-ke-rya-wo*'s donation is the richest because it includes a bull,
and shows the widest range of crops and animal products.

PY Er 880

.1   <u>e-]ke-rya[wo</u> ki-]ti-me-no , e-ke

.2   **sa-ra-pe-do[pe-]pu$_2$-te-me-no**

.3   to-so [pe-ma]GRA 30[ ]

.4   to-so-de , [   ]to , pe-ma GRA 42[

.5   to-sa , we-je[-we   ]1100[

.6   to-sa-de , su-za[   ]1000

.7   *vacat*

.8   ku-su-to-ro-qa , to-so , pe-ma 94

.9-10   *vacant*

.1   *E-ke-rya-wo* has two ki-ti-me-na estates

.2   at *Sa-ra-pe-do,* planted in trees and vines

.3   (On this estate) so much area measured in seed grain: GRA 30+ (probably 52)

.4   (On the other estate) and so much [ ]to area measured in seed grain: GRA 42+

.5   (On this estate) so many vines trained up trees: 1100

.6   (On the other estate) and so many fig trees: 1000

.7   empty line

.8   Total—so much area measured in seed grain: GRA 94

Er 880 shows the size of *e-ke-rya-wo*'s estates at *sa-ra-pe-do* (also measured in terms of GRA), and records fig trees and vines on them, but does not indicate what other crops or livestock might be on the land, or whether tenants cultivated a portion. The large numbers of trees and vines indicates that *e-ke-rya-wo* devoted part of his lands to large scale orchard husbandry, but still had enough land and labor to raise a range of other crops and animals, in particular cattle.

Another tablet series, the Mycenae Ge "spice" tablets, points to specialized production of herbs and spices. The pattern of entries recording deliveries by at least 5 named individuals, indicates that fresh herbs, many of them water-loving species, were delivered continuously through the growing season. This type of specialized production is possible in large irrigated gardens, and points to the pattern of agricultural diversity and focus on luxury foods found in elite estates, rather than general production throughout the countryside. I have argued that the individuals providing the fresh herbs were not workers on palace estates but rather large landholders, growing luxury plants in irrigated gardens on part of their own estates (Palmer 1999, 477-80). The sacrificial animals and wine assessed from the estate holders listed in Un 718 are also "luxury" commodities produced in quantity by wealthier landholders. Thus the palaces drew upon basic resources produced by all farmers, as well as luxury foods from the larger landholders.

The consensus view is that the destruction of the palaces completely upset this delicately balanced agricultural system based on specialized production, or alternately, stress upon the agricultural system might have led to the fall of the palaces (cf. Betancourt 1976). Hanson presents an extreme view of the palace administration directing agricultural strategies from above, creating an agricultural work force dependent on palace stores for food, and ignorant of agricultural know-how (Hanson 1995, 30-33), while Sallares thinks that the primitive crops being grown—emmer wheat, wild olive and wild flax—seriously hindered the range of productivity of Mycenaean agriculture (Sallares 1991, 15-16). From ca. 1300 to 1200 B.C.E. in Greece, settlement density and population reached the highest point in the Bronze Age. Pollen cores show that in the region from the palace at Pylos down to the bay, between ca. 1600 and 1400 B.C.E., up to 40% of the land was cleared and used for grazing, since the pollens of open steppe plants and low oak scrub predominate (Zangger et al. 1997, 589-92). Between 1400 and 1200, the oak pollen drops, and olive and other orchard tree pollen rises, indicating that some of the land has been planted in orchards, and so would be closed to common grazing practiced in the earlier period. This pattern of forest clearing for grazing, then for new cultivation fits well with the rise in population from 1600 to 1200 B.C.E. With high population density comes a landholding pattern of a few landholders (including the palaces) controlling a large amount of the land. In contrast, the majority of the population was engaged in intensive farming on plots of land perhaps too small to allow full self-sufficiency, constrained to provide crops and labor to the administration, and forced to depend on the local elite or the palace for help in times of need. However, even if these smallholders did not have the resources for more than a few animals, or crop trees, they would not have forgotten the strategies of mixed farming, because they would have been able to observe or even work with the flocks and orchards of the larger landholders in their communities.

Dark Age Agriculture

The destruction of the palaces would have caused great hardship for farming households whose surpluses had been collected by the palaces, leaving them no safety net from crop failure, and would have generated famine for workers fully dependent on palace stores. Constant warfare or raiding would disrupt agricultural activities, leading to food shortages. But the fall of the palaces probably had little effect on the actual agricultural tradition. The causes of the destructions and the sequence of population movements and desertions are different for each area, and should not be oversimplified.[6] Also after the destructions, each region developed separately, with varying degrees of outside contact. Lin Foxhall (1995, 247-48) postulates that towns with a strong local elite who had some autonomy to act for themselves survived the destructions better than the smallest sites, or those areas under direct palace control. One immediate effect of the destructions would be to make available arable land and other resources such as pasture and woods, which were formerly restricted to palace use. The reduced population could then raise animals as well as crops, to achieve full self-sufficiency. The pattern of agriculture where land is relatively plentiful and farmers are under no constraint to superiors is quite different from a landlord-tenant situation with land in short supply. When there is no pressure on land, the farmer aims to use his labor most efficiently through extensive agriculture. There may be no distinction between good and poor crop land, or crop land and grazing land; what matters is that just enough land has been put under cultivation to meet all subsistence needs (Fotiadis 1985, 68-71).

The greatest period of depopulation began at the end of LH and LM IIIC, over 100 years after the destruction of the palaces, so presumably the earlier IIIC populations had supported themselves through traditional mixed farming. The cause of the depopulation, or the size of the population at its lowest point, is unknown.[7] The population level apparently held steady for 200 years, until the growth of cemeteries indicates a rise in population ca. 800 B.C.E. (Snodgrass 1980, 22-23). The transformation of the Mycenaean *qa-si-re-u*, or local official, into the Dark Age *basileus* indicates that some vestiges of Mycenaean social hierarchy survived through the Dark Ages (Morris 1987, 172). Although most settlements would have been scattered and small, between 30 and 50 people, some centers such as Athens and Knossos show continuous habitation at a relatively high level of population through the LH IIIC and Dark Age period (Athens: Morris 1987, 1991; Knossos: Coldstream 1994). However, population estimates from supposedly populous Dark Age sites such as Athens, Knossos, Lefkandi and Argos are based on burials from cemeteries, not from information from settlements. This problem is central to our understanding of Dark Age agricultural practices, because settlements with low population, 100 or less, are more likely to allow open access for its members to arable land, pasture and other natural resources. Such a simple society would not have a fixed hierarchy, but rather a "big man" as leader, who achieved and maintained his position through his ability to attract followers through gifts and feasting (Antonaccio 1994, 409; Donlan and Thomas 1993, 65; Tandy 1997, 90). Snodgrass calculated population size at Lefkandi and Athens directly from number of datable burials per period, and concluded that these "large" settlements would have less than 200 people per generation (Snodgrass 1983, 168-69; Tandy 1997, 21-22). However, if as Ian Morris claims, the excavated cemeteries contain only elite burials, and the majority of the population disposed of their dead in less visible ways, this would indicate both a larger population and a well-defined hierarchy with hereditary *basilees* (Morris 1987, 173-79; 1991, 27, 42; Garnsey and Morris 1989, 99-100). Morris argues that from the beginning of the Protogeometric period in Athens, ca. 1050 B.C.E., the basis of this stratification was control of land, where the elite held large estates and the peasants were their serfs or tenants. In both reconstructions, the success of the leaders depends in part upon control of land and labor, and the use of animals as a sign of wealth. But the greater the population, the more unequal would be access to land, and the ability to achieve self-sufficiency through diversification.

Let us return to Snodgrass's criteria for the Dark Age which point to pastoralism: low population and short lived sites, meat in the heroic diet, bronze figurines of cows and sheep dedicated at Olympia and elsewhere in the tenth century, and the prevalence of cattle bones at Nichoria (Snodgrass 1980, 21-36; 1987, 193-210). The main problem as I see it is the lack of definition for pastoralism, and how, as Snodgrass implied (1980, 27), pastoralism would be adopted as a reaction against Mycenaean tradition. Pastoralism implies that a household is putting the greater part of land and labor towards raising animals and processing their products as staples, using them as the main source of nourishment, rather than grains, legumes or tree crops which were still being grown. Halstead (1996, 22-24) discusses different degrees of pastoralism practiced in Greece in recent times, showing that all pastoralism involves some component of plant cultivation. In the dry climate of southern Greece, livestock management as the main form of subsistence requires far more land and labor than grain production, which is why grain in Greece has always been the main staple (Cherry 1988, 21; Halstead 1996, 34). Transhumant pastoralists who do not have land to raise their own grain must exchange animal products for grain or flour, and for grazing rights (Halstead 1996, 22; Forbes 1995, 326). Furthermore, territorial rights to grazing land were always carefully defined and vigorously defended (Chang 1994, 359, 361-362); the wealthy men of the community were the ones who controlled the most land, and consequently had the most herds. Homeric heroes eat roast meat, not because it is the main staple, but because it is rare, and so indicating high status. The mixed farming tradition has always included some livestock, with the amount and type varying according to the resources of the household. Livestock can act as mobile food banks, to be slaughtered in times of need, but this was not the main reason for raising them; rather the primary function of animals is to generate and display wealth, not to be used for subsistence (Forbes 1995, 332). This is the pattern seen in the Linear B tablets, and in the Classical period; on what grounds would this pattern differ in the Dark Age? Snodgrass points to the prevalence of cow and sheep figurines in remote sanctuaries as indicating transhumant pastoralists herding animals for meat (Snodgrass 1987, 205-207). However, cattle are not usually included in transhumant herding because they need too much water and are usually grazed in wetlands (Isager and Skydsgaard 1992, 98). Furthermore, the cow figurines could represent plow oxen, signifying agricultural wealth, as well as meat animals (Burford 1993, 324 n. 11).

The Dark Age village of Nichoria is often cited as proof for pastoralism, primarily because it has the best published bone and plant analysis for a mainland site. The Dark Age settlement lasted for 175 years, so it was not a short term site, as Snodgrass considered typical of pastoral settlements. The bone material showed that while sheep and goats were the main meat sources, the percentage of cows slaughtered steadily rose to between 30 and 40% in the Dark Age phases, from 15 to 20% in the Bronze Age. Deer were also hunted in significant numbers, which implies that wasteland or woods were close to the settlement (Sloan and Duncan 1978, 64-69, 76; McDonald, Coulsen, and Rosser 1983, 323-24). The site of Nichoria lies near river bottomlands which would be suitable for grazing cows (Aschenbrenner 1972, 49). The relatively high percentage of cow bones from the Bronze Age settlement indicates that cattle were an important component of livestock raising at that period too, but were used primarily as draft animals, then slaughtered for meat at an advanced age (Mancz 1989, 115-124). The scanty seed material recovered show grains, grapes, olives, figs and peas were raised, just as in the Mycenaean period. Samples of charcoal from the Dark Age phases include pruned branches of olive, fig and grape, so tree crops were also cultivated at Nichoria (Shay and Shay 1978, 53-56).

Tandy uses the bone and plant material from Nichoria together with the pollen cores from the Pylos area to explain how the low level of population during the Dark Age was due to poor nutrition from a diet of red meat, olives and fig, with few grains or dairy products. He argues that the lack of pollen from domesticated grains and no physical evidence of granaries proves that grains were unimportant in Dark Age agriculture (Tandy 1997, 35-37). Evidence for built granaries in settlements is rare at best even in the Mycenaean period; most produce was stored in large earthen jars. Pollen cores by their very nature provide ambiguous information about crops.

Wetlands which have undisturbed areas suitable for taking cores are rare in modern Greece. Some cultivated plants spread their pollen for very short distances (Zangger et al. 1997, 580), so that if the area next to the marshland is not being cultivated, certain crop pollens will not appear in the core. Also tree crops require overall less labor than grains or legumes, but to produce an adequate crop of fruit, farmers need to work intensively at certain times of the year to dig around the roots, in order to clear out weeds and loosen the soil. Grain production requires less intensive spurts of labor, spread more evenly throughout the growing season. In terms of labor input, it is highly unlikely that Dark Age households concentrated on tree crops rather than on grains. Furthermore, it is more likely that Snodgrass's short-lived settlements engaged in grain growing rather than tree husbandry, because of the long period of time between planting tree crops and harvesting them profitably.

Nichoria presents a good example of the intensification of the herding component of the agricultural system under the right conditions, but there is not enough information to indicate if the people relied on animal products more than on grain. Also the higher percentage of cattle at Nichoria may not be typical of Dark Age sites in general, since the settlement is close to wetlands suitable for grazing cattle. The bone evidence from the sites at Kavousi, Crete also indicates a small rise in consumption of beef, but sheep and goats still made up 70 to 78% of the identifiable animals slaughtered (Klippel and Snyder 1991, 179-82). Bone material from sites is usually more plentiful and better preserved than plant remains, which survive best in sites when burned, and in pollen profiles which require undisturbed wetlands. While we can trace different strategies for use of livestock from Nichoria and Kavousi, the difficulty in finding and processing good samples of plant material makes it hard to prove conclusively that the Dark Age communities relied more on livestock for food, than on grains, legumes or tree crops.

The *Odyssey* is often used as evidence for Dark Age pastoralism. The main problems with this source lie in the problem of dating the poem, and its relevance to actual Dark Age society. Among recent scholars, the Homeric poems in their completed forms are usually considered to reflect Greek society ca. 800 B.C.E. or slightly later (Donlan 1997, 649; see Tandy 1997, 8-10, for an overview of other possible dates). The evidence for livestock management in the *Odyssey* points to short range transhumance of large herds, with herdsmen of low status working for the elite.[8] Odysseus and Laertes also own extensive orchards (*Odyssey* 24, esp. 336-344), but land cultivated in grains is not specifically mentioned, even though slave women grind grain every day, and bread accompanies meat at feasts. The pattern of livestock and orchards seen in the *Odyssey* is similar to the flocks and the orchards listed in the Linear B tablets (see above). In the *Odyssey*, owning land and herds was the mark of an aristocrat, and the status of a chief depended in part upon his ability to feast his followers (Antonaccio 1995, 225, 260). According to Tandy (1997, 106-10), examples from the *Iliad* and *Odyssey* indicate that the Dark Age *basilees* practiced redistributive mobilization. In particular, the case of Eumaios the swineherd of Odysseus who was given a homestead and a wife by his patron resembles the mid-level specialists in the Linear B texts who hold land in return for specialized services. In his reconstruction of the Homeric economy, Donlan assumes that arable farming was always the main means of food production in the Dark Age, but people owned as much livestock as they could support. The main crops and livestock raised were those exploited in the Bronze Age (Donlan 1997, 650, 654-55). Possession of flocks implied that the landowner had sufficient grain reserves to support his herdsmen. Odysseus's herds and trees represent the mixed farming system at its most extensive, where Odysseus has enough land and labor to specialize, yet still maintain diversified crops. The main differences between Mycenaean and Dark Age land use lay in the Dark Age emphasis on herds as wealth, and the extensive use of land for grazing, which was possible due to the low population, and lack of competition for land between crop cultivation and herding (655-56). The Mycenaeans valued herds, especially cattle, but had access to many other ways to display wealth—elaborate palaces, specialized luxury products, and imported finished goods and raw materials, which were rarely available to Dark Age elites.

Population Growth and Intensive Agriculture

Population growth is usually associated with intensification of agriculture. Howe's thesis that toward the end of the Dark Age, the adoption of grains as new crops directly caused the population to grow, just as potatoes in sixteenth-century Ireland did, is no longer considered valid. Instead population growth and increased reliance on grains work on each other to form a positive feedback loop. Only a few preserved deposits of grains from Dark Age sites have been found and studied; the Nichoria material has been discussed above. Snodgrass (1987, 207-208) cites pulse seeds from a Protogeometric level at Iolkos in Thessaly, and grain seeds from a Geometric level in the same site as supporting his model of pastoralism later changing to grain production. But unless a similar sequence of fodder plants in the early Dark Age, then grains a century or so later is found in southern Greece, this at best may indicate intensification of herding in Thessaly, famous for its well-watered plains in the historical period. Furthermore, pulses as a fodder crop fit into a pulse-grain rotation cycle of land-use (Hodkinson 1988, 39).

The other piece of evidence used to show the growing importance of grains in the later Dark Age is the model "granary" found as part of the grave goods of a wealthy female cremation burial in the Athenian Agora, dated ca. 850 B.C.E. The piece is a terracotta chest with removable lid, which has five onion domes each with a little window with flap near the point. Fragments of another freestanding dome with window and flap were also found in the grave. There is no definite proof that the domes on the chest represent a granary; it is simply the most probable interpretation. The burial contained many pieces of locally made gold jewelry, an imported faience necklace, and two ivory stamp seals (Smithson 1968, 78-81,93, pls. 24-27). The idea that the terracotta chest represents a granary complements the display of wealth which went into the burial; both luxury goods and wealth in staples emphasize the status of the deceased (cf. Tandy 1997, 102 and n.88).

Parallels to the terracotta "granary" domes found in this burial appear mostly in Late Geometric or Protoattic burials, 100 years or more later, but at least one other dome also dates to ca. 850 B.C.E. All appear to come from female burials (Smithson 92 n. 41, and 93). Evelyn Smithson also equates the terracotta model chests from Protogeometric burials with the model "granaries" of the Geometric period (Smithson 1968, 96; Coldstream 1977, 55, 314); they both represent the function of the lady of the household to guard the harvested crop, which implies producing enough grain to store over the winter. The sudden appearance of circular domes on the chest models can be ascribed to a change in pottery styles. The domes are essentially the same shape as the pointed pyxis, which potters invented in the Early Geometric period (Coldstream 1977, 26). The model chest with domes was made as part of the funerary equipment for the burial, since it was beautifully decorated by the same artist who painted the burial urn, yet was poorly fired (Smithson 1968, 82, 94). The chest was not a jewel box for its owner while she lived, but rather a purely symbolic connotation of the agricultural wealth under her care. The Protogeometric terracotta chests imply that grain-growing was also important in Athens between 1050 and 900 B.C.E.[9] The appearance of domes to represent granaries "need be no more indicative of an interest in a newly introduced technique of arable farming than, say, the manufacture of teapots in the shape of thatched cottages is of a new line in domestic dwellings" (Burford 1993, 234, n. 11).

If the domed circular shapes of the models truly represent granaries, then what were the size and construction method for the originals? The circular foundations in an eighth-century level at Lefkandi have been interpreted as footings for granaries which could hold up to 450 bushels of grain (Tandy 1997, 39 n. 91). They would be made of mud-brick rather than wood, and would function as silos, filled with grain from the top. This would imply the production and consumption of grain on a much greater order of magnitude than in an ordinary farm like the one Hesiod describes in *Works and Days* (see below). His granaries are wooden huts (*kaliai*) with store-jars (*angeia*) to hold the harvest (*Works and Days* 301, 307, 475, 600). Wooden bins or chests might also hold threshed grains or legumes. Once a jar or bin was opened, the household had to use the contents before mold or vermin spoiled the contents (cf. *Works and Days* 368-369). In contrast, grain in a silo type granary is not put in smaller containers. The grain by the walls and floor would be affected by damp and pests, but the greater volume in the interior would remain good, as long as it was used quickly.

The cemeteries show that Athens in the Protogeometric and Geometric periods before 800 B.C.E. had a relatively high population, which as it grew would lead to increased social stratification and unequal access to land. Once land was not readily available to all, households with smaller parcels of land would turn to intensive grain production, and cut down accordingly on livestock and crop trees. It is impossible to tell if new crops or techniques were introduced which might have facilitated population growth. The technique of grafting fruit trees probably came to Greece from the Near East in the historical period (Sallares 1991, 29). Grafting allowed faster propagation of favorable strains of fruit trees. Six row barley continued to be the most widely grown grain because of its tolerance for poor soils and lack of water, while the type of wheat may have shifted from hulled emmer wheat to naked (hull-less) durum wheat, because it is easier to process durum wheat to make bread (Sallares 1991, 347; Palmer 1992, 490-91). However, it is not yet possible to trace changes in varieties of cultivars because plant material from historical sites rarely has been collected and studied.

Hesiod's poem *Works and Days* is the last major piece of evidence used to point to the growing importance of grain agriculture at the end of the Dark Age. Hesiod is a proponent of intensive grain agriculture, but his advice does not constitute a "how to grow grain" manual for those who have not done it before. He is full of traditional wisdom on when to time tasks through the agricultural year, and on how to choose wood for farm equipment, but never mentions *which* grains are being grown, or the difference between barley and wheat in terms of soil types and of sowing and reaping. He mentions using mules to plow, but never says where to get them. He practices mixed farming, with sheep and goats for milk, hides, meat and wool, cattle for traction and meat, and vines for wine, as well as fields of grain. In this poem, Hesiod focuses on the proper attitude, or ethos of self-sufficiency in one's household, as well as proper relations with kin, neighbors, and the elite *basilees*.

Where do we place Hesiod's poems? The picture of god-nourished *basilees* at the head of a redistributive system of goods and services is set in the recent past, ca. 800 B.C.E. The *Theogony* is also a praise poem for the *basilees*, and shows the same social view as the Homeric epics; therefore the *Theogony* and *Works and Days* too are eighth-century (Tandy 1997, 13-14, 190-92). However, *Works and Days* presents an anti-aristocratic attitude toward the elite and their control of resources, and the poet Hesiod takes on the persona of a peasant mistrustful of the aristocracy (198, 206-208). Tandy proposes that in the eighth century, goods which the elite formerly assessed and circulated in a redistributive system, they now disposed of in market exchanges, causing scarcity and wide-spread debt among the poorer members of the community (ch. 5, 112-38). Instead of portraying the elite and the *polis* as worthy of praise, *Works and Days* teaches that the only relationship possible with gift-devouring *basilees* is a negative one. A household can rely only on itself for success, and reciprocity between kin and neighbors is valid only when the household has already achieved self-sufficiency. In the images on the Shield of Achilles (*Iliad* 18.541-572), men, women and children work cheerfully plowing and harvesting, and are rewarded with wine, or music and dancing (191). In Hesiod's depiction, farm work is a long, lonely struggle with few helpers. There are rewards: *Works and Days* 589-596 describes delicacies fit for a feast, wine, flatbread made with milk, tender beef and kid.[10] The successful farmer does not have to rely on the *basilees* for feasts. Where the elite would emphasize their animal wealth, implying also possession of land and staples to spare, in *Works and Days*, the need to be self-sufficient in grains is foremost, and the animals and vines are secondary in importance.

Conclusion

Dark Age agriculture had a large livestock component, not because of any reaction to or rejection of Mycenaean farming traditions, but because animal husbandry was a part of the traditional mixed farming system in all periods. The cultivation of grains was certainly not forgotten during the Dark Age.

Similarly the emphasis on grain cultivation in *Works and Days* seems to represent a return to intensive farming, in a time of growing population. The main questions then are not why did pastoralism develop in the Dark Age, then to be supplanted by grain cultivation, but why did population drop so severely in the late Mycenaean period, and then rise again in the ninth and eighth centuries?

The Mediterranean mixed farming tradition is very old and flexible; its various components can be manipulated and intensified according to available resources. But the more specialization occurs, the greater the risk of failure, so specialization was generally balanced by diversification. Livestock management, even elevated to the status of transhumant pastoralism, should always be considered as complementary to and dependent on plant cultivation. In fact the Linear B sheep tablets provide the best example of specialized pastoralism (Cherry 1988, 25; Halstead 1996, 33). Only the rich would have had the resources to invest in large herds. The majority of Mycenaean farmers would have practiced small scale mixed farming both under the palaces, and after their fall; but the ability to produce luxury foods such as meat and wine remained the social ideal. The supposed Dark Age pastoralism should be seen as a variant in the mixed farming tradition; depopulation left more land free for livestock than had been available before, but grain cultivation was still the most efficient way to produce energy. When the population grew, competition for arable land may have led to more restricted grazing, and a corresponding drop in livestock.

Above all, we must emphasize that change was never uniform throughout the Greek world, either in the Bronze Age, or the Dark Age. In the Bronze Age, palace control did not extend to all areas of Greece, and the nature and degree of control varied within the kingdoms. After the destructions of the thirteenth century, some areas experienced immediate depopulation, while in others, settlements continued and even grew temporarily in population. Communities such as Athens or Knossos with relatively large populations for the Dark Age would display more social hierarchy and unequal access to resources than a small settlement such as

Nichoria. The best way to understand the changes occurring between 1200 and 700 B.C.E. is through survey and excavation region by region (cf. Haggis 1993; Davis et al. 1997). Furthermore, we need more seed and bone evidence from Classical sites comparable to the material recovered from Bronze Age sites, so that interpretation of ancient Greek agriculture need not rely so much on literary evidence. David Reese (1994) lists first-millennium sites where bone and shell remains have been studied, but no equivalent list for plant material is available.

Finally, it is useful to look at the history of the models for agriculture in Mycenaean and historical Greece, to trace the source of the elements that make up the models. The great difference between how Mycenaean society and first-millennium *polis* society are portrayed is due just as much to differences in theoretical approaches between Bronze Age and Classical scholars, as to differences in material culture and patterns of social organization. In the 1970s and 1980s, Snodgrass revolutionized the view of the end of the Mycenaean period by showing that there was no clear evidence of outside invaders bringing new elements. This meant that the differences between Mycenaean, Dark Age and historical *polis* culture had to be analyzed in terms of internal change. Dark Age pastoralism was identified as one of the main changes from Mycenaean, palace directed agriculture. In one sense, Snodgrass is correct in ascribing the rise in animal husbandry in the Dark Age as a reaction to the pattern of Mycenaean agriculture, because the destructions of the palaces and subsequent depopulation left the survivors with open access to land, and under no constraint to provide labor or goods to the centers. The decade of the 1990s has seen a change in approach towards Greek agriculture. Most texts, both Mycenaean and Classical (including *Works and Days*), present information about agriculture from the point of view of the well-to-do. It is possible to take that bias into account, and to analyze agricultural strategies in terms of risk management for different levels of society through ethnoarchaeological parallels. Agriculture provides a strong element of continuity in Greece through the ages, and a fertile area for exchanging methodologies between Bronze Age and Classical scholars.

NOTES

This paper has gone through many changes. It developed from a paper entitled "From Mycenae to Homer: the continuity of Greek agriculture," given at the 1996 AIA meetings. In expanding and exploring aspects of the topic, I became interested in the history of the models of Mycenaean agriculture and Dark Age pastoralism. The terms used in the subtitle, "from the Mycenaean to the Historical Period," instead of "LH III B to Early Iron III," emphasize the heavy reliance on texts rather than archaeological material in reconstructing agricultural systems in second and first-millennium Greece. Many thanks to those who listened and read drafts, in particular Bill Owens, Vance Watrous and Carol Hershenson, and especially to David Tandy, whose *Warriors into Traders* provided valuable insights.

1. The definitions of the different agricultural strategies vary from author to author, and sometimes overlap. I present the following definitions as guidelines. Agriculture is a general term for any system of getting food to eat by raising and processing domesticated plants and animals. Mixed farming is a more specific term for a household raising a complementary range of domesticated plants and animals to diminish the risk of failure for any single component. Agrarian or arable farming implies that the household concentrates on raising annual crops, usually grains, in plowed fields (although hoes can also be used on smaller plots). Pastoralism is a strategy where the household puts the most effort into herding livestock and processing animal products. Transhumant pastoralism involves moving herds, usually large ones, for relatively long distances to fresh pastures when grazing runs out in the home territory. Pastoralists may raise crops too, if they have access to land, and arable farmers tend to have some livestock. Farmers who specialize in tree crops practice orchard husbandry. Subsistence farming is the practice of producing crops and animals for household consumption first, to meet all the household nutritional needs, rather than for market exchange or redistribution first. Subsistence farmers aim to produce a surplus, which then can be used for transactions outside the household. In the Mediterranean, it is easier to achieve subsistence by raising crops than by herding animals.

2. e.g., Osborne 1987, 57; Sallares 1991, 14-16, 64-65; Langdon 1993 (*From Pasture to Polis*) 9, 46; Hanson 1995, 27-31; Tandy 1997, 4, 23. These works do not focus upon the agricultural economy in the Mycenaean or Dark Age period, but upon aspects of Dark Age culture (sculpture, poetry, burial practices) or Classical agrarian culture, adopting whichever elements of Snodgrass's pastoralism model which suits them. Bronze Age scholars are just as one-sided since they rarely mention Dark Age economy.

Susan Langdon's exhibition *From Pasture to Polis* provides a good example of how the pastoralism model is used. Her commentary on the exhibition and the associated symposium assumes that the pastoralism model is correct, but not fully accepted, and that there is room for questions: "The exhibition's title was itself deliberately provocative: indeed the nouns touch upon current controversies. Not everyone agrees that the fall of the Bronze Age kingdoms threw Greece into a state of transhumance and pastoralism, nor is the eighth-century origin of the *polis* widely accepted." (Langdon 1997, 2). Hurwit's overview of Dark Age society in *From Pasture to Polis* follows Snodgrass 1987, in presenting a society where pastoralism was more important than plant cultivation, but unlike most of the other discussions of Dark Age pastoralism, Hurwit emphasizes that Greek society was never purely pastoral or agrarian. Both Mycenaean and Dark Age agriculture were mixed, but the proportions of the mix differed in each case (Hurwit 1993, 21 n. 20).

3. Handbooks by their very nature present simplified overviews, and rarely discuss the nature of the evidence upon which these views are based. Those handbooks which do discuss the Mycenaean period and the transition to the Dark Age present the pastoralist model as uniformly applying to all Greece, and usually refer to Homer's heroic diet of roast beef as proving the model. The elements of Snodgrass's model concerning regional variation, and the nature of the material evidence are usually not mentioned.

4. The exact relationship between the palace and the collectors in charge of various flocks, weaving and perfume workshops remains subject to much discussion. Speculation upon their status and function ranges from being the highest nobility granted the proceeds from the flocks by the palace as their stipend to being minor palace bureaucrats acting as tax farmers. See the articles by Bennet, Godart, Driessen and Carlier in Olivier 1992, and Killen 1995. What remains clear is that the flocks and the cloth produced from their wool are so closely monitored by the central administration, that they must ultimately belong to the palace.

5. Foxhall (1995, 243) notes that flax requires well-watered soils, which are also suitable for grains and garden plants. The standard amount of flax required from a land-holding group in the Pylos Na series is 30 units of flax, where a unit represents a bundle or bale, not a weight (*Docs* [2], 468-469). It is not clear how large the unit of flax is, or if it consisted of raw stalks or already processed flax fibers. PY Nn 831 lists assessments of flax (expressed as the ideogram SA) from individuals or groups at ko-ri-to; most give between 1 and 4 units, but the *ko-re-te* (mayor) is assessed at 24 units (*Docs* [2], 296). The question then is whether the amount assessed from each donor represents a portion of what each would normally raise, or whether the donors planted flax because the palace requested it.

6. The destruction of a palace need not result in long-term impoverishment or movement of people; the traditional date for the destruction of Knossos, ca. 1380 B.C.E., was followed by an extended period of prosperity for Crete, and the continued use of Linear B script on stirrup jars for the export trade.

7. Richard Sallares's thesis in his 1991 book, *The Ecology of the Ancient Greek World*, is that population in Greece experiences long-term fluctuations. When population reaches a peak where even intensive agriculture cannot support it, social mechanisms restricting population growth such as emigration, delaying marriage, and infanticide, go into effect a generation or two *after* the population has reached its peak. Natural mechanisms, such as disease or malnutrition, may also limit fertility (Sallares 1991, 69-78). Sallares discusses mainly the increase in population during the Classical period that peaked in the fourth century B.C.E., but by implication his theory applies to the end of the Bronze Age with its high population level surpassed only by the fourth-century population. The continual drop in population between 1200 and 1100 could have resulted from strict checks on fertility, which had achieved their full effect in the tenth century. Sallares proposes that the Dark Age population remained low because of an age-class system similar to the ones practiced in Sparta or Crete, that restricted access between men and women (84).

8. Odysseus has 12 herds each of cows, sheep, pigs and goats on the mainland, and more on Ithaka itself. Either slave herdsmen or guest-friends of Odysseus (other elites) are in charge of the herds (*Odyssey* 14. 100-104.)

9. Merle Langdon (1976, 88-91) also argues in favor of widespread grain cultivation in Attica during the Dark Age, on the basis of the Protogeometric and Geometric pottery found at the sanctuary of Zeus on Mt. Hymettos, a shrine dedicated to Zeus the rain-bringer. Langdon thinks that farmers praying for rain to nourish the crops left the pottery on Hymettos as dedications. According to Hesiod, *Works and Days* 487-490, in the planting season, rain is needed at specific times and amounts for the crop to germinate successfully. Langdon then argues against Howe's reconstruction of pastoralism in Mycenaean and Dark Age Greece, and cites the granary models as the main proof for an emphasis on grain production. However, worshippers could also have come to the shrine to pray for rain for pastures, so the evidence does not unilaterally point to worshippers who practiced only grain agriculture.

10. The context of this passage raises interesting questions. The poet begins the passage with an optative "let there be," and then gives the list of luxury foods. In line 592-596, the syntax turns to indirect statement. The person enjoying these delicacies is masculine singular, but not necessarily the narrator. The impression is of a single man sitting in the summer shade, eating and drinking in solitary enjoyment. But feasts should be shared, if not among neighbors (cf. 342-343), at least within the household.

BIBLIOGRAPHY

Antonaccio, Carla. 1994. *Contesting the past: Hero cult, tomb cult and epic in early Greece*. American Journal of Archaeology 98:389-410.

————. 1995. *An archaeology of ancestors: Tomb cult and hero cult in early Greece*. Lanham, Md.: Rowman and Littlefield.

Aschenbrenner, Stanley E. 1972. A contemporary community. In McDonald and Rapp 1972, 47-63.

Bennet, John. 1992. "Collectors" or "Owners?" In Olivier 1992, 65-101.

————. 1995. Space through time: Diachronic perspectives on the spatial organization of the Pylian state. In Laffineur and Niemeier 1995, 587-602.

Betancourt, Philip P. 1976. The end of the Greek Bronze Age. *Antiquity* 50: 40-46.

Bintliff, John. 1982. Settlement patterns, land tenure and social structure: A diachronic model. In *Ranking, resource and exchange*, edited by Colin Renfrew and Stephen Shennan, 106-11. Cambridge: Cambridge University Press.

Blegen, Carl W. 1939. Excavations at Pylos, 1939. *American Journal of Archaeology* 43:557-76.

Burford, Alison. 1993. *Land and labor in the Greek world*. Baltimore: Johns Hopkins University Press.

Carlier, Pierre. 1992. Les collectors son-ils des fermiers? In Olivier 1992, 159-66.

Chang, Claudia. Sheep for the ancestors: Ethnoarchaeology and the study of ancient pastoralism. In Kardulias 1994, 353-71.

Cherry, John. 1988. Pastoralism and the role of animals in the pre- and protohistoric economies of the Aegean. In Whittaker 1988, 6-34.

Coldstream, J. N. 1977. *Geometric Greece*. New York: St. Martin's.

———. 1994. Urns with lids: The visible face of the Knossian "Dark Age." In *Knossos, a labyrinth of history: Papers in honour of Sinclair Hood*, edited by Don Evely, Helen Hughes-Brock, and Nicoletta Momigliano, 105-121. London: British School at Athens.

Davis, Jack L., Yannos G. Lolos, Susan E. Alcock, Cynthia W. Shelmerdine, and John Bennet. 1997. The Pylos region archaeological project, part I: Overview and the archaeological survey. *Hesperia* 66:391-494.

Dickinson, Oliver. 1998. The Bronze Age palace societies. In *Greek Civilization: An Introduction*, edited by Brian Sparkes, 38-53. Oxford: Blackwell Publishers.

Donlan, Walter. 1997. The Homeric economy. In *A New Companion to Homer*, edited by Ian Morris and Barry Powell, 649-67. *Mnemosyne* Supplement 163. Leiden: Brill.

Donlan, Walter, and Carol G. Thomas. 1993. The village community of ancient Greece: Neolithic, Bronze and Dark Ages. *Studi Micenei ed Egeo-anatolici* 31: 61-71.

Driessen, Jan. 1993. "Collector's items": Observations sur l'élite Mycénienne de Cnossos. In Olivier 1992, 197-214.

Finley, Moses I. 1954. *The world of Odysseus*. London: Penguin. 2d rev. ed. 1978.

———. 1957. Mycenaean palace archives and economic history. *Economic History Review* ser. 2, 10: 128-41. Reprinted and cited from Finley 1983, 199-212.

———. 1983. *Economy and society in ancient Greece*, edited by Brent D. Shaw and Richard Saller. London: Penguin.

Forbes, Hamish. 1995. The identification of pastoral sites within the context of estate-based agriculture in ancient Greece. *Annual of the British School at Athens* 90:325-38.

Fotiadis, Michael. 1985. *Economy, ecology and settlement among subsistence farmers in the Serres Basin, northeastern Greece, 5000-1000 B.C.* Ph.D. diss., Indiana University.

Foxhall, Lin. 1995. Bronze to iron: Agricultural systems and political structures in late Bronze Age and early Iron Age Greece. *Annual of the British School at Athens* 90:239-50.

Garnsey, Peter, and Ian Morris. 1989. Risk and the *polis:* The evolution of institutionalized responses to food supply problems in the ancient Greek state. In Halstead and O'Shea 1989, 98-105.

Godart, Louis. 1992. Les collectors dans le monde égéen. In Olivier 1992, 257-83.

Haggis, Donald. 1993. Intensive survey, traditional settlement patterns, and Dark Age Crete: The case of early Iron Age Kavousi. *Journal of Mediterranean Archaeology* 6:131-174.

Halstead, Paul. 1981. Counting sheep in Neolithic and Bronze Age Greece. In *Pattern of the past: Studies in honour of David Clarke*, edited by Ian Hodder, 307-39. Cambridge: Cambridge University Press.

———. 1989. The economy has a normal surplus: Economic stability and social change among early farming communities of Thessaly, Greece. In Halstead and O'Shea 1989, 68-80.

———. 1990/91. Lost sheep? On the Linear B evidence for breeding flocks at Knossos and Pylos. *Minos* 25-26:343-65.

———. 1992a. Agriculture in the Bronze Age. In *Agriculture in ancient Greece*, edited by Berit Wells, 105-15. Goteborg: Paul Åströms Förlag.

———. 1992b. Mycenaean palatial economy: Making the most of the gaps in the evidence. *Proceedings of the Cambridge Philological Society* 38:57-86.

———. 1996. Pastoralism or household herding? Problems of scale and specialization in early Greek animal husbandry. *World Archaeology* 28:20-42.

Halstead, Paul, and John O'Shea, eds. 1989. *Bad year economics: Cultural responses to risk and uncertainty*. Cambridge: Cambridge University Press.

Hanson, Victor Davis. 1995. *The other Greeks: The family farm and the agrarian roots of western civilization*. New York: Free Press.

Hodkinson, Stephen. 1988. Animal husbandry in the Greek *polis*. In Whittaker 1988, 35-74.

Hope Simpson, Richard. 1965. *Gazetteer and atlas of Mycenaean sites*, Bulletin Supplement 16. London: Institute of Classical Studies.

Howe, Thalia Phillies. 1958. Linear B and Hesiod's breadwinners. *Transactions of the American Philological Association* 89:44-65.

Hurwit, Jeffrey. 1993. Art, poetry, and the *polis* in the age of Homer. In Langdon 1993, 14-42.

Isager, Signe, and Jens Erik Skydsgaard. 1992. *Ancient Greek agriculture*. London: Routledge.

Kardulias, P. Nick, ed. 1994. *Beyond the site: Regional studies in the Aegean area*. Lanham Md.: University Press of America.

Killen, J. T. 1985. The Linear B tablets and the Mycenaean economy. In *Linear B: A 1984 Survey*, edited by Anna Morpurgo-Davies and Yves Duhoux, 241-305. Bibliotheque des Cahiers de l'Institut de linguistique de Louvain 26. Louvain-la-Neuve: Cabay.

———. 1995. Some further thoughts on "collectors." In Laffineur and Niemeier 1995, 213-24.

———. 1998. The role of the state in wheat and olive production in Mycenaean Greece. *Aevum* 72:19-23.

Klippel, Walter E., and Lynn M. Snyder. 1991. Dark Age fauna from Kavousi, Crete: The vertebrates from the 1987 and 1988 Excavations. *Hesperia* 60:179-86.

Laffineur, Robert, and Wolf-Dietrich Niemeier, eds. 1995. *Politeia: Society and the state in the Aegean Bronze Age*. Aegaeum 12. Brussels: Université de Liège.

Langdon, Merle. 1976. *A Sanctuary of Zeus on Mt. Hymettos*. Hesperia Suppl. 16. Princeton: American School of Classical Studies.

Langdon, Susan, ed. 1993. *From pasture to polis: Art in the age of Homer*. Columbia: University of Missouri Press.

———, ed. 1997. *New light on a dark age: Exploring the culture of Geometric Greece*. Columbia: University of Missouri Press.

Lorimer, Hilda L. 1950. *Homer and the monuments*. London: Macmillan.

Mancz, Elizabeth Ann. 1989. *An examination of changing patterns of animal husbandry of the Late Bronze and Dark Ages of Nichoria in the southwestern Peloponnese*. Ph.D. diss., University of Minnesota.

McDonald, William A., and Richard Hope Simpson. 1972. Archaeological Exploration. In McDonald and Rapp 1972, 117-47.

McDonald, William A., and George Rapp, Jr., eds. 1972. *The Messenia Minnesota expedition.* Minneapolis: University of Minnesota.

McDonald, William A., William D. E. Coulson, and John Rosser. 1983. *Excavations at Nichoria. Vol III. Dark Age and Byzantine Occupation.* University of Minnesota Press, 1983.

Morris, Holly J. 1986. *An economic model of the late Mycenaean kingdom of Pylos,* Ph.D diss., University of Minnesota.

Morris, Ian. 1987. *Burial and ancient society: The rise of the Greek city-state.* Cambridge: Cambridge University Press.

———. 1991. The early *polis* as city and state. In *City and country in the ancient world,* edited by John Rich and Andrew Wallace-Hadrill, 24-57. London: Routledge.

Olivier, Jean-Pierre, ed. 1992. *Mykenaïka.* Actes du IXe Colloque international sur les textes mycéniens et égéens. *Bulletin de Correspondance Hellénique* Suppl. 25. Paris: de Boccard.

Osborne, Robin. 1987. *Classical landscape with figures: The ancient Greek city and its countryside.* London: G. Philip.

Palmer, Ruth. 1992. Wheat and barley in Mycenaean society. In Olivier 1992, 473-95.

———. 1994. *Wine in the Mycenaean palace economy. Aegaeum* 10. Liège: Université de Liège.

———. 1999. Perishable goods in Mycenaean texts. In *Floreant Studia Mycenaea,* edited by Sigrid Deger-Jalkotzy and Georg Nightengale, 463-85. Proceedings of the Tenth International Colloquium on Mycenaean and Aegean texts. Salzburg: Institut für alte Geschichte.

Polanyi, Karl. 1944. *The great transformation: The political and economic origins of our time.* New York: Holt Rinehart.

———. 1957. The economy as instituted process. In *Trade and market in the early empires,* edited by Karl Polanyi, Conrad M. Arensberg, and Harry W. Pearson, 243-70. Glencoe, Ill.: Free Press. Reprinted in Polanyi 1968, 139-74.

———. 1960. On the comparative treatment of economic institutions in antiquity with illustrations from Athens, Mycenae and Alalakh. In *City Invincible,* Carl H. Kraeling and Robert M. Adams, 329-50. Chicago: University of Chicago Press. Reprinted in Polanyi 1968, 306-34.

———. 1968. *Primitive, archaic and modern economies: Essays of Karl Polanyi,* edited by George Dalton. Boston: Beacon Press.

Postgate, J. N. 1992. *Early Mesopotamia: Society and economy at the dawn of history.* London: Routledge.

Rapp, George T., and S.E. Aschenbrenner, eds. 1978. *Excavations at Nichoria.* Vol I: *Site, environs, and techniques.* Minneapolis, University of Minnesota.

Reese, David. 1994. Recent work in Greek zooarchaeology. In Kardulias 1994, 191-221.

Renfrew, Colin. 1972. *The emergence of civilisation: The Cyclades and the Aegean in the third millennium B.C.* London: Methuen.

Sallares, Richard. 1991. *The ecology of the ancient Greek world.* Ithaca: Cornell University Press.

Shay, Jennifer M. and C. Thomas Shay. 1978. Modern vegetation and fossil plant remains. In Rapp and Aschenbrenner, 41-59.

Skydsgaard, Jens Erik. 1988. Transhumance in ancient Greece. In Whittaker 1988, 75-86.

Sloan, Robert E., and Mary Ann Duncan. 1978. Zooarchaeology of Nichoria. In Rapp and Aschenbrenner 1978, 60-77.

Smithson, Evelyn Lord. 1968. The tomb of a rich Athenian lady, ca. 850 B.C. *Hesperia* 37:77-116.

Snodgrass, Anthony M. 1971. *The Dark Age of Greece.* Edinburgh: Edinburgh University Press.

———. 1980. *Archaic Greece: The age of experiment.* Berkeley: University of California Press.

———. 1983. Two demographic notes: The size of Lefkandi; Population in late eighth-century Attica. In *The Greek renaissance of the eighth century B.C.: Tradition and innovation,* edited by Robin Hägg, 167-71. Stockholm: Paul Åströms Förlag.

———. 1987. *An archaeology of Greece: The present state and future scope of a discipline.* Berkeley: University of California Press.

Tandy, David W. 1997. *Warriors into traders: The power of the market in early Greece.* Berkeley: University of California Press.

Ventris, Michael, and John Chadwick. 1953. Evidence for Greek dialect in the Mycenaean archives. *Journal of Hellenic Studies* 73:84-103.

———. 1956. *Documents in Mycenaean Greek.* Cambridge: Cambridge University Press. 2d ed. 1973 = Docs2.

Vickery, Kenton Frank. 1936. *Food in early Greece.* Urbana: University of Illinois Press.

Whittaker, C.R., ed. 1988. *Pastoral economies in classical antiquity.* Cambridge Philological Society Suppl., vol. 14. Cambridge: Cambridge University Press.

Zangger, Eberhard, Falko Kuhnke, Michael E. Timpson, Jost Knauss, and Sergei B. Yazvenko. 1997. The Pylos regional archaeological project, part II: Landscape evolution and site preservation. *Hesperia* 66:549-641.

Chapter Three

ETHNIC IDENTITY
AND *ALTERTUMSWISSENSCHAFT*

Jeremy McInerney

In his lectures at Columbia University in the late 1940s, Karl Polanyi asserted that in the text of Hesiod's *Works and Days* we can detect "the rise of the individual" away from his dependence on the collective, on the tribe (Polanyi 1977, 147-57). In this paper, I want to look at this phenomenon that Polanyi articulated in his own (as usual) special way and see how our perception of early Greek tribes was shaped by events and cultural trends of the nineteenth and twentieth centuries. Ancient History, as an intellectual discipline, and as distinct from mere antiquarianism, did not undergo a long period of gestation during the years of the enlightenment but emerged fully formed from the head of the Prussian Minister of Education in 1807. It was in that year that Wilhelm von Humboldt declared:

> In the Greeks we have before us a nation in whose fortunate hands everything, which, according to our deepest feelings, sustains the noblest and richest aspects of human existence, matured to the utmost perfection...To know them is for us not just pleasant, advantageous and indispensable (*nicht bloβ angenehm, nützlich und notwendig*); only in them do we find the ideal of that which we ourselves should like to be and to produce.[1]

It was in this same year, not coincidentally, that Fichte delivered his *Address to the German Nation.* This was an epochal year. Napoleon had just defeated the Prussian army at Jena, and in the wake of this disaster the aims and content of the Prussian educational system were to be completely revolutionized. The study of classics would be placed at the heart of the curriculum not because learning dead languages was considered good exercise for the mind but because the new *Bildung* was going to rebuild Prussian society in the image of its more perfect antecedent, ancient Greece.

The importance of these conditions for the subsequent development of *Altertumswissenschaft,* as the new discipline was called, have often been overlooked. This is unfortunate, not merely because the intellectual history of the nineteenth century is itself fascinating, but also because many of the ideas and patterns of thinking that were a part of nineteenth-century Ancient History still exert a powerful influence today, often the more so for not being recognized. Foremost among the notions we have inherited from the historians of the last century are assumptions concerning Greek ethnicity. The reasons for this are complex, and include a tendency in post-colonial society to look upon tribes as ancient and traditional, as opposed to that locus of alienation, modern society. Tribes are often thought to be closed social systems that mold the identity of their members by virtue of their age-old ties of blood and custom. In fact, tribes and tribal identity are now known to be anything but set and inflexible, and are better thought of as situational, that is, adaptable and relatively fluid. But aside from sharing this general tendency to misunderstand the nature of tribes and ethnicity, Greek historians have also inherited misconceptions about Greek tribes, *ethne,* that are specifically due to the fact that nineteenth-century German historians colonized the historical imagination of European scholarship. What they established was the view that Greek political evolution was the earliest example of the triumph of national character. Grappling with the problem of German identity and the tensions between separatism and unification, these historians tried to find in the Greek material answers to their own dilemmas. Tribes were treated semi-mystically as the carriers of a genius under whose influence the Greeks achieved those cultural accomplishments which put them at the fountainhead of European culture. The political system which evolved in the

Classical age was infused with this spirit and, paradoxically, made tribes redundant as political organisms. National character expressed the genius of the people, but, it was believed, the people outgrew their tribes. In fact, the political evolution of the various Greek states, both *poleis* and *ethne*, in the Archaic period was not dictated by antecedent ethnic divisions. Rather, these divisions shaped the discourse on ethnicity that unfolded throughout Greece after 800 B.C.E. In this paper I propose to show how the early practitioners of *Altertumswissenschaft* established a pattern in the interpretation of Greek ethnicity that persists today. Then, drawing on recent studies in Anthropology and African Studies, I hope to demonstrate that a more nuanced approach to the *ethnos* is possible, allowing us to see the Archaic period of Greek history as a time of political experimentation, for which the *ethnos* was an especially adaptable form.

Von Humboldt's manifesto should come as no surprise since the idealization of Greece is the dominant *leitmotif* running through German intellectual and cultural life throughout the late eighteenth and early nineteenth centuries.[2] Aesthetic romanticism constantly used the Greeks as a touchstone. Schiller, for example, was captivated by Winkelmann's work and saw in the Greeks a paradigm of humanity. Like von Humboldt, Schiller was explicit about the relationship between the Greeks and the Germans, claiming in the Sixth Letter of his tract *On the Aesthetic Education of Man*, that "[the Greeks] are at the same time our rivals (*unsre Nebenbuhler*), indeed often our models (*unsre Muster*) in those very excellences with which we are wont to console ourselves for the unnaturalness of our manners" (Schiller 1967, 6.2). In contrast to Europeans in general and Germans in particular, the individual Greek, for Schiller, represented his entire society. This theme of personal integration as a mirror of society was picked up by Herder, who also found in the Greeks a synthesis of human qualities absent in his own society. In the *Denkmahl Johann Winkelmanns* he called for a "rebirth of the Greek spirit in Germany" (Herder 1778, 436). Hölderlin's poetry reflects a similar sense of awe before the Greeks, not only for their separate qualities but for their capacity to integrate them into a single, seamless culture. In 1793 he composed the "Hymne an die Genius Griechenlands" and in *Hyperion* he explicitly contrasted the brilliance of the Greeks with the world of his own contemporaries, saying, "I can think of no people as torn apart as the Germans" (Hölderlin 1992, 754). The same interpretation, according to which the Greeks were the positive image of Germany's negative, was developed by Hegel. In Athenian society he saw a realization of the harmony lacking in the spiritually and socially fragmented lives of contemporary Germans. Two years before von Humboldt was to set about remaking Prussia in the image of Athens, Hegel declared that the Greek *polis* was a work of art, an ideal and harmonious entity (Hegel 1931, 251).

The consistent emphasis on Greece as a fully realized, integrated whole, capable of nurturing its citizens and producing a culture of genius holds the key to the attraction of philhellenism to the poets and thinkers of German romanticism. The Greece of their imagination stood in sharp contrast to the Germany of their own day. In France and England political unification had been accomplished centuries earlier, but Germany was still divided, and, despite the revolutions of 1830 and 1848, would remain so until the triumph of Bismarck's policies in the period 1866-1871. The country was made up of over 300 separate states, ranging from the kingdoms of Prussia and Bavaria to the Bishopric of Osnabrück. So entrenched were these various principalities, dukedoms and kingdoms that one historian has called particularism (*Kleinstaaterei*) "the very essence of German political life of the period (Plant 1972, 25). Those, then, who spoke of the German nation (as Fichte did in 1807), were using "a hortatory figment of the ethical imagination" (Kelly in Fichte 1968, xxxi). Political fragmentation was matched by religious divisions, but a shared culture offered glimpses of a more deeply embedded unity. The urge to overcome the debilitating effects of regionalism spurred an interest in those elements of culture that produced, or at least betokened, unity, such as the common folklore of the German people recorded and assembled by the Brothers Grimm. The romantic conceits of *Volk* and *Geist* were especially serviceable in this enterprise, expressing the imagined essence of German unity.[3] The Greeks were attractive to those concerned with these issues, because they were the proof that national genius could produce a sublime culture regardless of political unification.

Despite the fact that romanticism was more often associated with radicals and liberals, German philhellenism was essentially conservative. It advocated a cultural, not a political transformation. Aesthetic romanticism led the Philhellenes to set Classical Greece up as a spiritual model, but they never proposed abolishing the institutions of the German states in favour of Athenian-style democracy.[4] Schiller, for example, was horrified to find that his poem "Die Götter Griechenlands" had been interpreted as a political statement and revised it, emphasizing the metaphysical aspects of his philosophy (Marchand 1996, 3). In this respect the German use of Greece was utterly different from the French use of Rome. Indeed, the perfect image of Greece which Germans encountered in the mirror of history was much less politically charged than the Rome which the French encountered in the pages of Livy. The power of their identification with Rome is displayed in the flood of neoclassical works that poured out of the atelier of Jacques-Louis David. Later, when the revolution lapsed into the absolutism of Napoleon's rule, the same historical identity could still be plundered, allowing Napoleon to present himself as consul and finally as the new Augustus, the first emperor. As the revolution first dissolved into terror and then recast itself in strongly nationalistic colours, the association of French radicalism with the Romans inspired in reaction an even deeper German identification with the Greeks (Fichte 1968, 7.388-90, 495).

Von Humboldt's *Bildung* and the science of *Altertumswissenschaft* that came into being at the same time were therefore influenced by a combination of factors. Romantic idolization of Greece had already been a feature of German intellectual life for a generation. It had identified Greece as Germany's ideal *Doppelgänger* in a way that was seemed apolitical, but which was conservative precisely because it eschewed any revolutionary overtones. The elevation of Greece to the level of a cultural obsession had been facilitated by the fact that both cultures were constructed around the tension between cultural unity and political fragmentation. In this climate, and already convinced of the status of the Greeks as demi-gods, von Humboldt and the new German professoriate created an educational system whose purpose was to gather and analyze all that could be known about the history and culture of the Greeks, but whose function was to ensure the security of Prussia's social and political institutions. In fact, there were radical seeds in this programme, but the harvest did not come in 1848. Von Humboldt's programme would become a blue-print for the cultural unification and spiritual renaissance of Germany, culminating in the events of 1872.

What distinguished *Altertumswissenschaft* from the earlier panegyrics of the Romantics was that the German professoriate did not rely on intermediaries such as Winkelmann or Cicero to bring the Greeks to life for them. Their research entailed detailed historical investigation of the primary sources, based on an exhaustive reading of the literary texts, soon to be supplemented by the new disciplines of epigraphy and papyrology. This would result in prodigious feats of scholarship, making possible the work of men like Jacoby and Fraenkel in this century. In the works of the first generations of scholars produced by this system, however, the framework into which many of the "facts" of history were arranged was borrowed from the contemporary German struggle to reconcile a national identity with political fragmentation.

Ancient Greece was figured as the precursor of Germany in form as well as spirit. This is conspicuous in Niebuhr's 1853 *Lectures on Ancient Ethnography and Geography* in which he repeatedly uses German *Länder* to interpret Greek *ethne*. For example, to explain the importance, in ancient Greece, of the Dorians, Niebuhr notes that the homeland of Doris was only the size of the Swiss canton of Uri, with a population of 12,000. And to explain how the people of so small a territory could become so influential, he compares Doris and the Dorians to Angeln in Schleswig and its original inhabitants, the Angli (Niebuhr 1853, 135). Just as tribes and territory were similar in both cultures, so too historical events in one could show how episodes in the other's history should be interpreted. The Sacred War

(356-346 B.C.E.), for example, had been improperly named, according to Niebuhr, because it was not a dispute over sacred territory at all. It had been stirred up by the Thessalians and Boiotians against the Phokians, who were driven to the desperate defense of their country, and who ravaged the territory of their hostile neighbours, just as the Hussites of fifteenth-century Bohemia spread devastation far and wide throughout Bavaria, Franconia and Saxony (Niebuhr 1853, 133).

The two most influential treatments to make early Greece an analogue of Germany were Karl Otfried Müller's *Die Dorier* and Ernst Curtius's *Griechische Geschichte*. Müller's work served as the foundation for an immensely popular interpretation of Greek culture, according to which the Dorians were supposed to have exhibited the innate genius responsible for the cultural accomplishments of the Greeks (Müller 1820-1824). The same theory was advanced by Curtius, Müller's student, and gained wide currency beyond the academy. His history went through six editions and was translated into English. (Some measure of the popularity of the Dorian thesis can be seen in the fact that as recently as 1986 serious scholarly treatment of the Dorians still began with a critique of Müller's racial theories; see Musti 1990, xii-xiv.) Teacher and student alike took for granted that tribes had distinct, fixed, and identifiable characteristics, and that early Greek history was shaped by the fusion of Ionian and Dorian spirit. But reading Curtius's treatment of dialect differences between the two Greek tribes, one wonders whether he is describing Ionians and Dorians or Prussians and Bavarians.

> In [Doric Greek's] full and broad sounds we recognize the chest strengthened by mountain air and mountain life; its characteristics are brevity of form and expression, such as suit a race which, in the midst of the labors and privations of its daily life, has neither much care nor time for long speeches (Curtius 1867, 35).

And as for Ionian:

> Here life was easier, the acquisition of property readier to hand, the incitements from without more numerous and various. The tendency

to ease expresses itself in the restriction of the number of aspirate sounds, a collision of which is especially avoided; t is thinned down into s: the sounds are formed less frequently in the back of the mouth and the throat; in short, men take things easily (Curtius 1867, 35).

One might just as easily have been distinguishing between the hard and soft pronunciations of "Ich" in Berlin and Munich. But for Müller and Curtius, what was at stake was not simply a question of pronunciation. Rather, they read the differences between the Greek dialects as indicators of two distinct sets of national characteristics, a view which reflected Herder's belief that the uniqueness of a people was reflected both in its culture and its language.

Differences in dialect pointed to other fundamental oppositions, such as the physical environment and national character that complemented each dialect. In particular, the Dorians were studied. Aside from their laconic speech the two aspects of the Dorians most emphasized were the healthy, alpine environment in which they were nurtured and the unique quality of their contribution to Greek culture. Curtius saw them as rugged highlanders:

The very nature of the northern highlands forces their inhabitants to live in their narrow, well-watered valleys as peasants, shepherds, and hunters; to steel their strength by the Alpine air, and to preserve it intact amidst their simple and natural conditions of life, until the time shall have come for them to descend into the regions farther to the south, the more subdivided and manifold formation of which has, in turn, assigned to them the mission of becoming a theatre for the creation of states, and of leading their inhabitants in an eastward direction into the maritime and coast intercourse of a new and wider world (Curtius 1867, 19).

The environmental determinism in this passage is no less remarkable than its messianic theme. The Dorians and Ionians were, after all, both Greek, but the contrast between the tough simplicity of the mountains and the variegated topography of the south allowed Curtius to attribute to Dorians and Ionians different and complementary rôles. Faced with adverse conditions the

Dorians turned conservative. Preserving simplicity and a natural life was their response to the challenge of a harsh environment. The Ionians, meanwhile, were conditioned by variety, movement, and experimentation. They built states, created commerce, and took to the water. The blending of these two would result in Greek culture.

According to this scheme the two complementary ethnicities were physically united as a result of the migrations of the heroic period recalled in myth and poetry. At an early stage in these population movements the term Hellas had applied only to part of Thessaly. This is how Homer uses the name. Based on this fact Curtius located the homeland of Greek culture there and imagined that the extension of the name Hellas to include all of Greece was evidence of the diffusion of Greek culture from a single birthplace in northern Greece. It was in Thessaly, then, that the emergence of national identity took place, and Thessaly, therefore, became a Dorian locale:

> Thessaly long remained the proper country of Hellenes, who with undying veneration revered Olympus as the home of their gods, and the valley of the Peneus as the cradle of their political development. The service rendered by the Dorian tribe lay in having carried the germs of national culture out of Thessaly, where the invasion of ruder peoples disturbed and hindered their farther growth, into the land towards the south, where the germs received an unexpectedly new and grand development (Curtius 1867, 130).

Here we see Curtius using the geography of legendary Greece in two ways: to historicize the movement of the Dorians from the north into their eventual home in the Peloponnese, and to legitimize the claim of a uniquely Dorian contribution to Greek culture. The first of these aims found support not only in the well-attested distribution of the Greek dialects but also in epichoric myth. The return of the Herakleidai, in particular, suggested a mythopoetic rendering of an historical migration into the Peloponnese. It was, however, on the question of the Dorian genius that Müller's disciples pushed positivism to the limit. Schoemann asserted that there was a clear spiritual difference between Dorian and Ionian, evidence for which, he proposed, could be found in the areas of art, architecture, and music (Schoemann 1855, 88). The essential characteristics of this Dorian spirit (*Geist*) he identified as *Zweckmäßigheit* (purposefulness), *Festigheit* (constancy) and *Solidität* (firmness). Others would go much further. Not content with isolating static qualities Curtius attempted to reconstruct an entire heroic history for central Greece which would foreshadow the accomplishments of the Classical age and prove that they were inspired by the Dorians. He began with the assertion that the Dorians "possessed an innate tendency towards the establishment, preservation and spread of fixed systems" (Curtius 1867, 125). In their Thessalian phase, Curtius believed, the Dorians had pioneered the idea of federalism. They had made this a reality by founding the Delphic Amphiktyony, "the combination of all the tribes of the same descent from Olympus to the bay of Corinth" (Curtius 1867, 125). Here was a federation that embraced many tribes, and acknowledged their common blood. It achieved unity without imposing the political domination of any single state. In the context of German political and intellectual debate of the mid-nineteenth century, when the same problems of unification and separatism were real and immediate issues, Curtius's Amphiktyony can only have seemed ideal. It exemplified the operation of *Gemeinschaft*, and offered a solution to the contemporary dilemma of *Einheit*.

Central to the unification of the northern tribes was the position of Delphi. Not only was it imagined to be the physical meeting place for the Amphiktyony but also, as the site of Apollo's oracle, it was its heart and soul. In Curtius's mystical vision of Dorian genius Delphi was transformed from an oracular shrine into the earthly setting for a complete and morally superior religious system. Race and religion would authorize and shape the course of state formation: "Preeminently the Apolline religion derived from the majesty of its moral ideas and the spiritual superiority of its professors (the Dorians) the mission of assembling around it, and uniting amongst themselves, the various districts of the land" (Curtius 1867, 124). This synthesis of ethnicity and politics was important in the scheme proposed by

Curtius because he also envisaged these ethnic accomplishments as a necessary precondition to the emergence of a truly universal Greek culture:

> The whole vital action of a people lies in its races, by them all great performances are accomplished: and accordingly fall into the divisions of Doric and Ionic art, Doric and Ionic systems of life, political constitutions and philosophy...The separate life of the individual races had to be exhausted before a common Hellenic type could assert itself in language, literature and art (Curtius 1867, 38).

In Curtius's interpretation, then, it was the particular and fixed characteristics of the earlier tribe which created distinct culture and paved the way to the realization of national culture. It need hardly be said that this entire reconstruction of the heroic period amounts to no more than a flight of imagination. There is no evidence that the Amphiktyony was under the control of the Dorians, either directly or indirectly, nor is it clear that the tribal Amphiktyony was in any way a political union. And one can only wonder what is meant by "the majesty of the moral ideas" of Apolline religion. But Curtius's fanciful reading of early Greek history proved immensely popular, and a major reason for this is that it paralleled so closely the Germans' experience of their own ethnic identity. Like the Greeks the Germans shared an Indo-European language that was broken into various dialects. The Germans were fond of imagining themselves as a single *Volk*, but acknowledged the existence of many ethnic sub-divisions (*Unterstämme*), such as Saxons, Hessians, and Friesians, much as for the Greeks the term "Hellene" encompassed Dorian, Ionian, Aiolian, and, at another level, Lokrian, Boiotian and Arkadian. Both cultures were nurtured by a rich myth-history expressed in epic poetry that told of an heroic age. The Müller-Curtius interpretation of legendary Greece was, in fact, a figuring of the distant Greek past on the model of an equally romanticized German past.

The particular value of legendary Greece lay in the fact that it validated contemporary belief in a *Volksgeist*.[5] As an expression of at least one kind of unity this was reassuring for a German society which, despite its cultural homogeneity, was still politically fragmented. It was also an inherently conservative idea since it marginalized political debate over real constitutions by subordinating such debate to the search for the chimera of national identity. For German historians the Greeks legitimized this use of *Volksgeist* by offering a prestigious precedent for treating as distinct the matters of ethnic character and constitutional form. They had established dozens of separate democracies and oligarchies, which, despite being divorced from each other, were united at the deeper levels of blood and language. Thus the cultural accomplishments of the Greeks could serve as proof that constitutional differences were less important than the mysterious bonds of ethnicity. True greatness arose from within the race.

By the end of the century some historians had recoiled from the excesses of Müller and his followers, but even when George Grote and Karl Beloch rejected the Müller-Curtius reconstruction as fundamentally unsound they did so for reasons of methodology. They did not question the underlying notion that ethnicity was fixed. Grote, for example, in describing the structure of the Amphiktyony, says that its members were all counted as races, adding parenthetically that, "if we treat the Hellenes as a race, we must call these subraces" (Grote 1899, 246). Grote was not troubled by the belief in a specifically Greek genius, but by the fact that there were no adequate criteria by which one could assess the historicity of legendary material.[6] Beloch was more ferocious in his criticisms of his predecessors and charged that almost the entire course of nineteenth-century scholarship had been ruined by Müller and Niebuhr.[7] Despite this he too was capable of declaring that national individuality was, in the first instance, contingent upon speech (Beloch 1912, 67). Language reflected national character. Beloch accepted that this national character was innate and unique, existing at a level more primal even than language. The very fact that a foreigner who acquired a language did not thereby acquire nationality proved that national character preceded language. In a chilling footnote Beloch observed,

> Speech alone does not constitute national character. An English speaking Black is still far from being an Englishman; and a Jew who

spoke Greek as his mother-tongue counted in antiquity as Greek as little as today for us a German-speaking Jew counts as German (Beloch 1912, 67, n. 1).

This understanding of innate national character emphasized exclusivity. It was therefore impossible for Beloch to imagine the tribes located on the northwestern periphery of the central Greek world as ethnic states that had assimilated Greek culture through trade or contact. They simply either were or were not Greek. Of the Amphilochians, for example, he says, "The tribe has a genuinely Greek name."[8] He notes the Greek names of their towns and points out that Thucydides reported the inhabitants of the capital spoke Greek, but this was because they were colonists from Ambrakia, while the indigenous inhabitants were barbarian. Since the barriers between such distinct groups were insurmountable, Beloch could only surmise that they coexisted, but not as equals. Instead, the Greek speakers necessarily dominated a backward peasant class. Though Belch conceded the remote possibility of a mixing of the Greek and non-Greek populations, he preferred a scenario in which a Greek city exercised control over a non-Greek countryside. "This is exactly what happened among the Amphilochians, just as it has happened in every region and in every time period."[9]

While German historians were exploring the racial dimension of Greek history in the heroic period, French historiography was pursuing a more scientific approach. In 1864, Fustel de Coulanges published *La Cité Antique*, and, in the context of the time of its publication, a remarkably distinctive feature of the work is the absence of a racial theory to explain the origin of Greek culture. Instead of race or tribe, Fustel de Coulanges saw the family at the heart of ancient society. The family was "enlarged and extended" by religion into ever greater institutions: *gens*, phratry, and tribe (Fustel de Coulanges 1979, 13). State formation was here envisaged as an evolutionary process, beginning with the smallest social unit of human existence and progressing towards increasingly larger and more complex aggregates. The last stage of this process saw the emergence of the *polis*: "But just as several phratries were united in a tribe, several tribes might associate together, on

condition that the religion of each should be respected. The day on which this
alliance took place the city existed" (Fustel de Coulanges 1979, 127). Here
the emphasis was on gradual growth through a series of stages, each leaving
its mark in the fossil record of social institutions. However, it was not blood
which tied the ever larger groups together, but religion. Fustel de Coulanges
understood the importance of religion as a form of dialogue between human
groups and saw every social unit larger than the family not as an extension of
the kinship group but as a social construct, formed by the mutual consent of
all if its constituent parts.

Here was an approach that banished Romantic essentialism and offered
a way forward for those Germans who, like Eduard Meyer, rejected the racial
determinism of the previous generation. Meyer's work first appeared in 1884
and would later be praised by Beloch for its treatment of the religious history
of the Greeks and their spiritual life (Beloch 1926, 17). In this respect Meyer
showed himself to be the heir to Fustel de Coulanges. What is especially
apparent when Meyer's history is read against those of his predecessors is his
great concern with establishing a reliable methodology for the study of
history. Cautious of the elaborate *Sprachwissenschaft* used by Müller and
Curtius to assert the innate characteristics of Dorians and Ionians, Meyer
reminded his readers that the roots of the words supplied no more than
"abstrakte Hilfskonstruktionen" (Meyer 1907, 4). Where earlier historians
looked for unchanging qualities, rooted in race, Meyer emphasized the
mutability of human groups. Warfare, raiding, and enslavement, not to
mention trade, commerce, and the social intercourse ritualized by
guest-friendship, were all elements, in Meyer's view, in the constant
intermingling at the heart of Greek life. Hence, the key to the historical
development of the Greeks was not isolation, which was an aberration, but
the continuous mixing of new elements into new combinations:

> As rarely as the single man existed, so too the single group and the
> single state existed in isolation occasionally; but the perpetual
> exchange (*Austausch*), and the intermittent physical and psychological
> interchanges with other similar systems (*Gebilden*)…produced larger,

homogeneous cultures (*Bildungen*) of which it (the single state) was a part (Meyer 1907, 72).

Although Meyer refrained from an outright attack on Müller and Curtius such as Beloch would later write, his silence was just as telling. In a lengthy chapter with subheadings such as "Rasse, Sprachstamm, Volkstum" Meyer simply made no mention of Ionians or Dorians. In fact, his only reference to the great tribal divisions of early Greece emphasized the active process of ethnogenesis: "The larger, populous tribes and states differentiated themselves (scheiden sich) into two groups" (Meyer 1907, 72). His interpretation did not deny the existence of tribes, or even national character, but situated these within the larger setting of states and cultural zones:

> The individual state, however, never existed in isolation, but stood, even if it completely encompassed the characteristics of the people (*Volkstum*) and bore a national character, within a state-system, where procedures within the one state were constantly interacting with those in all the others, and later within a cultural zone (*Kulturkreise*); and in addition the various state-systems and cultural zones remained in contact with each other through exchange and reciprocal relations (Meyer 1907, 197).

Despite the modern outlook of Meyer's work—his understanding of relations between communities reads very much like the contemporary theory of peer-polity—his view of Greek history demanded a tribal phase to be followed by a *polis* phase. In a lecture delivered in 1904 at the University of Chicago, Meyer offered this overview, beginning with Mycenae:

> The result of this first epoch of the history of the Aegean world is undoubted: the earlier race, with whom the art originated, was absorbed by the Greek tribes, who adopted that civilization...But their states were internally weak, and their civilization died away; and at last they were overthrown by that invasion of ruder but stronger tribes from the mountains which is known by the name of the Doric migration (Meyer 1910, 223).

It is only after the tribal age that political development occurs:

> So the Greek world split into those innumerable political atoms which
> were the cause at the same time of its political weakness and of the
> versatility of the nation and the harmonious and manifold
> development of its civilization (Meyer 1910, 223-24).

Meyer may have avoided the Aryan fantasies of his predecessors, but the
underlying model for his scheme remained the same as the one used by each
of his German predecessors: a pre-*polis* society, characterized by separate
and distinct ethnic units. Subsequent generations have tended to interpret the
ethnos similarly. A good example of this is Schober's explanation of the
origins of the Phokians. Based on the classification of the Phokian dialect as a
mixture of Doric and Aiolic elements, he concluded, "The Phokians belong
to the group of northwestern Greeks who were neighbours of the Dorians
(*der den Dorern nahestehenden Gruppe der Nordwestgriechen*), and were
closely related to the inhabitants of Epeiros, Akarnania, Aitolia, south
Thessaly and Lokris."[10] According to the dialect hypothesis, the Boiotians led
the first wave of migrations into southern Central Greece. Next came the
Lokrians who were followed, and split, by the Phokians as they made their
way into the Kephisos valley. As recently as 1984 Schachermeyr used the
same dialect map to assert: "While it was probably the Lokrians who first
advanced out of Aitolia into the middle of central Greece, next came the
Phokians from the north. They seized for their own, as Phokis, the central
portion of Lokrian territory (Schachermeyr 1984, 236 n.12). In these
conventional reconstructions of the tribal phase of pre-*polis* socio-political
development, *ethne* are seen as separate and distinct units of fixed
membership. According to this essentialist reading of tribes, by no means
confined to Greek history, they were "fundamentally cultural groups that
had virtually impermeable boundaries."[11]

The linking of tribal migrations with the subsequent rise of cities
remains the most tangible legacy of two hundred years of German
historiography on the early historical period. It can be seen most clearly in

the work of Michael Sakellariou, who has offered a definition of state formation that is in a direct line from Hermann's work: "as soon as blood-related societies established permanent dwelling places, then contiguity began to have a stronger influence than kinship. . . . These groups acquired a political existence while ties based on kinship grew weaker."[12] According to this scheme the *ethnos* is a tribal unit that grows organically out of kinship networks, but is then superseded by the *polis*.[13] *Polis* and *ethnos* become expressions of fundamentally opposite socio-political phenomena. Since the *polis* exists in both a physical and a political dimension, expressed in the formation of an urban centre and some manner of synoicism, the *ethnos* has been inferred to have had the opposite characteristics. The definition suggested by Snodgrass is a good example: "In its purest form the *ethnos* was no more than a survival of the tribal system into historical times: a population scattered thinly over a territory without urban centres, united politically and in customs and religion, normally governed by means of some periodical assembly at a single centre, and worshiping a tribal deity at a common religious centre" (Snodgrass 1980, 42). At the same time, this conception of the *ethnos* as opposite to and earlier than the *polis* rests on the same assumptions that have governed studies of state formation in the Archaic period for the last one hundred years, namely, that the *ethnos* was a real extended kinship group, a natural extension of the ties of blood incorporating all those families who shared not just a common culture but also a common lineage.

Under the influence of these historians we continue to treat the *ethne* of Greece as vestiges of an earlier, less advanced system which was founded squarely on real and distinct ethnic groupings. The *ethnos* is figured as a social group based on kinship and blood ties, an aggregate of families, and the essential point in the political evolution of the Greeks is felt to be the break from the principle of kinship and the establishment of the principle of cohabitation. In other words, the tribe is rendered obsolete by the growth of communities not bound by blood. Then towns and cities can replace hamlets and villages, and the social and political evolution of the community can proceed as it turns to deal with matters of justice and the power of the state.

In reality, this is not how tribes function at all, and any reconstruction of the processes at work in Archaic Greece based on this conception is flawed. As Fredrick Barth has demonstrated, ethnic groups are dynamic and ethnicity is not a matter of biological inheritance but rather a conscious process of identification with a particular social group. For Barth, ethnicity is a process of differentiation between one set of people and another; it is a political act. It appeals to the *idea* of ineluctable cultural difference, but "in fact, people can readily invent cultural differences if it is in their political interest to do so. Ethnicity is the pursuit of political goals—the acquisition or maintenance of power, the mobilization of a following—through the creation of cultural commonness and difference."[14]

This applies not only to ethnic minorities in large modern states. There is a growing body of evidence to suggest that the ethnicity of tribal groups is also more elastic than was once imagined. In African studies, for example, field work and theoretical studies of the last generation have consistently emphasized the ambiguous nature of the tribe and have questioned the "earlier idea of the tribe as a simple and clearly bounded entity" (Southall 1970, 71). In his studies of the Alur, a Nilotic speaking people living in Uganda and Zaire, Aidan Southall has determined that behind the homogeneity and fixity suggested by a label such as "the Alur tribe" there lurks a reality that is heterogeneous and unstable. For centuries Alur chiefdoms incorporated various other people through migration, conquest, intermarriage, peaceful absorption, the founding of new communities only partially Alur in origin, and even through arbitration between non-Alur groups. New subclans were formed, changed allegiance, and died out. Fighting and feuding between groups ebbed and flowed, but all the while the slow process of incorporation went ahead and the Alur "tribe" took shape. Even then, because the Alur were formed by centuries of incorporation, there remained different levels of identification in Alur society. Some groups maintained traditions of separate ethnic origins but adopted Alur language, some accepted Alur rule but spoke their own language, some were assimilated completely. Southall has also examined Evans-Pritchard's famous studies of the Nuer and Dinka and has questioned the very use of these names, suggesting that they served as useful labels for the purposes of categorization but that it is unclear that there was ever a sense of ethnic identity among these groups "until the colonial administration told them who they were." Fixed tribal entities were in fact the creation of complex processes of differentiation both within these groups and partially imposed from without. The Dinka actually call themselves Jieng, the Nuer call themselves Naath, and within these groups, members from one subgroup visiting another might be treated as complete strangers. Early anthropology consistently downplayed the heterogeneity of "primitive" societies, giving us *the* Nuer, and *the* Talensi, because the main concern of these studies was to understand non-Western societies as isolates (ethnography) or as a universe of such units (cross cultural comparison). In employing these categories anthropologists were often following the lead of others. Politicians and administrators, for example, helped to create some of the best known American Indian tribes, such as the Navajo, Ute and Cheyenne, who were originally made up of autonomous bands, by driving them onto reservations. The groups that made up these tribes were often quite distinct, not even speaking the same language. One western historian has recently observed that the "Whites needed to invent a tribe so someone could sign the treaties."[15]

Colonialism entailed the greater codification of indigenous societies into categories and units capable of manipulation by colonial masters. At the same time, the creation of tribes where previously there existed shifting patterns of loyalty and identification could also become a collaborative exercise involving the active participation of local leaders. John Iliffe has termed this "progressive traditionalism" because it meant inventing tribal groups but concealing the process as a revitalization of a putatively dormant tribal identity. In his study of early twentieth-century Tanganyika he has demonstrated that some headmen cooperated with colonial authorities in this fiction because it was a mutually beneficial arrangement. The new, larger tribal entities enhanced the new chiefs' prestige and power while for the administrators amorphous and fluid social groupings were replaced by fixed, standardized tribal groups (Iliffe 1979, 318-41). Increasingly we are coming to realize that we have focused so relentlessly on the tribe as a category that we have lost sight of the tribe as a structure. We see a concrete entity, when the real essence of the tribe is its very fluidity. Summing up the problems of the older approach and the new directions offered by a different understanding of ethnicity, Terence Ranger has offered trenchant criticisms of African history that ought to be read by anyone interested in the issue of Greek ethnicity:

> The trouble with this [traditional] approach was that it totally misunderstood the realities of pre-colonial Africa. These societies had certainly valued custom and continuity but custom was loosely defined and infinitely flexible. Custom helped to maintain a sense of identity but it also allowed for an adaptation so spontaneous and natural that it was often unperceived. Moreover, there rarely exists in fact the closed, corporate, consensual system which came to be accepted as characteristic of "traditional" Africa. Almost all recent studies of nineteenth-century pre-colonial Africans moved in and out of multiple identities, defining themselves at one moment as subject to this chief, at another as member of that cult, at another moment as part of this clan, and at yet another moment as an initiate in that professional guild (Ranger 1983, 247-48).

Increasingly we are coming to realize that we have focused so relentlessly on the tribe as a category that we have lost sight of the real essence of the tribe: its very fluidity. Similarly Greek *ethne* were not closed kinship groups, but flexible systems incorporating many smaller, quite disparate groups. The Aitolians were made up of at least three lesser tribes, the Apodotoi, Eurytanes, and Ophiones, and possibly a fourth, the Agraioi. The Triphylians in the Peloponnese took their name from three distinct *phylai* who were unrelated to each other: indigenous Epeians, settlers from Minyan Orchomenos in Boiotia, and Elians from further north in the Peloponnese. Eventually Triphylia was annexed by the southern expansion of the Elian *ethnos* that also swallowed up the Pisatans and the Kaukones, an *ethnos* of whom Strabo remarks, somewhat paradoxically, "not even the name survived." It is often noted that Dorian communities all share the same tribal structure, as if this were proof that all Dorian communities were agnatically linked, but one of the three ubiquitous Dorian tribes was named Pamphyloi, suggesting that it was the tribe to which individual new-comers were assigned. Entire communities could change their ethnic affiliation. Megara, for example, became Dorian according to Pausanias after the Peloponnesians took it from Athens and gave it to the Korinthians (Pausanias 1.39.5). A better known example is Sikyon, where Kleisthenes ejected Dorian cults and abolished the Dorian tribal names, replacing them with Hyatai (Pig-Men), Oneatai (Ass-Men) and Choireatai (Swine-Men) (Herodotos 5.67). Perhaps not surprisingly, Kleisthenes was only partially successful, and sixty years after his death the Sikyonians returned to their old Dorian tribal names, but they added a fourth tribe named Aigialeoi. This was an inspired compromise between Dorian and Ionian because Aigialeoi had two etymologies: according to the Dorian genealogy Aigialeus was the son of Adrastos, but Aigialos was also an ancient name for the coastal strip of Achaia, between Elis and Sikyon, whose inhabitants were known as Aigialean Ionians (Pausanias 7.1.1; Strabo 8.1.2). The name Aigialeoi was suitably ambiguous.

Perhaps the best proof that ethnicity was flexible is Herodotos's well-known account of the Ionians. He reports that there are twelve Ionian cities because the Ionians built twelve to correspond to the twelve segments of the Ionian Peloponnese. This detail was evidently used by the inhabitants of the Ionian cities to bolster the claim that their twelve cities were more genuinely Ionian than anyone else's, a claim that Herodotos dismisses as foolish because there were so many non-Ionians among those who colonized the eastern Aegean. These non-Ionians include Abantes from Euboia, "who are not even called Ionian," Minyans from Orchomenos, Kadmeians,

Dryopes, Phokian seceders, Molossians, Pelasgian Arkadians, Dorians from Epidauros, and many other tribes (Herodotos 1.146). Each of the tribes he names is associated with territory north of the isthmus, outside of the pre-Achaian, Ionian Peloponnese, and a Dorian component from Epidauros. For Herodotos the Ionians were a bastard race: one could not point to a tribal homeland from which all "real" Ionians ultimately derived.

Nevertheless Herodotos appears to recognize two straightforward criteria of Ionian legitimacy when he observes they are truly Ionian who are descended from Athenians and who celebrate the Apatouria (Herodotos 1.147). But even this is undercut as he recounts the tale of these Athenian-born Ionians. These men had not brought women with them but had taken Karian wives whose parents, husbands and sons the Athenians slaughtered. The term used by Herodotos in his account of pure Ionian ancestry is *katharos*, but what did it mean to concede that the Athenian-born Ionians were *katharos* when their grandmothers were Karian and their grandfathers were killers? In both senses of the word *katharos*, meaning "pure-bred" or "undefiled," these Ionians were anything but. As for the shared religious practice of the Apatouria, Herodotos notes an exception immediately: the Ephesians and Kolophonians do not celebrate this festival because of an act of bloodshed. As for linguistic unity Herodotos explains that their dialects fall into four separate groups. As for common practices Herodotos goes out of his way to explain that the origins of the Panionion lay not in a decision to include all those who called themselves Ionian, as we might expect given the name, but rather from a decision taken by the twelve cities who were not ashamed of being called Ionian to exclude other Ionians, like the men of Smyrna who had to petition for admission to the Panionion. The city had been Aiolian. A similar story of switching ethnicity is recorded by Pausanias, who says that the Phokaians petitioned for entry to the Panionion and were initially rebuffed because they were "by blood and by descent" from Phokis, and hence not Ionian (Pausanias 7.3.10). They were admitted only when they agreed to accept kings of the blood of Kodros. Thus were they Ionized.

What Herodotos is capable of doing, and what more recent historians often fail to do, is to separate the question of the historical origins of an ethnic entity from the subsequent manipulation of the ethnic identity as a vehicle for self-definition and the focusing of group loyalty. To use the example of the *ethne* of central Greece once again, the splitting of Lokris by the Phokians into two distinct groups is a curious phenomenon, but even more telling is the fact that when Pausanias traveled around Phokis he found that the Phokians had not one but two eponymous heroes, both with their own complete genealogy, and that in each Phokian town he visited the local inhabitants acknowledged their common descent from Phokos as well as their unique descent from the Abantes, the Phlegyans, the Aiolians, the Argives, or the Thrakians. Phokian ethnic identity was a fiction used in support of the political unification of the communities of the Parnassos district.

Even when it did not result in the formation of a new political entity, such as a federal league, the discourse on ethnicity could function as part of the communication between neighboring, even rival groups. The Messenians and Spartans provide a good example of this. The Messenians came to accept Dorian domination, in part because of the decision of the Dorian kings to pay honour to the pre-Dorian cult of Zeus on Mr. Ithome as well as to venerate Messene as a heroine, so that by the time of the First Messenian War the Messenians had come to think of themselves as thoroughly Dorian, an identity reinforced by the Lakonian decision to allow the Messenians a share in the Dorian cult of Artemis Limnatis (Pausanias 4.3.9, 4.4.2). When war broke out the Messenians sought arbitration from the Argives whom they asserted were related to both sides and castigated the Spartans for attacking fellow Dorians and committing sins against the Dorian gods (Pausanias 4.8.2). So despite the fact that they became implacable foes both Spartans and Messenians were engaged in a dialogue that used common ethnicity as a way of expressing common interest. A population whose myth-history went back to the age before the Return of the Herakleidai was quite capable of assuming the same ethnic identity as its conquerors and its perennial foes.

If, then, we approach the *ethnos* as an open and changing structure, and ethnicity as an elective affiliation, the Archaic period takes on quite a different appearance. Instead of seeing the rise of the *polis* as marginalizing the *ethnos*, we are forced to see it too as part of the political experimentation of the Archaic period. During a time of tumultuous change emerging communities were fashioning identities not only at the local level, but regionally and beyond. Colonization made this especially important since the very act of founding a community with no prior history made all the more pressing the need to assert a common ethnic identity, ultimately derived from the mother-city, thereby establishing order and cohesion within, and defining the community against its non-Greek environment. So groups were forced to find common ground and we see this in the profusion of heroic genealogies in Akusilaos, Pherekydes and Apollodoros from as early as the eighth century purporting to anchor each of these ethnic groups to a heroic past. These genealogies are not historical documents of the Bronze Age but cultural artifacts of the eighth century and later, manufactured to give legitimacy to the present by connecting it with the past. They were produced independently and locally but are the substrata of panhellenism, allowing different groups to establish connections through fictitious lineages.[16]

Benedict Anderson once observed that "[A]ll communities larger than primordial villages of face to face contact (and perhaps even these) are imagined. Communities are to be distinguished not by their falsity/genuineness but by the style in which they are imagined" (Anderson 1983, 15). Judged in these terms we are forced to see Greek ethnic identity as an especially inventive response to the pressures of state formation, reconciling the urge for autonomy and the need for unity.

NOTES

An earlier version of this paper was delivered at the 1996 meeting of the American Philological Association, and was improved by my participation in the 1997 colloquium on ancient ethnicity organized on behalf of the Hellenic Center by Irad Malkin. My thanks to my fellow participants in that colloquium and to my colleagues in the Department of Classical Studies at the University of Pennsylvania.

1. W. von Humboldt, *Geschichte des Verfalls und Unterganges der griechischen Freistaaten,* cited in Nippel 1993, 12. Von Humboldt expressed similar sentiments in his tract *Über das Studium des Alterthums, und des griechischen insbesondre* (1793). On von Humboldt, the origins of *Altertumswissenschaft* and the Dorian interpretation of Greek history see also Bernal 1987, 281-94. Bernal's investigation of *Altertumswissenschaft* goes a great deal further than charting the problematic philhellenism of German culture in the eighteenth and nineteenth centuries and posits a deliberately racist suppression of the African (Egyptian) and Semitic (Phoenician) origins of Greek culture. Most criticisms of Bernal's work have concentrated on his capricious use of ancient evidence but his discussion of the German scholarship is similarly flawed; see Norton 1996, 403-10.

2. Butler 1935. For a more recent and comprehensive study of the "Aesthetic State" that demonstrates the intensity of this German Hellenism, see Chytry 1989. Graf (1987, 15), describing Heyne's interest in mythology, speaks of the second half of the nineteenth century as the period during which the Greek world exercised an unparalleled hold over the spiritual life of Germany. An excellent study of the relationship between German philhellenism and Romantic aestheticism can be found in Marchand 1996, 3-35.

3. In 1764, over one hundred years before political unification, Kant published the *Beobachtungen über das Gefühl des Schönen und Erhabenen,* with a chapter on the national characteristics of the Germans, French, English, Spanish and Dutch. "Die Deutsche Frage" remains a central feature of political discourse in German life, no less so since the most recent reunification; see Geiss 1992. On the brothers Grimm see Graf 1987, 29.

4. The lack of political aims among German Philhellenes is noted by Marchand (1996, 6).

5. For the continuing importance of the terms *Volk* and *Geist,* see Brumlik 1990, 179-90.

6. In the first volume of his work, which he entitled *Legendary Greece,* Grote wrote: "[A]ttempts to *explain* (as it is commonly called) the mythes (sic) (i.e. to translate them into some physical, moral or historical statements suitable to our order of thought) are, even as guesses, essentially unpromising"(353 n.1). Later (409 n.2) he adds "My position is that, whether there be matter of fact or not, we have no test whereby it can be singled out, identified, and severed from the accompanying fiction." On this aspect of Grote's work see Momigliano 1952, 21.

7. "It is the fault of the approaches established by Otfried Müller that all work in the field of ancient Greek history remains virtually useless until the end of the nineteenth century. Scholars continued to tread in the tracks which Niebuhr had laid" (Beloch 1926, 11).

8. Der Stamm hat einen rein griechischen Namen (Beloch 1893, 35).

9. Es ging eben in Amphilochien, wie es in allen Ländern und zu allen Zeiten gegangen ist (Beloch 1926, 35).

10. Schober 1924, 55. Aiolic elements include dative plural in -*essi* and patronymic adjectives such as *Pantaineta*. The place name Aiolidai (from near Delphi) recalls the connection with Aiolis.

11. Atkinson 1994, 14. Atkinson's remarks concern definitions of ethnicity and the view of the *ethnos* implied by them. His discussion deals primarily with African ethnicity and its representation under colonial rule. It is worth comparing the German treatment of the *ethnos* with the wide-spread notion in contemporary western thinking regarding tribal societies, summarized by Skalnik (1988, 68): "they represent an earlier stage in human social evolution when people belonged to tribes rather than modern nations." A helpful essay summarizing the shift in attitudes in recent anthropological approaches to ethnicity is found in Tapper 1989, 232-46.

12. Sakellariou 1989, 39. On the records of these groups see Sakellariou 1990b.

13. See Sakellariou 1989, 37-39. On this tendency see also the criticisms of Morgan 1990, 4.

14. Skalnik 1988, 79-80. For other definitions of ethnic groups and ethnicity see Cohen 1978, 387; Tapper 1989, 232-46; Reminick 1983, 8-13; Toland 1993, 3.

15. Richard White in Horn 1990, 62.

16. For a useful introduction to Greek genealogical works see West 1985.

BIBLIOGRAPHY

Anderson, Benedict. 1983. *Imagined communities: Reflections on the origins and spread of nationalism*. London: Verso.

Atkinson, Ronald Raymond. 1994. *The roots of ethnicity: The origins of the Acholi of Uganda before 1800*. Philadelphia: University of Pennsylvania Press.

Barth, Fredrik, ed. 1969. *Ethnic groups and boundaries: The social organization of culture difference*. Boston: Little, Brown.

Beloch, Karl Julius. 1912. *Griechische Geschichte*, 2d ed., vol. 1, pt. 1. Strassburg: K.J. Trübner.

———. 1926. *Griechische Geschichte*, 2nd ed., vol. 1, pt. 2. Strassburg: K.J. Trübner.

Bennett, John W. 1975. *The new ethnicity: Perspectives from ethnology*. St. Paul, Minn.: West Publishing.

Bernal, Martin. 1987. *Black Athena: The Afroasiatic roots of classical civilization*, vol. 1. New Brunswick, N.J.: Rutgers University Press.

Bommeljé, Sebastiaan, Peter K. Doorn, et al. 1987. *Aetolia and the Aetolians: Towards the interdisciplinary study of a Greek region*. Utrecht: Parnassus Press.

Brillante, Carlo. 1981. *La leggenda eroica e la civiltà micinea*. Rome: Edizioni dell'Ateneo.

Brumlik, M. 1990. Die Entwicklung der Begriffe "Rasse," "Kultur" und "Ethnizität" im sozialwissenschaftlichen Diskurs. In *Ethnizität: Wissenschaft und Minderheiten*, edited by Eckard J. Dittrich and Frank-Olaf Radtke, 179-90. Opladen: Westdeutscher Verlag.

Butler, Eliza Marian. 1935. *The tyranny of Greece over Germany*. Boston: Beacon Press.

Chytry, Josef. 1989. *The aesthetic state: A quest in modern German thought*. Berkeley: University of California Press.

Cohen, Ronald. 1978. Ethnicity: Problem and focus in anthropology. *Annual Review of Anthropology* 7:379-403.

Curtius, Ernst, 1867. *The History of Greece.* 4 vols. Translated by Adolphus William Ward. New York: C. Scribner's Sons.

Danforth, L.M. 1993. Claims to Macedonian identity. *Anthropology Today* 9.4:3-10.

Devereux, George. 1975. Ethnic identity: Its logical foundations and its dysfunctions. In De Vos and Romanucci-Ross 1975a, 42-70.

De Vos, George. 1975. Ethnic pluralism: Conflict and accommodation. In De Vos and Romanucci-Ross 1975a, 5-41.

De Vos, George, and Lola Romanucci-Ross, eds. 1975a. *Ethnic identity: Cultural continuities and change.* Palo Alto, Calif.: Mayfield Publishing.

―――. 1975b. Ethnicity: Vessel of meaning and emblem of contrast. In De Vos and Romanucci-Ross 1975a, 363-90.

Epstein, A.L. 1978. *Ethnos and identity: Three studies in ethnicity.* London: Tavistock.

Fichte, Johann Gottlieb. 1968. *Addresses to the German nation,* translated by R.F. Jones and G.H. Turnbull. Westport, Conn.: Greenwood Press.

Fustel de Coulanges, Numa Denis. 1864. *The ancient city,* translated by Willard Small. Reprint: Gloucester, Mass.: P. Smith, 1979.

Geiss, Imanuel. 1992. *Die deutsche Frage 1806-1990* Mannheim: B.I.-Taschenbuchverlag.

Gonsalez, N.L. 1975. Patterns of Dominican ethnicity. In Bennett 1975, 110-23.

Graf, Fritz. 1987. *Griechische Mythologie.* Munich: Artemis.

Grote, George. 1899-1900. *History of Greece,* New York: Peter Fenelow Collier.

Hegel, Georg Wilhelm Friedrich. 1931. *Jenenser Realphilosophie.* 2nd ed. Leipzig: Hoffmeister.

Herder, Johann Gottfried. 1778. *Denkmal Johann Winkelmanns.* In volume 8 of his *Sämmtliche Werke,* edited by Bernhard Suphan, 436-83. Berlin: Weidmannische Buchhandlung, 1892.

Hölderlin, Friedrich. 1992. *Sämtliche Werke und Briefe.* Edited by Michael Knaupp. Munich: Carl Hanser Verlag.

Horn, M. 1990. "How the West was really won," *U.S. News and World Report* May 21, 1990: 56-65.

Iliffe, John. 1979. *A modern history of Tanganyika.* Cambridge: Cambridge University Press.

Just, Roger. 1989. Triumph of the ethnos. In Tonkin, McDonald, and Chapman 1989, 71-88.

Lefkowitz, Mary, and Guy McLean Rogers, eds. 1996. *Black Athena revisited.* Chapel Hill: University of North Carolina Press.

Marchand, Suzanne L. 1996. *Down from Olympus: Archaeology and philhellenism in Germany, 1750-1970.* Princeton: Princeton University Press.

Meyer, Eduard. 1907. *Geschichte des Altertums.* 2d ed. Bd. 1.1, *Einleitung: Elemente der Anthropologie.* Stuttgart: J.G. Catta'sche Buchhandlung.

―――. 1910. The development of individuality in ancient history. In *Kleine Schriften,* 213-30. Halle: Max Niemeyer, 1924.

Momigliano, Arnaldo D. 1952. George Grote and the study of Greek history. In *A.D. Momigliano: Studies in modern scholarship,* edited by G.W. Bowersock and T.J. Cornell, 15-31. Berkeley: University of California Press, 1994.

Müller, Karl Otfried. 1820-24. *Geschichten hellenischer Stämme und Städte.* Vol. 1, *Orchomenos und die Minyer,* Vols. 2 and 3, *Die Dorier.* Breslau: J. Max.

Musti, Domenico, ed. 1990. *Le Origini dei Greci: Dori e mondo egeo.* Rome: Laterza.

Niebuhr, Barthold Georg. 1853. *Lectures on ancient ethnography and geography.* Vol 1 translated by Leonard Schmitz. London: Walton and Maberly.

Nippel, Wilfried. 1993. *Über das Studium der alten Geschichte.* Munich: Deutcher Taschenbuch Verlag.

Norton, Robert E. 1996. The tyranny of Germany over Greece?: Bernal, Herder and the German appropriation of Greece. In Lefkowitz and Rogers 1996, 403-10.

Plant, Raymond. 1972. *Hegel: An introduction.* 2d ed. Oxford: Blackwell.

Polanyi, Karl. 1977. *The livelihood of man.* Edited by Harry W. Pearson. New York: Academic Press.

Ranger, Terence. 1983, The invention of tradition in colonial Africa. In *The invention of tradition,* edited by Eric Hobsbawm and Terence Ranger, 211-62. Cambridge: Cambridge University Press.

Reminick, Ronald A. 1983. *Theory of ethnicity: An anthroplogical perspective.* Lanham, Md.: Univ Press of America.

Sakellariou, Michael B. 1989. *The polis-state: Definition and origin.* Meletemata 4. Paris: de Boccard.

———. 1990. *Between memory and oblivion: The transmission of early Greek historical traditions* Meletemata 12. Paris: de Boccard.

Schachermeyr, Fritz. 1984. *Griechische Frühgeschichte.* Vienna: Verlag der Osterreichischen Akademie der Wissenschaften.

Schiller, Friedrich. 1967. *On the aesthetic education of man.* Edited and translated by Elizabeth M. Wilkinson and L.A. Willoughby. Oxford: Clarendon Press.

Schoemann, Georg Friedrich. 1855. *Griechische Alterthümer.* Vol 1, *Das Staatswesen.* Berlin: Weidmann.

Schober, Friedrich. 1924. *Phokis.* Crossen a. d. Oder: Richard Zeidler.

Skalnik, Peter. 1988. Tribe as colonial category. In *South African keywords: The uses and abuses of political concepts,* edited by Emile Boonzaier and John Sharp, 68-78. Cape Town: D. Philip.

Snodgrass, Anthony M. 1980. *Archaic Greece: The age of experiment.* London: J.M. Dent.

Southall, Aidan. 1970. Ethnic formation among the Alur. In *From tribe to nation in Africa,* edited by Ronald Cohen and John Middleton, 71-92. Scranton, Cal.: Chandler.

Tapper, Richard. 1989. Ethnic identities and social categories in Iran and Afghanistan. In Tonkin, McDonald, and Chapman 1989, 232-46.

Toland, Judith D. 1993a. Dialogue of self and other: Ethnicity and the state building process. In Toland 1993b, 1-20.

Toland, Judith D., ed. 1993b. *Ethnicity and the state.* Political and Legal Anthropology 9. New Brunswick, N.J.: Transaction.

Tonkin, Elizabeth, Maryon McDonald, and Malcolm Chapman, eds. 1989. *History and ethnicity.* London: Routledge.

West, Martin L. 1985. *The Hesiodic "Catalogue of women": Its nature, structure, and origins.* Oxford: Clarendon Press.

Chapter Four

"IN FERTILITY CYPRUS IS NOT INFERIOR TO ANY ONE OF THE ISLANDS": A PROLEGOMENON TO CONSTRUCTING THE ECONOMY OF IRON AGE CYPRUS

David W. Rupp

Introduction

The study of the economy of an ancient culture using archaeological evidence as the primary source is a challenge even in data-rich situations. The fortuitous presence of contemporaneous or near-contemporaneous documentary and/or literary sources can augment as well as help to fill in numerous gaps in coverage of the typically lean construction crafted by the archaeologist (Deetz 1988). The normal approach of archaeologists is a descriptive one, in the first instance at least, as few holistic or comprehensive economic models exist for pre-industrial, traditional societies for one to use to organize and to analyse the data. Put another way, if an archaeologist has any interest in discussing the economy beyond the circumscribed realm of trade and exchange networks, he or she has few firm bases on which to rely or build. With the exception of the economy of the Roman Late Republic and Empire such a broader interest in the totality of an ancient Mediterranean economy is the exception rather than the norm. The situation in Cypriote studies follows this pattern well except for the Late Cypriote period (ca. 1600/1550 - 1125/1100 B.C.E.) (Karageorghis and Michaelides 1997).

What is an archaeologist to do if he or she seeks to attempt to construct the economy of an ancient society? Such a goal is made even more difficult if the chosen society has an unevenly documented archaeological record and there are few if any written or other sources to use for supplementary information, which is the case of Early Iron Age (hereafter EIA) Cyprus (ca. 1125/1100 - 600 B.C.E.) (Rupp 1997). Until recently the archaeologist had few choices. Rhoda H. Halperin, in her *Cultural Economies: Past and Present* (1994), claims to provide a workable solution for such a common dilemma. But can her proposed model be applied successfully to the construction of an ancient economy as recalcitrant as that of the EIA in Cyprus?

The Generic Model of the Economy

Halperin defines the economy in all societies, past and present, as "the material-means provisioning process" (1994, 8). From this, using the ideas and concepts of Karl Marx and Karl Polanyi, she crafts a more refined version of Polanyi's "Generic Model of the Economy" in order to enable one to analyse all economies as they are embedded in their unique cultural contexts in a consistent and systematic fashion (Halperin 1994, 34-54) (Figure 1). Using Marx's "Institutional Paradigm" (and elaborated on by Polanyi) with the structure and institutions of a society as the basic units of analysis (Halperin 1994, 34-40, fig. 1), she focuses on the basic economic processes of production, distribution, storage, and consumption (Halperin 1994, 50-51, fig. 3). In this formal and hierarchical model these processes are controlled in the next tier, either separately or jointly in some fashion, by two analytically distinct kinds of production, *appropriational movements* (Marx's *relations of production* and Polanyi's *changes of hands*) and *locational movements* (Marx's *forces of production* and Polanyi's *changes of place*) (Halperin 1994, 50, fig. 2). The former movement covers the ecological and the latter the institutional dimensions of the economy. The "specific forms [of these movements] vary from one kind of economy to another" (Halperin 1994, 51). At a lower level of abstraction are Polanyi's forms of economic integration, reciprocity, redistribution, market exchange, and householding, which represent recurring patterns of appropriational and locational movements (Halperin 1994, 50, figs. 2-3). The specific "character of the movements is determined by the structure(s) within which they occur" (Halperin 1994, 52).

Halperin's choice of the Institutional Paradigm as the "overarching framework" for these analyses is a conscious one. By eschewing the competing "methodological individualism" approach with individual behavior and action (or agency) as the unit of analysis, she believes that with the Institutional Paradigm one can compare and contrast more effectively the economies of different cultures and their economic processes (Halperin 1994, 13-21).

Figure 1: Karl Polanyi's "Economic Processes and the Generic Model of the Economy" According to R.H. Halperin (1994: Figs. 2 and 3)

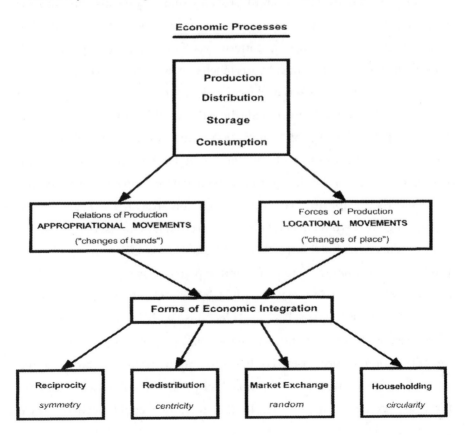

Where Does One Go From Here?

The effective application of Halperin's theses on the Generic Model of the Economy to specific data sets derived mainly from archaeological research is not readily apparent. She offers no detailed and connected recipe-like exegesis for doing this. Her case studies focus primarily on ethnographic research where there is "thick description." Hunter-gatherer societies and contemporary North American subcultures predominate in these discussions. Agrarian and pre-industrial complex societies are less frequently examined. Thus, Halperin's concrete thoughts on how one could go about "teasing out" the nature and structure of a society's economy in situations where one has only "thin descriptions" derived from "messy" or "dirty" and incomplete archaeological data are, in general, lacking.

A careful examination, however, of Halperin's discussion of storage as an economic activity (1994, ch.6) provides some useful insights into the general patterning of economic processes in a society. Her attempts to visualize graphically recurring patterns via flow charts (Halperin 1994, 188-90, figs. 4-5) offer archaeologists much to contemplate. In essence, these charts show how the material objects and the residues of production can enter the archaeological record and where this would most likely occur. The resulting patterning is, of course, a product of the overall level of sociopolitical organization of the society under scrutiny. This, in turn, determines the nature of the appropriational and locational movements and, consequently, the forms of economic integration present. The exact form(s) of the integration would depend on the nature and function(s) of the good or item produced. Colin Renfrew's (1975) graphic visualizations of possible production, distribution, and consumption patterns, as well as the those for exchange networks, resonate well with Halperin's. Combining the distinctive features of both approaches provides one with more complex and encompassing flow charts with which to visualize the major permutations of the basic economic processes. To these different patterns one can assign the probable appropriational and locational movements involved as well as the forms of economic integration. In this way, one could begin to trace potentially the life cycle of each type of good or item produced in a society. Figures 2-4 are preliminary attempts to construct the potential life cycles of foodstuffs and products in a society that has a certain level of hierarchy, such as one would expect to see in chiefdoms and early states. From individual constructions such as the ones illustrated here, one could then speculate on the overall characteristics of the economy and the ways in which it was organized. The resulting tentative model could be tested by further analysis of the extant data sets as well by newly acquired archaeological information.

EIA Cyprus: A Potential Case Study Using the Generic Model of the Economy?

The challenge of constructing the economy of Cyprus in the EIA, that is from ca. 1125/1100 to 600 B.C.E., is almost beyond comprehension.[1] This pivotal epoch in the island's cultural development corresponding to the archaeologically defined periods labelled Late Cypriote IIIB (ca. 1125/1100 - 1050 B.C.E.; Iacovou 1994, 149-50), Cypro-Geometric I through III (ca. 1050-750 B.C.E.) and Cypro-Archaic I (ca. 750 - 600 B.C.E.) (Figure 5), lies within the realm of prehistory and protohistory from a documentary source perspective. There are limited non-Cypriote documents referring to the affairs of the island beginning at the end of the eighth century. These are supplemented somewhat by the even more meagre Cypriote documents that have survived. Archaeological evidence, while more voluminous in comparison to the written material, is nevertheless severely limited in a chronological and a thematic sense (Rupp 1998). That is, the excavated remains tend to cluster in the eleventh century and to a greater extent in the later eighth through seventh centuries.

The main focuses of this chronologically bipolar distribution are burial assemblages throughout the entire time span and urban sanctuaries plus rural shrine deposits in the later peak. Settlement data are poorly represented, especially in the earlier peak.

*Figure 2: The Material-Means Provisioning Process For: High-Bulk /
Low-Value Commodities (Cereals)*

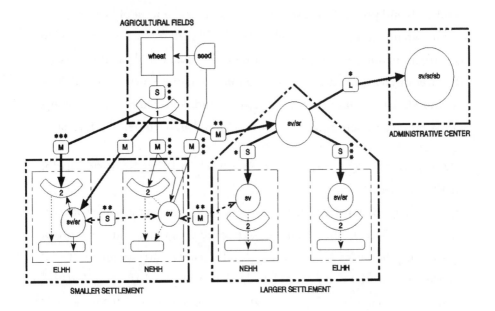

*Figure 3: The Material-Means Provisioning Process For: High-Bulk /
Low-Value Products (Kitchen and Storage Wares) Produced by a Craft
Specialist on a Seasonal Basis*

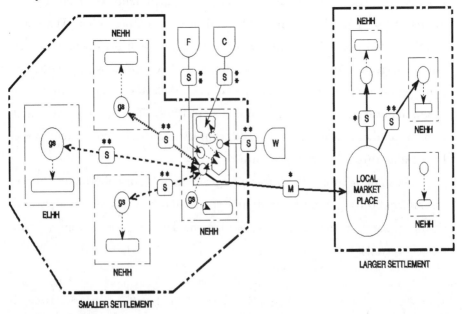

Figure 4: The Material-Means Provisioning For: Medium-Bulk / Medium-Value Products (Simply Decorated Vessels For Wine Storage, Serving and Consumption) Produced by a Craft Specialist on a Seasonal Basis

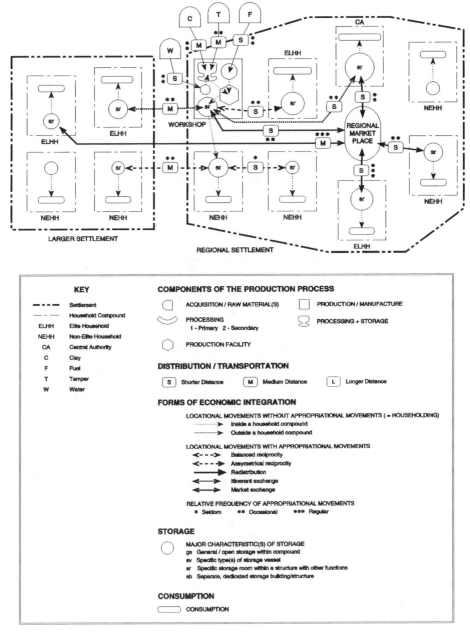

Figures 2, 3, and 4 Created by David W. Rupp and Loris Gasparotto

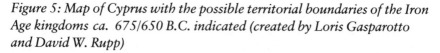

Figure 5: Map of Cyprus with the possible territorial boundaries of the Iron Age kingdoms ca. 675/650 B.C. indicated (created by Loris Gasparotto and David W. Rupp)

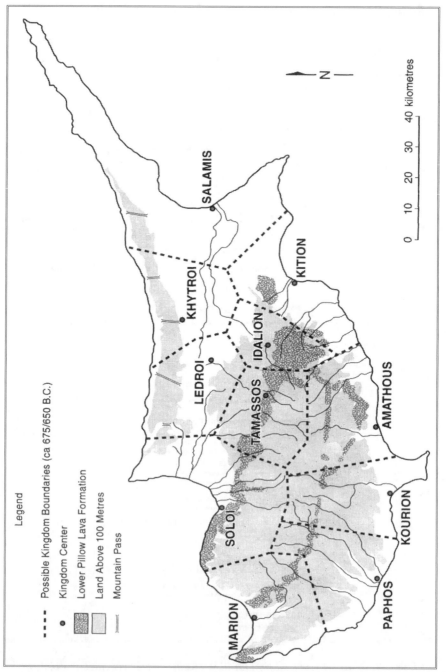

Generally, the evidence is scanty for at least five reasons:

1. The continuous inhabitation of the settlements from this epoch until the Late Roman/Early Byzantine period and/or the fact that they lie beneath modern villages, towns or cities;

2. The large-scale pillaging of cemeteries and sanctuaries by nineteenth-century putative antiquarians and by modern looters;

3. The continuing predilection of many professional archaeologists and art historians to seek out primarily the highly visible artifactual and architectural products of ancient elite consumption behaviors rather than a broader view of the society as a whole;

4. The general lack of attention to the systematic recovery and analysis of paleobotanical and paleofaunal remains, as well as, paleoenvironmental data for the construction of subsistence patterns and the environment; and

5. The cultural and political agendas of current governments in the region for use of the past to bolster ideological positions, which limit our knowledge and understanding of the exact nature and components of EIA Cypriote society, as well as, their interrelationships.

Until broader and more fine-grained data sets are assembled systematically with explicit attention to the island's economic system, its development and its operating mechanisms (Rupp 1997), this present tentative and highly speculative *prolegomenon* cannot be tested for its overall validity nor its specific constructions.[2] With these observations and caveats in mind, what light does the Generic Model of the Economy shed on the nature and workings of the EIA Cypriote economy?

The Possible Structure and Operating Processes of the EIA Cypriote Economy

The general format used by Halperin to visualize graphically the hierarchical relationships among the economic processes, the "movements" of production and the forms of economic integration (Figure 1) will be employed here to analyse the structure and economic processes at work during the Cypriote EIA.

1. Economic processes

1.1 Production

Subsistence

There is little tangible, direct evidence for the agro-pastoral base of the economy for the period under consideration. Given the artifactual evidence and the visual depictions, as well as what is known about the Late Bronze Age (Knapp 1994, 396-97) and the sixth through first centuries B.C.E., one can surmise what the economy probably was like between ca. 1125 and 600 B.C.E. Except for the perfection of "utilitarian iron" in the twelfth and eleventh centuries B.C.E. as the metal of choice for tools (Sherratt 1994), there does not appear to have been any major technical advances in either the production or the extraction and processing spheres of agricultural pursuits. As there is no evidence for irrigated agriculture, dry farming using oxen pulling an aard must be assumed. The terracing of hill slopes to increase the area of cultivable land may have occurred in the more mountainous areas of the island, but there is no direct evidence for this. The survival and well-being of its members is one of the basic aims of any society. The subsistence base, therefore, must ensure this through adequate food resources and long-term economic stability. The inevitable interseasonal and interannual variation in the food supply results in risks and uncertainties for every sedentary agrarian society. Besides attempting to produce storable surpluses every year to dampen the effects of temporal fluctuations in the food supply (Halstead 1989), one of the risk-management strategies available is diversification (Halstead and O'Shea 1989b, 123-24). In Cyprus this mechanism appears to have been the norm. The "Mediterranean triad" of cereals (buckwheat, emmer, naked and hulled barley), olives, and grapes would have formed the core of the diversified agricultural base. Pulses (especially lentils) would also have been important. Animal husbandry of sheep and goats would have formed another key element. The cultivation of fruit (fig, citrus, pomegranate) and of nut (almond, pistachio, hazel) trees, as well as the collection of wild plant resources, would have supplemented the major food sources. Hunting (Persian fallow deer, wild boar, hare, birds) probably was a limited food source and possibly was a restricted activity for the larger animals. Given the general pattern of settlement (Rupp 1989), offshore fishing and the onshore collecting of marine life would have been marginal food sources except in a few port settlements. Flax may have been cultivated for its fibres. They may have engaged in apiculture too (Bonet Rosado and Mata Parreño 1997; Crane 1983).

These subsistence activities would have produced the following foodstuffs and products as well as derivative products. There is no substantive evidence to gauge the scale of this production. Inasmuch as the island in the Hellenistic and Roman periods was considered to be very fertile (Strabo 14.6), the scattered, mostly small settlements during the EIA must have generated a more than adequate yield under normal conditions.

"Heavy industry"

Table 1: Subsistence Sources

Key: *storable; storable & exchangeable*; → = derivative product		
cereals *grain*	→	bread and/or porridge → *wheat cakes*
pulses	*dried seeds*	→ porridge
olive trees	*olives*	→ *olive oil* → *flavored or perfumed oils and/or ungents*
grapevines	grapes	→ *raisins* → *wine*
fruit trees	fruit	→ *dried fruit*
nut trees	*nuts*	
sheep	wool	→ *yarn* → *plain fine fabric* → decorated fine fabrics*
	meat	

goats	milk	→ ferment milk products
		→ *cheese*
		→ *coarse fibres* → *coarse fabrics*
pig	meat	
	hides	→ *pigskin*
wild plants	greens	
	fruits	
	fibers	
	seasonings	
	medicines	
	baskets	
fishing	fresh fish	→ *dried/smoked fish*
marine bottom life	small, edible foods	
	shells	
hunting	fresh meat	
	leather	
	antlers	
	skins	
	feathers	
oxen	*hides*	→ *leather*
	meat	
flax	*fibers*	→ *linen* → *sails*
bees	*honey combs*	→ *flavor for wine, oil and/or ungents*
	honey	

The primary "heavy industry" for which there is direct and, more often, indirect archaeological evidence is metallurgy. Copper-ore mining on a small, decentralized scale must have continued unabated from the Late Bronze Age (Fasnacht et al. 1989; 1990; 1991). The primary smelting of the ores took place in or immediately adjacent to the areas of mineralization in the Lower Pillow Lava formation around the Troodos Mountain and in the area of Troulli near Kition (Kouchy and Steinberg 1989; Fasnacht et al. 1992, 60-67), secondary smelting in and around the primary settlements (Gaber 1995, 33). Iron probably was a byproduct of these operations as the

island is rich in iron oxide ores and the addition of iron compounds as fluxes
to the charge of copper smelting furnaces would reduce them accidentally to
metallic iron (Kassianidou 1994, 78-79). Gold and silver may have been
produced in small quantities.

The construction "industry" normally constitutes a significant element
of the economy of most early states. The evidence for buildings and other
constructions is extremely scarce on the island before the mid-eighth century
B.C.E. The core building technique used was sun-dried mudbrick on an
unworked rubble socle. The small-scale rectilinear structures had flat roofs
constructed with wooden beams, reeds and clay. Only with the construction
of the so-called "Royal Tombs" at Salamis (Rupp 1988) and the lower
portions and gates of the fortification walls around some of the kingdom
centers does dressed ashlar stone masonry reappear on the island (Rupp
1987). Some use of this technique was made in sanctuary structures during
the Cypro-Archaic I period. This evidence suggests that the construction
industry did not play a major role in the economy until the later eighth
century, and then only in the major settlements.

Given the distribution of Cypriote artifacts outside of the island and the
presence of terracotta ship models (Karageorghis 1993, 74-76; 1995,
128-31; 1996, 72-77), the only other heavy industry that would appear to
have existed was ship building, which would have used the trees of the
forested mountains, and would have been localized in the major port
settlements. The apparent lack of the importance of fishing in the diet, as well
as the limited number of truly coastal settlements, would suggest that the
scale of this industry was minor. It is also possible that, apart from small,
inshore boats, there was no indigenous offshore ship building industry and
that all of the large ships associated with the island were built in Phoenicia
and/or in the Aegean.

Consumer products

The objects and materials required to enact and to actualize the economic,
social, political, and ideological realms of Cypriote society comprise the

overwhelming portion of the archaeological record that we possess. These are the artifacts and "art" that archaeologists and others recover from the ground. It is difficult to gauge what approximate percentage any one aspect of these diverse items represented in terms of the total economy. The location and concentration, the organizational structure and context, the technical skills and technology involved, and the frequency, intensity, and scale of the production (Costin 1991, table 1.1; Van der Leeuw 1977) would vary depending on the object or material under consideration, the chronological/cultural phase in which it occurred, and the intended consumer.

An analysis of the consumer products by the primary material used in their manufacture provides the information in Table 2.[3]

*Table 2: Consumer products   Key: **exchangeable***

Wood:	utensils and containers	Fibers:	**plain cloth**
	tools		**plain clothing**
	furniture		**decorated cloth**
	carts and chariots		**decorated clothing**
	weapons		**cordage**
	small boats		**baskets**
			sails
Leather:	hides	Ceramic	plain storage wares
	clothing and foot coverings	Vessels:	plain food preparation wares
	animal trappings and gear		plain food/beverage serving and consumption wares
	sailing gear		**serving and consumption wares**
			decorated food/beverage serving and consumption wares
			decorated religious, votive, funerary and/or ceremonial vessels and items
Terra Cotta:	**votive figurines and models**	Stone:	containers and basins
			figurines
	statuettes and statues		**statuettes and statues**

Bronze:	tools and hardware knives, weapons and armor utilitarian vessels religious and/or ceremonial stands and vessels jewelry horse trappings chariot decoration figurines	Iron:	tools and hardware knives and weapons firedogs and spits
Silver:	jewelry beverage consumption vessels religious and/or ceremonial vessels and items furniture decoration	Gold:	jewelry clothing decoration religious and/or ceremonial items
Ivory:	jewelry furniture decoration religious and/or ceremonial items figurines	Semi-precious stones:	jewelry seals religious and/or ceremonial items

1.2 Storage

In agrarian societies storage is one of the four basic coping strategies available to dampen the effects of seasonal and interannual variability in the food supply (Halstead and O'Shea 1989b, 123-24). Storage can take many forms, from direct, shorter-term mechanisms to indirect, longer-term ones. There are many limitations to each approach, of course. Direct storage of foodstuffs is unreliable over many years. Indirect storage of them by feeding the surpluses to livestock entails massive losses of energy (Halstead 1989, 79). The need for some form of storage container and/or storage facility and the logistical arrangements to get a food product to such a facility would depend on a number of factors (Halperin 1994, 167-90). The inherent storability of the item, the relative quantity of the item involved, the location of production or manufacture, the available transportation means, the reason(s) for production or manufacture, the intended function(s) and purpose(s) of the item, the timing or scheduling of the consumption or use of the item and the relative value of the item are some of the factors that would need to be considered, since the storing mechanisms are highly variable. Another way to "bank" the surpluses is to turn them into durable tokens of value to be given to others and, thereby, establishing some sort of entitlement for future reciprocation. This "social storage" process of creating value-added food products or objects from the agricultural surpluses would permit one to recoup them later on a time-scale longer than normally possible through direct storage alone (Halstead and O'Shea 1982; Halstead 1989, 75-79).

In the various storing mechanisms appropriational and/or locational movements come into play. The possibilities for the interaction of the two types of movements in the context of the distribution and the consumption of a food product or a manufactured object are multifold (Halperin 1994, 189-90, fig. 5). In the case of the Cypriote EIA the chronological/cultural phase in which the storage took place is another important consideration in constructing the life cycle of a food product or a manufactured object. Therefore, not all foodstuffs or objects would require storage.

In the preceding subsection on subsistence products those foodstuffs and items which are most likely to be stored were indicated (Table 1). There exist in the Cypriote archaeological record various small scale ceramic vessel forms which could be used to store both dry food stuffs and/or liquids. The almost complete disappearance of large storage *pithoi* from the ceramic repertory after Cypro-Geometric IA (ca. 1050-1000 B.C.E.; Pilides 1996, 110, 119-20), indicates, however, that the quantity of food stuffs stored and the organization of the storage had changed dramatically since the Late Bronze Age. Until the mid-eighth century there is no evidence for communal or state storage facilities even in the major settlements. The appearance of large White Painted III/IV and Bichrome III/IV as well as Black-on-Red I + II (III + IV) storage *amphorae* in (normally elite) funerary contexts and Plain White IV ware transport *amphorae* as well as other transport shapes (Gjerstad 1948, 242-247, fig. 51) at the end of Cypro-Geometric III/beginning of Cypro-Archaic I (ca. 775/725 B.C.E.) suggests that the storage and the transport of foodstuffs and liquids had increased in importance and in quantity.

1.3 Distribution

Three of Polanyi's four forms of economic integration (reciprocity, redistribution, market exchange,[4] but not householding [Halperin 1994, 45, fig. 2; 51, fig. 3]) are germane to the construction of the EIA Cypriote economy; the two most important factors are which food product or object is involved and in which chronological/cultural phase within the EIA one or more of these mechanisms of distribution may have taken place. As the ideal for any household unit was self-sufficiency, the overwhelming majority of the food stuffs and animal products would have remained in the hands of the primary producers in the rural villages, in order to sustain themselves and their families. Surpluses could have been stored in various ways for future needs. Balanced reciprocity between kin, among the non-kin families in a village, and/or among villages in a region could have served to address differences in landholdings and variability in local productivity. This is one of low-level coping mechanisms to deal with "bad year economics" (O'Shea and Halstead 1989b, 123-24). The surpluses could also have been exchanged by means of redistribution and/or regional market exchange. For the latter to happen, however, a certain level of transportation technology would have been needed to enable the products to be moved and a requisite level of sociopolitical complexity achieved, such as a chiefdom or a state.

The archaeological and representational evidence suggests that donkeys or mules with panniers on their sides were the principal non-human means of transporting goods. A network of simple paths would suffice for their effective movement. Equids carrying ceramic vessels on their backs was another means of moving foodstuffs around (Karageorghis 1993, 94; 1996, 28-29). While two-wheel carts pulled by equids existed (Monloup 1984, 158, 161; Crouwel 1985), it is not clear if there were in this period intraregional and interregional road networks which they would require for their effective use (Bekker-Nielsen 1993, 189-90). If suitable roads did not exist then the carts would have had a very limited value in the movement of goods long distance through the landscape.[5] Two- or four-horse chariots are attested by the mid-eighth century (Crouwel 1987). They appear to have been used solely by warriors for militaristic and elite display purposes. There is no direct evidence to suggest that ships were used to convey products between the few truly coastal settlements, although this would have been the most effective means to transport low-value/high-bulk foodstuffs.

In this context the questions of whether or not redistribution and market exchange occurred and, if so, which foodstuffs and which objects were involved, as well as when it occurred must be answered. To do this properly, however, requires detailed information on the location and the manner of production of each item as well as evidence of where it was consumed.

1.4 Consumption

I have touched upon the subject of consumption at various points in the previous pages. Before we can explore this economic process further a few points need to be emphasized. First, EIA Cypriote society does not appear to have been highly urbanized. The regional (and later the fortified kingdom) centers would have been the closest approximations to "cities" in the ordinary sense of the term. Despite the typically large area enclosed by the defensive walls of these settlements there is no indication that all or even a significant portion of the enclosed area was, in fact, built-up. It seems highly unlikely, then, that large numbers of people lived in these main settlements. Second, based on the location and extent of the visible surface artifact concentrations most settlements (or "villages") were small in size and dispersed across the arable landscape. A few other intermediate-sized ones (or "towns"?) also may have existed and served as secondary nodes in the regional settlement system (Rupp 1987).[6] The overwhelming majority of the population, therefore, must have lived in these "rural" settlements. Third, the patterns of distribution (hence consumption) of various artifact classes are not constant but vary over space and time.

If the bulk of the population lived off the land and practised economic self-sufficiency as much as possible, then these rural, non-elite households located in small villages would have been the primary nodes of food production and of "utilitarian" consumption in EIA Cyprus. As noted above, balanced reciprocity among the households in a village and others in the region would have supplied normally requisite foodstuffs and manufactured objects which were in short-supply or lacking for whatever reason. Based on the spatial patterning of prestige/high status goods (Rupp 1989), it would appear that elite residence was concentrated in the major regional centers and probably to a lesser extent in the secondary settlements. The major settlements would have contained both non-elite and elite households, as well as that of the monarch at a later time (Rupp 1998). The requisite foodstuffs for such a larger settlement with a mixed population may have exceeded the carrying capacity of its immediate economic territory.

Figure 6: Simplified model of socioeconomic interaction/relationships in complex chiefdoms and early state societies (created by David W. Rupp and Loris Gasparatto)

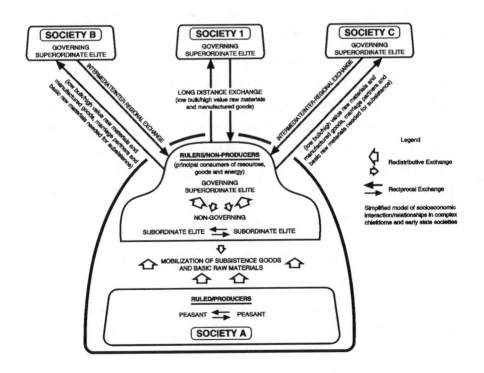

The resulting shortfall, plus any additional demand by the central authority to support its sociopolitical activities and aspirations, would have to come from the surpluses produced by the non-elite inhabitants in the smaller settlements in the countryside of the region. Some form of redistribution would have been the most likely means to achieve this effectively. Given the nature of the available transportation technology and the lack of evidence during this period for centralized storage facilities, the scale of this redistribution could not have been large. It is important to note here that it is in these regional centers that most of the consumption of non-utilitarian/prestige goods would have taken place (Rupp 1989) (Figure 6). As a direct consequence, most of the production of these specialized goods must have taken place in and immediately adjacent to these settlements.

2. Locational and appropriational movements

Locational movements or "changes of place" involve the interaction between humans and their natural environment where people and/or goods move from one locus to another. They can consist of one or more of the following: (1) *transfers from one physical space to another*, involving (a) physical transfers of goods or of people from one place to another, as in movement of work crews, or (b) physical transfers of productive resources, such as tools; (2) *physical changes* in the material stuff of livelihood, for example, changes in the physical condition of a food stuff (raw to cooked, whole to divided, seeds to plants); (3) *energy transfers*, such as the relocation of resources and storage facilities from one place to another or the relocation of a village vis-à-vis ecological zones (Halperin 1994, 59).

From the discussions of the four economic processes one can see many possibilities for locational movements in the EIA Cypriote economy. The extent to which they occurred is difficult to determine archaeologically. Extensive provenience studies would have to be undertaken to begin to understand what is local and what is non-local. The perishable organic materials are, in most cases, beyond such ascertainments.

Appropriational movements or "changes of hands," by contrast, involve the technical arrangements which institutionalize the locational movements. In this sense the two types of movements are inseparable. They

> ...consist of (1) *organizational changes*, or (2) *transfers of rights*. Organizational changes involve changes in the principles allocating resources or goods, e.g., a shift from communal land tenure to private property. Butchering game is a locational movement, but sharing the meat is an appropriational movement. Even if butchering and sharing occur at nearly the same time, the two kinds of movements, locational and appropriational, can and must be separated analytically. Transfer of rights change people's access to and control over goods and resources. The ability to control goods and resources used in production of surpluses to maintain large populations and the ability to acquire goods for simple and direct consumption by producers are both examples of appropriational movements (Halperin 1994, 59).

Again, there are many possibilities here for EIA Cyprus. The complexity of sociopolitical organization of Cypriote society at any given phase would determine what types of appropriational movements took place as well as where and when. A clear understanding of the nature of the island's political structure and institutions is required, therefore, before one can begin to suggest what appropriational movements there could have been.

3. Forms of economic integration

As was shown in the discussion of distribution certainly two (reciprocity and redistribution) and probably three (market exchange) of the four forms of economic integration occurred during the Cypriote EIA. The bulk of the materials produced by the inhabitants of Cyprus would have been organic ones for subsistence. Hence, after their storage and/or consumption there would be very few, if any, identifiable residues to detect in the archaeological record. In theory, many but not all of the manufactured goods would be archaeologically detectable. However, as I stated above, the research orientation and the archaeological data recovery strategies of those studying the EIA on the island determine to a great extent what we chose "to see" in the archaeological record (Rupp 1997). Thus, there is an inherent difficulty in attempting to construct plausibly the circulation patterns or life cycles of the foodstuffs and of the manufactured objects.

The circulation of subsistence products and utilitarian goods, apart from the autarchic production and consumption by individual households, would have been facilitated by some form of reciprocity and/or redistribution. Reciprocal exchanges between households in the same small, agrarian village for scarce foodstuffs or goods would be limited, since their landholdings would occupy mostly the same ecological niche. Intercommunal exchanges in which each settlement was situated in a different ecological setting would be more advantageous and thus more likely (Halstead and O'Shea 1982, 95). The need for exogamy in such villages would have created contacts in distant villages through the establishment of marriage partnerships and alliances. Over time interwoven chains and networks of long-distance interactions based on reciprocity would have evolved (Halstead 1989, 74). With a more complex, hierarchical level of sociopolitical organization, such as chiefdoms or states, foodstuffs and utilitarian goods could have been collected in tribute from the non-elite producers, stored, and then redistributed to the members of the elite, officials, assorted dependents, regional administrators, attached specialist craft people, or corvée laborers by what has been termed "staple finance" (D'Altroy and Earle 1985; Keswani 1993, 76). For one to argue for this form of redistribution, however, there must be evidence for large-scale storage facilities with limited means of access to them.

The form(s) of economic integration that produced the observed distribution patterns for the various manufactured objects, especially those considered to be prestige/high status ones (Rupp 1989), probably involved some form of market exchange at some point in their life cycles. The primary settlement in any region must have served as the principal production and consumption node for a wide range of objects. These with low-bulk/high-value non-utilitarian goods, produced by craft specialists, could have been given by the central authority to the elites and others as a form of remuneration for services rendered, loyalty, etc. This form of redistribution is often termed "wealth finance" (D'Altroy and Earle 1985; Keswani 1993, 76). Nevertheless, the various possible redistributive activities choreographed in some fashion from this main settlement could not have accounted for all of the observed spatial movement of these objects within the settlement itself, its region or between regions.

Another point should be made here. Redistribution implies a centralized and hierarchical society. The lack of evidence for this, especially in the tenth and ninth centuries B.C.E., may mean that the political economies of the island's regions were not, in fact, centralized. Some form of decentralized/non-centralized or heterarchic system (or systems) may have existed both within each region and among the regions (Keswani 1997, 216-17; Crumley 1995). If this existed, then redistribution would not be the dominant form of integration. Finally, the movement of imported exotica within the island such as Greek (Coldstream 1986, 321; 1988, 38-44; 1989a, 92, 94; 1995a; 1995b, 212; Sørensen 1988, 20-22) or Phoenician (Bikai 1987, 70; 1994, 34-35) painted fine wares, as well as the export from the island of low-bulk/high-value objects (Jones 1986, 693-96; Markoe 1992, 73-74, 81; Popham 1994, 28; Waldbaum 1994, 53-54, 58; Reyes 1994, 148-50; Hoffman 1997, 5, 21-22, 116, 133-35, 143-44, 177-78, 257), cannot be simply the result of gift exchange (balanced reciprocity), prestige chains, or administered trade among different elite groups at varying distances (Renfrew 1975) (Figure 6).

Discussion

This analysis of the characteristics of the EIA Cypriote economy must now be put into its broader historical context (Rupp 1989; 1998; Petit 1992; *contra* Snodgrass 1988; Steel 1993; Iacovou 1994; 1995). In light of the points made previously one can argue that the economy of Cyprus between ca. 1125/1100 and 600 B.C.E. progressed through four stages of development. The first stage, ca. 1125-1000 B.C.E. (or LC IIIB–CG IA), saw the final demise of the Late Bronze Mediterranean interaction sphere and the emergence of many of the features which were to characterize the evolving Iron Age Mediterranean world system (Sherratt and Sherratt 1991). At the same time there appears to have been a decrease in the level of sociopolitical complexity (Coldstream 1989b; Rupp 1989; Morden 1995). During the second stage, ca. 1000-850/825 B.C.E. (or CG I–end CG IIB/beginning CG IIIA), Cyprus reverted to a semi-autarchic agro-pastoral economy with limited signs of internal complexity and external contacts (Coldstream 1985; Sherratt and Sherratt 1993). From ca. 850/825 to 707 B.C.E. (or end CG IIIB/beginning CG IIIA–CA IA), the inherent potential of the island's economy began to be mobilized again and production was intensified. This was in direct response to Phoenician economic pressure and demands as part of the growth of both the Mediterranean and the Neo-Assyrian interaction spheres (Markoe 1992; Sherratt and Sherratt 1993; Rupp 1998). The system of territorial kingdoms (see Figure 5) must have emerged during this phase (Rupp 1988; 1989; 1998). From ca. 707 to 600 B.C.E. (or roughly speaking CA I), the island's economy saw extensive development and increased production while it was a peripheral tertiary level player and tribute-paying vassal in the Neo-Assyrian world system (Lipinski 1991; Postgate 1992; Gitin 1995; 1997, 77-81). Its economic ties to the Aegean basin and participation in the Mediterranean interaction sphere were not as important in this fourth stage (Sørensen 1988, 20-21; Coldstream 1988, 41-43; 1995, 212).

From this historical perspective, the known spatial and chronological distributions of the artifacts and of the architectural features on the island are not random, chaotic occurrences. They are palimpsests of the EIA Cypriote economy in action. Reviewing the scant available evidence, one could propose that, while Cyprus as a whole had one unified economy as it was an island without significant topographical barriers, it was subdivided geographically into regional economies. The overwhelming percentage of each region's "GNP" would have derived from semi-autarchic agro-pastoral pursuits. Throughout the EIA, balanced reciprocity would have been practised as a risk-buffering mechanism. When there was a higher level of sociopolitical complexity various forms of redistribution would have linked the non-elite producers in the countryside with the elite consumers in the regional center. Primarily in and around this settlement a third form of economic integration must have operated as well, namely market exchange. This would have been dependent upon the other two but at the same time separated from them, as the majority of the consumers/purchasers in this market exchange would have been members of the elite pursuing their personal socio-economic agendas. Part- and full-time craft specialists would have produced value-added manufactured goods for elite consumption. Although some of these could have been attached to elite patrons, thereby negating the need for market exchange, most probably were independent producers. The size of this quasi-independent market exchange in terms of the overall economy must have been relatively small. Each regional market node would have been connected to one or more of the other regional nodes by inter-elite gift exchange (i.e., balanced reciprocity) and market exchange. Thus, the island's economy would have been comprised of a series of essentially self-sufficient regional ones linked in various ways through elite interaction spheres to form "small-world networks" or "peer polities" (Renfrew 1986). The major settlements with direct access to the sea along major Mediterranean transportation corridors, such as Amathus, Kition, and Salamis (see Figure 5), would have served as "gateway communities" (Hirth 1978; Hodges 1982) to one or more of the broader, mostly coastal, networks of interdependent market exchanges which constituted one of the forms of integration that made up the Neo-Assyrian and the Mediterranean interaction spheres.[7] Once again balanced reciprocity (i.e., gift exchange) and market exchange would have been the dominant forms of integration. This last component of the island's economy, however, could not have been a very significant one in any phase, the high level of attention given to it by archaeologists notwithstanding.

Conclusions

This preliminary macroanalysis of the EIA Cypriote economy using Halperin's augmented presentation of the four basic economic processes in the context of Polanyi's Generic Model of the Economy has been revealing. For EIA Cyprus it reveals how little we really know about the island's overall "material-means provisioning process" during a time period in which its inhabitants made two crucial and major transitions in their cultural evolution. It also reveals the gaps in our knowledge and limits of our understanding of the production, distribution and consumption of prestige/high status goods, both locally made and imported. The discussion of the possible mechanisms behind the manufacture and the export of "Cypriote" low-bulk/high-value objects to the Levant and to other regions of the Mediterranean as well as the role(s) of this production in terms of the totality of the island's economy is still at a very preliminary stage.[8] In short, at this point one can only present speculative *prolegomena* on various well-documented aspects rather than construct a plausible and inclusive model of the total economy. To reduce this high level of speculation many things must be done (Rupp 1997). The systematic retrieval of paleobotanical and paleofaunal data to construct the subsistence base is essential. The manner, means, scale and location of production of the manufactured objects are key topics for discerning the forms of economic integration in use at any given time (Knapp and Cherry 1994). Detailed knowledge on the manner of use and the social organization of space at the household, community, and "off-site" or regional levels would provide many insights on how the economy operated (Trigger 1968). In short, a fine-grained "landscape archaeology" for the EIA is needed here to complement the evolving one for the latter part of the Cypriote Bronze Age (Knapp 1997).

Halperin's thesis that one can study and compare effectively cultural economies in the past as well as the present using the Generic Model of the Economy reveals the limits of such an approach, at least for the past. Her emphasis on distribution and storage at the expense of production and consumption prevents one from seeing the holistic nature of all four. This imbalance continues with her extended discussions of householding and the informal economy. For past economies these two interrelated topics are very difficult, if not impossible, to discern unequivocally in the archaeological record. It should be obvious that the locational and appropriational movements work at the same time both on the level of the intertwined economic processes and on the level of the forms of economic integration. As suggested previously, for foodstuffs and for manufactured objects there are a large number of possible paths from production to consumption, each involving different combinations of locational and appropriational movements and forms of economic integration (Figures 2-4). From this perspective, Halperin's treatments of production and of consumption are superficial. The complexities of these initiating and terminating processes require further scrutiny on her part, in particular for complex societies, as well as systematic reference to the existing literature (Knapp 1985). Even her discussion of storage has significant gaps in its coverage. As it stands, *Cultural Economies* is too conceptual and uneven to enable other "scholars and practitioners" to use its ideas and insights easily, as she had hoped (Halperin 1994, 13).

Despite these criticisms and caveats the Generic Model of the Economy offers archaeologists a useful formal model within which to analyse his or her data sets as they relate to a culture's economy. The use of the Institutional Paradigm instead of the more common Methodological Individualism approach allows one to examine the workings of institutions and processes in an economy in order to ascertain its overall structure. Thus, the hierarchical levels of the model help to focus one's attention on the necessity of attempting to explain the totality of the economy, the interrelationships among its components, as well as how it probably operated.

NOTES
The quotation is from Strabo, *Geographica* 14.6. An earlier version of this paper, entitled "A *prolegomenon* to the construction of the economy of Iron Age Cyprus," was given at the Sixth International Karl Polanyi Conference at Concordia University in Montreal in November, 1996. The insightful comments of David Tandy and A. Bernard Knapp have enabled me to progress on the crafting of this article in a more effective fashion. Michael Wedde and Metaxia Tsipopoulou have assisted in making this version more readable. They, collectively or individually, are not responsible in any way, of course, for my eclectic substantivist/formalist/Neo-Marxist leanings on the topic of the "ancient economy," my usual speculative ruminations, or my creative use of the evidence.

The article is dedicated to my students in CLAS 4V20: Economic Archaeology (Winter 1998) at Brock University, who patiently helped me distill the useful insights contained in Halperin's book (Halperin 1994).

1. This crucial point is reinforced dramatically by the fact that the April 1995 international symposium in Nicosia, Cyprus, on the development of the Cypriote economy from the prehistoric period to the present day (Karageorghis and Michaelides 1996) had no paper which addressed this topic directly. Only one paper, on olive oil production (Hadjisavvas 1996), touched on one aspect of the period's economy.

2. These limitations for the Iron Age are most evident in the sporadic and peripheral treatment of economic topics and issues in Karageorghis's (1982, 108-156) standard general overview of the island's cultural development and history. A.T. Reyes's (1994, 26-28, 101-121, 138-151) treatment of the various sectors of the Cypro-Archaic economy represent a significant step forward in this regard.

3. It should be obvious that many objects were made from more than one raw material. For this discussion, however, this important point is not considered germane.

4. In "market exchange" prospective sellers go to a set location and wait for potential buyers to come and attempt to negotiate an exchange at some set equivalency. This, however, is not the only form of exchange that can take place. As prospective sellers can go around looking for potential buyers at their households or on the road and prospective buyers can go out to the household or workshop of a potential seller or search for them on the road, another type of exchange which is not marketplace specific exists, called here (Figure 3) "itinerant exchange."

5. A fifth-century (?) B.C.E. Bichrome Ware model of a vehicle with two solid wheels which supported a large globular-shaped *pithos* (Museum of Ancient Mediterranean Art, Stockholm) would suggest that there was at least a rudimentary road network at the regional level by the end of EIA.

6. In this context it should be noted, however, that Diodorus Siculus (16.42.2), writing in the first century B.C.E. about the sixth century, mentions only a major city and subordinate villages for each territorial kingdom.

7. The questions of the existence, the nature, forms, and duration of interaction spheres or "world systems" in the Late Bronze Age and Iron Age of the Old World are under spirited debate (cf. Frank 1993 with comments). It should be noted that the presumed existence of such world systems for the Late Bronze Age Mediterranean and the Iron Age Mediterranean and Near East (cf. Sherratt and Sherratt 1991, 1993; Gitin 1995, 1997; Sherratt 1998, 301-307) lies behind many of the assumptions made in this paper.

8. A significant portion of the original paper dealt with these topics and the nature of the extant evidence to base a construction on. This will be explored in an expanded fashion in another paper.

BIBLIOGRAPHY

Bekker-Nielsen, Tnnes. 1993. Centres and road networks in Cyprus. In *Centre and Periphery in the Hellenistic World*, edited by Per Bilde, Troels Engberg-Pedersen, Lisa Hannestad, Jan Zahle, and Klavs Randsborg, 176-91. Aarhus: Aarhus University Press.

Bikai, Patricia Maynor. 1987. *The Phoenician pottery of Cyprus*. Nicosia: A.G. Leventis Foundation.

———. 1994. The Phoenicians and Cyprus. In Karageorghis 1994, 31-37.

Bonet Rosado, Helena, and Consuelo Mata Parreño. 1997. The archaeology of beekeeping in pre-Roman Iberia. *Journal of Mediterranean Archaeology* 10:33-47.

Coldstream, J.N. 1985. Archaeology in Cyprus 1960-1985: The geometric and archaic periods. In *Archaeology in Cyprus 1960-1985*, edited by Vassos Karageorghis, 47-59. Nicosia: Department of Antiquities, Cyprus.

———. 1988. Early Greek pottery in Tyre and Cyprus: Some preliminary considerations. *Report of the Department of Antiquities, Cyprus (Pt. 2)*:35-44.

———. 1989a. Early Greek visitors to Cyprus and the eastern Mediterranean. In *Cyprus and the eastern Mediterranean in the Iron Age*, edited by Veronica Tatton-Brown, 90-96. London: British Museum Publications.

———. 1995a. Amathus tomb NW 194: The Greek pottery imports. *Report of the Department of Antiquities, Cyprus*:187-98.

———. 1995b. Greek geometric and archaic imports from Amathus II. *Report of the Department of Antiquities, Cyprus*:199-214.

Costin, Cathy Lynne. 1991. Craft specialization: Issues in defining, documenting, and explaining the organization of production. In *Archaeological Method and Theory* 3:1-56.

Crane, Eva. 1983. *The archaeology of beekeeping*. London: Duckworth.

Crouwel, J.H. 1985. Carts in Iron Age Cyprus. *Report of the Department of Antiquities, Cyprus*:203-11.

———. 1987. Chariots in Iron Age Cyprus. *Report of the Department of Antiquities, Cyprus*:101-18.

Crumley, Carole L. 1995. Heterarchy and the analysis of complex societies. In *Heterarchy and the analysis of complex societies*, edited by Robert M. Ehrenreich, Carole L. Crumley, and Janet E. Levy, 1-5. Archaeological Papers of the American Anthropological Association 6. Arlington, Va: American Anthropological Association.

Deetz, James. 1988. History and archaeological theory: Walter Taylor revisited. *American Antiquity* 53:13-22.

D'Altroy, Terence N., and Timothy K. Earle. 1985. Staple finance, wealth finance, and storage in the Inka political economy. *Current Anthropology* 26:187-206.

Fasnacht, Walter, et al. 1989. Excavations at Ayia Varvara-*Almyras*. *Report of the Department of Antiquities, Cyprus*: 59-76.

———. 1990. Excavations at Ayia Varvara-*Almyras*: Second preliminary report. *Report of the Department of Antiquities, Cyprus*:127-39.

———. 1991. Excavations at Ayia Varvara-*Almyras*: Third preliminary report. *Report of the Department of Antiquities, Cyprus*:97-108.

———. 1992. Excavations at Ayia Varvara-*Almyras*: Fourth preliminary report. *Report of the Department of Antiquities, Cyprus*:57-74.

Frank, Andre Gunder. 1993. Bronze age world system cycles. *Current Anthropology* 34:382-429.

Gaber, P. 1995. The history of Idalion: A history of interaction. In Wallace 1995, 32-39.

Gitin, Seymour. 1995. Tel-Miqne-Ekron in the 7th century B.C.E.: The impact of economic innovation and foreign cultural influences on a neo-Assyrian vassal city-state. In *Recent excavations in Israel: A view to the west*, edited by Seymour Gitin, 6-79. Dubuque, Iowa: Kendall-Hunt.

———. 1997. The neo-Assyrian empire and its western periphery: The Levant, with a focus on Philistine Ekron. In *Assyria 1995*, edited by S. Parpola and R.M. Whiting, 77-103. Helsinki: The Neo-Assyrian Text Corpus Project.

Gjerstad, Einar. 1948. *The Cypro-geometric, Cypro-archaic and Cypro-classical periods: The Swedish Cyprus expedition*, Vol. 4, Pt. 2. Stockholm: The Swedish Cyprus Expedition.

Hadjisavvas, S. 1996. The economy of the olive. In Karageorghis and Michaelides 1996, 127-37.

Halperin, Rhoda H. 1994. *Cultural economies: Past and present*. Austin: University of Texas Press.

Halstead, Paul. 1989. The economy has a normal surplus: Economic stability and social change among early farming communities of Thessaly, Greece. In Halstead and O'Shea 1989a, 68-89.

Halstead, Paul, and John O'Shea. 1982. A friend in need is a friend indeed: social storage and the origins of social ranking. In Renfrew and Shennan 1982, 92-99.

Halstead, Paul, and John O'Shea, eds. 1989a. *Bad year economics: cultural responses to risk and uncertainty*. Cambridge: Cambridge University Press.

Halstead, Paul, and John O'Shea. 1989b. Conclusions: Bad year economics. In Halstead and O'Shea 1989a, 123-26.

Hirth, Kenneth G. 1978. Interregional trade and the formation of prehistoric gateway communities. *American Antiquity* 43:35-45.

Hodges, Robert. 1982. The evolution of gateway communities: their socioeconomic implications. In Renfrew and Shennan 1982, 117-23.

Hoffman, Gail L. 1997. *Imports and immigrants: Near eastern contacts with Iron Age Crete*. Ann Arbor: University of Michigan Press.

Iacovou, Maria. 1994. The topography of eleventh century B.C. Cyprus. In Karageorghis 1994, 149-65.

———. 1995. Kypriaki protoistoria: I Kypros prin apo ta basileia. *Report of the Department of Antiquities*:95-110.

Jones, R.E. 1986. *Greek and Cypriot pottery: A review of scientific studies*. Fitch Laboratory Occasional Paper 1. Athens: British School at Athens.

Karageorghis, Vassos. 1982. *Cyprus from the Stone Age to the Romans*. London: Thames and Hudson.

———. 1993. *The coroplastic art of ancient Cyprus, II. The late Cypriote II-Cypro-geometric III*. Nicosia: A.G. Leventis Foundation/University of Cyprus.

———. 1995. *The coroplastic art of ancient Cyprus, IV. The Cypro-archaic period: Small male figures*. Nicosia: A.G. Leventis Foundation/University of Cyprus.

———. 1996. *The coroplastic art of ancient Cyprus, VI. The Cypro-archaic period: Monsters, animals and miscellanea*. Nicosia: A.G. Leventis Foundation/University of Cyprus.

Karageorghis, Vassos, ed. 1994. *Cyprus in the 11th century B.C.* Nicosia: A.G. Leventis Foundation/University of Cyprus.

Karageorghis, Vassos, and Demetres Michaelides, eds. 1996. *The development of the Cypriot economy: From the prehistoric period to the present day*. Nicosia: University of Cyprus/Bank of Cyprus.

Kassianidou, V. 1994. Could iron have been produced in Cyprus? *Report of the Department of Antiquities, Cyprus*:73-81.

Keswani, Priscilla Schuster. 1993. Models of local exchange in late Bronze Age Cyprus. *Bulletin of the American Schools of Oriental Research* 292:73-83.

————. 1996. Hierarchies, heterarchies, and the urbanization processes: The view from Bronze Age Cyprus. *Journal of Mediterranean Archaeology* 9:211-50.

Knapp, A. Bernard. 1985. Production and exchange in the Aegean and eastern Mediterranean: An overview. In *Prehistoric production and exchange: The Aegean and eastern Mediterranean*, edited by A. Bernard Knapp and Tamara Stech. Los Angeles: Institute of Archaeology, University of California, Los Angeles.

————1994. The prehistory of Cyprus: Problems and prospects. *Journal of World Prehistory* 8:377-453.

————. 1997. *The archaeology of late Bronze Age Cypriot society: The study of settlement, survey and landscape*. Glasgow: Department of Archaeology, Glasgow University.

Knapp, A. Bernard, and John F. Cherry. 1994. *Provenience studies and Bronze Age Cyprus: Production, exchange and politico-economic change*. Monographs in World Archaeology 21. Madison: Prehistory Press.

Koucky, Frank L., and Arthur Steinberg. 1989. Ancient mining and mineral dressing on Cyprus. In *American Expedition to Idalion, Cyprus, 1973-1980*, edited by Lawrence E. Stager and Anita M. Walker, 275-327. Chicago: Oriental Institute of the University of Chicago.

Lipinski, Edward. 1991. The Cypriot vassals of Esarhaddon. In *Ah, Assyria: Studies in Assyrian history and ancient Near Eastern historiography presented to Hayim Tadmor*, edited by Mordicai Cogan and Israel Eph'al, 58-64. Jerusalem: Magnis Press/Hebrew University.

Markoe, Glenn E. 1992. In pursuit of metal: Phoenicians and Greeks in Italy. In *Greece Between East and West: 10th-8th Centuries B.C.*, edited by Günter Kopcke and Isabelle Tokumaru, 61-84. Mainz am Rhein: von Zabern.

Monloup, Therese. 1984. *Les figurines de terre cuite de tradition archaique*. Paris: de Boccard.

Morden, M.E. 1995. The function of foreign imports in early Iron Age tomb assemblages. In Wallace 1995, 40-50.

Peltenburg, Edgar, ed. 1989. *Early society in Cyprus*. Edinburgh: University of Edinburgh Press.

Petit, Thierry. 1992. L'origin des cités-royaumes cypriotes à l'Age du Fer: Le cas d'Amathonte. In *Etudes d'histoire*, 5-17. Sainte-Etienne: Université de Sainte-Etienne.

Pilides, Despina. 1996. Storage jars as evidence of the economy of Cyprus in the late Bronze Age. In Karageorghis and Michaelides 1996, 107-20.

Popham, Mervyn R. 1994. Precolonization: Early Greek contact with the East. In *The Archaeology of Greek Colonization. Essays dedicated to Sir John Boardman*, edited by Gocha R. Tsetskhladze and Franco De Angelis, 1-46. Oxford University Committee for Archaeology Monograph 40. Oxford: Oxford University Press.

Postgate, J.N. 1992. The land of Assur and the yoke of Assur. *World Archaeology* 23:247-63.

Renfrew, Colin. 1975. Trade as action at a distance. In *Ancient civilization and trade*, edited by Jeremy A. Sabloff and C.C. Lamberg-Karlovsky, 3-59. Albuquerque: University of New Mexico Press.

————. 1986. Introduction: Peer polity interaction and socio-political change. In *Peer polity interaction and socio-political change*, edited by Colin Renfrew and John F. Cherry, 1-18. Cambridge: Cambridge University Press.

Renfrew, Colin, and Stephen Shennan, eds. 1982. *Ranking, resource and exchange: Aspects of the archaeology of early European society.* Cambridge: Cambridge University Press.

Reyes, A.T. 1994. *Archaic Cyprus: A study of the textual and archaeological evidence.* Oxford: Clarendon Press.

Rupp, David W. 1987.*Vive le roi*: The emergence of the state in Iron Age Cyprus. In *Western Cyprus connections: An archaeological symposium,* edited by David W. Rupp, 147-68. Studies in Mediterranean Archaeology 77. Goteborg: Paul Åströms Förlag.

————. 1988. The "royal tombs" at Salamis (Cyprus): Ideological messages of power and authority. *Journal of Mediterranean Archaeology* 1:111-39.

————. 1989. Puttin' on the Ritz: Manifestations of high status in Iron Age Cyprus. In Peltenburg 1989, 336-62.

————. 1997. Constructing the Cypriot Iron Age: Present praxis, future possibilities. *Bulletin of the American Schools of Oriental Research* 308:69-75.

————. 1998. The seven kings of the land of Ia', a district of Ia-ad-na-na: Achaean bluebloods, Cypriot parvenus or both? In *Stephanos: Studies in honor of Brunilde Sismondo Ridgway,* edited by Kim J. Hartswick and Mary C. Sturgeon, 209-22. University Museum Monograph 100. Philadelphia: The University Museum, University of Pennsylvania.

Sherratt, Andrew, and Susan Sherratt. 1991. From luxuries to commodities: The nature of Mediterranean Bronze Age trading systems. In *Bronze Age trade in the Mediterranean,* edited by Noel H. Gale, 351-86. Studies in Mediterranean Archaeology 90. Jonsered: Paul Åströms Förlag.

Sherratt, Susan. 1994. Commerce, iron and ideology: Metallurgical innovation in 12th-11th century Cyprus. In Karageorghis 1994, 59-107.

————. 1998. "Sea peoples" and the economic structure of the late second millennium in the eastern Mediterranean. In *Mediterranean peoples in transition: Thirteenth to early tenth centuries BC,* edited by Seymour Gitin, Amihai Mazar, and Ephraim Stern, 292-313. Jerusalem: Israel Exploration Society.

Sherratt, Susan and Andrew Sherratt. 1993. The growth of the Mediterranean economy in the early first millennium B.C. *World Archaeology* 24:361-78.

Snodgrass, Anthony. 1988. *Cyprus and early Greek history.* Nicosia: Bank of Cyprus Cultural Foundation.

Sørensen, Lone Wriedt. 1988. Greek pottery found in Cyprus. *Acta Hyperborea* 1:12-22.

Steel, Louise. 1993. The establishment of city kingdoms in Iron Age Cyprus: An archaeological commentary. *Report of the Department of Antiquities, Cyprus*:147-56.

Trigger, Bruce G. 1968. The determinants of settlement patterns. In *Settlement archaeology,* ed. by Kwang-chih Chang, 53-78. Palo Alto: National Press Books.

Van der Leeuw, Sander E. 1977. Towards a study of pottery making. In *Ex horreo,* edited by B.L. van Beek, R.W. Brandt and W. Groenman-van Waateringe, 68-76. Amsterdam: Universiteit van Amsterdam.

Waldbaum, Jane C. 1994. Early Greek contacts with the southern Levant, ca. 1000-600 B.C.: The eastern perspective. *Bulletin of the American Schools of Oriental Research* 293:53-66.

Wallace, Paul W., ed. 1995. *Visitors, immigrants, and invaders in Cyprus.* Albany: Institute of Cypriot Studies, State University of New York.

Chapter Five

NAUKRATIS,
OR HOW TO IDENTIFY A PORT OF
TRADE

Astrid Möller

When Naukratis, lying in the Western Delta of the Nile, was discovered and
excavated at the end of last century, it immediately became famous by its
masses of excavated material: Archaic Greek sherds of hitherto unknown
styles, frequently with dedicatory inscriptions in Archaic local alphabets,
statuettes, faiences, and many more small finds. Such a place, however, full of
Greek finds and lying on Egyptian territory, is not easy to interpret. In 1892,
Percy Gardner, the Professor of Classical Archaeology at Oxford, wrote
about the busy excavations that followed the bombardment of Alexandria by
the British fleet:

> Mr. Petrie…has discovered and excavated…the site of Naukratis, the
> meeting-point in the seventh century B.C., of Egyptian and Greek, and
> the fulcrum by which the enterprising Hellenic race brought the
> power of their arms and of their wits to bear on the most ancient and
> venerable empire in the world…We moderns can see that a Greek in
> Memphis or Thebes as much represented a higher race and a nobler
> order of ideas, as a Spaniard in Mexico, or an Englishman in Canton.
> With him lay the future, with the Egyptians only the past…Thus
> Naukratis might be compared to a tender plant growing in an
> uncongenial soil, and surrounded on all sides by hardier shrubs ever

ready to encroach upon its narrow domain (Gardner 1892, 187, 191, 213)

Of course, this example of unquestioned western superiority can only raise our eyebrows today, but if we look for less imperialistic overtones we may still find more implicit examples of such assumed superiority of Greek culture. This consequently led scholars to interpret Naukratis as a Greek colony in Egypt. If we have, however, Karl Polanyi's concept of the port of trade in mind, we can no longer assume that the Greeks indeed were the driving force at Naukratis. In the following pages, I wish to show how Polanyi's concept of the port of trade can be used to clarify the status of Naukratis. In addition, I would like to offer a catalog of criteria which help to identify ports of trade. This should display at the same time into which directions Polanyi's concept developed as I worked with the material from Naukratis. That the further development of the model is quite a natural process can be explained by taking Polanyi's port of trade as a Weberian *Idealtypus*.

Ideal-type constructs are conceptual abstractions attained by reducing the wealth of empirical data to its supposed core components.[1] These are gained by singling out and accentuating those features which are held to be central or basic to the institution in question and by suppressing those features that are considered marginal to it. As the term itself reveals, the ideal type cannot be found in reality; it only approximates social reality. I assume that this is the very procedure which Polanyi applied in his work on economic anthropology. He collected data from different cultures and attempted to create his anthropological models of economic action by emphasizing single features. His well-defined patterns of integration cannot be found in social reality in their pure shape, but these models help to ask the right questions and to understand the design of empirical data much more precisely.

To form a model in such an inductive way, its material basis is of crucial significance. Accordingly, the ideal type usually keeps changing its shape while working with additional material. I have sorted out nine aspects or facets which delineate my ideal-typical port of trade:

1. geographical situation,

2. separation from the hinterland,

3. the political and economic structures of the trading partners,

4. the form of foundation,

5. administration,

6. infrastructure,

7. population structure,

8. kinds of goods exchanged, and

9. non-economic functions.

These aspects are based on (a) Polanyi's own formulations and observations, (b) further data found in research by other scholars dealing with prospective examples of ports of trade, and (c) the results gained by examining the Greek *emporion* Naukratis.[2] However, to identify a place in question as a port of trade, it is not necessary that indeed all nine facets can be found, although some are more decisive than others.[3] However, this model has to be seen in the context of Polanyi's other concepts; accordingly, it is essential to enquire in each case as to the background, the political and economic structures, of the respective trading partners. Polanyi regarded the economic institution of the ports of trade—a neutral checkpoint facilitating exchange under pre-market economy conditions—as a functional alternative to market institutions (Polanyi 1963, 30; cf. Humphreys 1978, 53-57; Dalton 1978, 102f.). It guaranteed that traders could go about their business with no fear of danger; that foreigners, for their part, did not become a danger for the hinterland; and that competition and rivalry played a minor role in trading. Polanyi explicitly linked the port of trade with administered trade, the most important institution of which it represents.[4] Let us now discuss the nine aspects to be considered in order to identify a port of trade.

1. Geographical situation

For Polanyi, one condition for a port of trade was a seaside or riverbank location, one of such a nature that favourable geographical circumstances would aid further transport on land (Polanyi 1963, 30-31). This point will presumably have played a role in the case of the majority of trading centres—understood here in a more general sense than the specific port of trade—and can only be seen as a necessary, not a sufficient, condition for the existence of a port of trade. However, it is the political geography that determines a port of trade; the fact that the port of trade lies on the margin of a controlled territory seems to be one of its most important features.

Polanyi used the term port of trade not only to describe isolated settlements on the edge of an "empire," but also for those lying outside town walls or separated from the city territory proper like the classical Greek *emporion* as part of a city-state's harbour (Polanyi 1963, 34). The latter kind is probably specific to societies in which the town was the centre of political power. In ancient Greek usage, two types of *emporia* can be distinguished: on the one hand, chiefly in Herodotus (1.165; 2.179; 3.5; 4.17, 20, 24, 108, 152; 7.158; 9.106), it is used to describe a settlement the inhabitants of which are involved in trade. On the other hand, it refers to places of external exchange in the harbour area of a *polis*. But we should not automatically assume that every *emporion* approximates a port of trade,[5] for both concepts easily tend to resemble each other. Not all *emporia* served as a device of administered trade or were at least controlled by a hinterland power.

Naukratis lay completely isolated on the Canopic branch of the Nile—that is the most Western one—and its location was inviting to sailing ships. It represented an *emporion* of the first type, being an isolated settlement of which the majority of the population was busy with trade. The assumption that the *emporion* of Naukratis was part of a *polis* Naukratis, recently taken up again by Hugh Bowden, can be dismissed—last but not least by the archaeological evidence. Neither the buildings nor the finds indicate such a separation between an *emporion* and a *polis*.[6]

2. Separation from the hinterland

Polanyi regarded the separation of external long-distance trade and local exchange as one of the most important prerequisites for the existence of a port of trade (Humphreys 1978, 54). Therefore, to talk about the integration of a port of trade into the hinterland by considering its rôle for the internal exchange framework would contradict Polanyi's approach. However, this point takes an important rôle in studies involving models like the gateway community or the solar central place, which cannot be considered true alternatives to the port of trade, for they either link external trade to internal trade, or emphasize precisely the existence of those markets that Polanyi rejected, or perform no economic function with regard to external exchange.[7]

Polanyi emphasized the extent to which the neutrality of the port of trade was an important condition for its existence (Polanyi 1963, 30, 33f.; cf. Revere 1957, 51f.). However, as a primary device of administered trade, the port of trade cannot be neutral and belongs to those powers controlling the coast and the hinterland. The idea of neutrality seems to be based on Polanyi's assumption that the port of trade had developed from the prehistoric *emporion* as defined by Lehmann-Hartleben (1923, 31) and was a derivative of silent trade. We might, however, define another type of port of trade which is stronger characterized by neutrality.

The separation between external and internal trade and the complete exclusion from the hinterland at Naukratis is evidenced by Herodotus (2.179), who describes its exceptional position in that Greeks were only allowed to disembark at this spot. The archaeological material confirms this segregation in that the Naukratis survey by William Coulson and Albert Leonard Jr. has revealed that there are virtually no Archaic Greek sherds to be found in the wider environs of Naukratis.[8]

3. The political and economic structures of the trading partners

To identify a port of trade as a device of administered trade, it is essential to consider the background of the trading partners involved. Polanyi saw the port of trade as a neutral checkpoint—or interface—between two societies of differing economic organization (Humphreys 1978, 53). However, as a primary device of administered trade, the port of trade cannot be neutral, belonging as it does to those powers controlling the coast and the hinterland.

The port of trade must often have been an instrument of passive trade, the state offering protection to foreign traders entering its land with goods, albeit under conditions of strict supervision, without itself becoming active. In guaranteeing the inflow of prestige items, it could be assured of the preservation of its elite.

Egypt is a very clear example of a redistributive system. It conducted its external trade through state officials who collected tributes or provided ports of trade such as Iquen at its Nubian border or Naukratis at its northern border.[9] There was no central political power in Greece, and Greek traders traveled on their own account. The archaic Greek economy developed very much along reciprocal lines; it acquired some market elements, but interdependent markets were not the result.[10]

4. Form of foundation

Being an institution of administered trade, the port of trade should exist on the condition of some ceremonial act of authorization or agreement. While it is not always possible to prove this in certain individual cases, its absence could also indicate the temporary nature of a settlement. It was necessary to secure safety through such agreements with those powers controlling the coast and the hinterland. In most cases of permanent ports of trade, divine protection was also present, in the form of temples or cults inside the port of trade.[11]

In the case of Naukratis we have Herodotus's testimony (2.178) that the Pharaoh Amasis gave (*edoke*) Naukratis to the Greeks; this would mean a date of about 570 B.C.E. If we take Herodotus to mean that Amasis founded Naukratis, this information is contradicted by the archaeological evidence, starting with Corinthian transitional style dated traditionally to around 630 B.C.E. The so-called burnt stratum, the earliest layer above virgin soil, can be dated to the late seventh century on account of Greek pottery fragments found by Petrie in the stratum, although later scholars ignored this.[12] Instead of solving the contradiction between Herodotus and the archaeological evidence by downdating the pottery chronology, I favour the argument that

Amasis settled Naukratis's status and/or reorganized it. However, Herodotus's testimony does not justify the downdating of the orthodox pottery chronology,[13] since he had the tendency to ascribe favours towards the Greeks to this pharaoh.

5. Administration

Polanyi regarded the port of trade as principally an instrument of administered trade, one thereby avoiding market mechanisms (Polanyi 1957, 262; cf. Chapman 1957, 116; Leeds 1961, 27f.). Hence, for Polanyi, price regulation constituted the most important administrative task. The state operating the port of trade as an institution of its external trade—and usually also combining it with fiscal interests—could perform these administrative duties via the state's officials. However, matters concerning inhabitants were often delegated to their own representatives.

The *prostatai tou emporiou,* "guardians of the trading post," in Naukratis would be an example of this internal organization. On the Egyptian side, we know of Nekhthoreb who was "Overseer of the Gate to the Foreign Lands of the Great Green" at the time of Amasis; he controlled duties and taxes (Tresson 1931; Posener 1947).

The stele of Nektanebis I, dated to 380 B.C.E., gives us an idea of the taxes levied in the fourth century. The remark "in addition to that which pertained before" is likely to refer to older regulations, now being augmented, but as yet unknown to us. There was a 10% tax on imported goods such as gold, silver, timber and worked wood, and of manufactured goods not specified (Lichtheim 1980, 86-89).

6. Infrastructure

We are concerned here with the question of whether such elements as storage facilities, quays for ships, and accommodation facilities can be found. Obviously, production for local consumption has to be considered. A marketplace within the port of trade will presumably have supplied the needs of the resident population, and will not itself have been the locus of long-distance trade.

At Naukratis, a workshop has been discovered in which Egyptian, Egyptianizing and Greek faience scarabs, scaraboids and amulets were produced. These products are found widely dispersed in the Mediterranean, though only in small quantities (Feghali Gorton 1996, 91ff., 177ff.). Also, it appears very likely that Chian pottery was produced on the spot, in some cases probably with imported clay (Boardman 1980, 123; 1986, 252f.). This production met the needs of Greek dedicators at the sanctuaries.

7. Population structure

Studies have revealed that the port of trade was populated either by members of the indigenous people, working there as officials and labourers or else by foreigners. It was also possible that the inhabitants took on a group identity of their own, as in the case of the medieval *portus* (Polanyi 1963, 36; Pirenne 1956, 102f., 107f.; cf. Hodges 1988, 80). Besides their ethnic identity, occupations may be established in connection with service functions in ports of trade.

At Naukratis, Greeks retained their old ethnic identities as long as it can be regarded a port of trade, describing themselves in dedicatory inscriptions as Teians, Chians or Mytilenians. Herodotus (2.178) testifies that there were two groups, those who wanted to trade and those who wanted to live there permanently in Egypt, although there are no traces in the archaeological material which would enable us to distinguish these groups. However, we know of famous *hetairai* ("courtesans") who very likely stayed at Naukratis for a while to pursue their business.[14] The identified faience workshop and the assumed pottery production point to the fact that there were groups of craftsmen living at Naukratis for extended periods of time.

Besides the Greeks there might have been Phoenicians and Cypriots. However, they are hard to discern in the material. Phoenician and Cypriote *amphorae* and Cypriote statuettes can also have been transported by Greeks. At closer inspection, many of the statuettes considered Cypriote appear to be of Mixed Style, although there might now be a chance to distinguish a Cypriote group within the Mixed Style.[15]

8. Kinds of goods exchanged

The question of the exchange of prestige items and/or the requirements of everyday life provides indications regarding the socioeconomic background of the trading partners involved. The offer of a port of trade frequently serves to preserve the power of the ruling elite, in that prestige items are exchanged here by passive trading. If the port of trade was linked to a redistributive system, then this device represented the foreign trader's only possibility of acquiring such goods as grain, slaves and metals, since these were collected by political power and not traded in the marketplaces of the hinterland. When interpreting archaeological finds, one must always bear in mind the fact that perishable goods might have been involved, and that those objects found in the port of trade were perhaps not intended for exchange with the outside trading partner.

Apart from speculations, it is almost impossible to tell definitely what kinds of products were exchanged at Naukratis in the archaic period. Most likely, the Greeks sought grain and the Egyptians wanted silver. The aforementioned stele of Nektanebis I refers to gold, silver, timber and worked wood for the fourth century B.C.E. Before we can say that the Egyptian elite was also interested in wine and olive oil, we would need more literary evidence or remains of Greek *amphorae* in purely Egyptian contexts.[16] The overwhelming amount of pottery was found in the Greek sanctuaries, dedicated to Greek gods and not intended to be traded with the Egyptians.

9. Non-economic functions

In addition to its chief function as the locus of long-distance trade under pre-market conditions, the port of trade also performed other, non-economic functions, among them the regulation of cultural contacts, the oversight of religious activities, and the circulation of information. The significance of non-economic functions is a possible way of determining whether the settlement under study was indeed a port of trade or whether other models—such as that of the solar central-place—should be enlisted.[17]

The archaeological remains of Naukratis clearly show its importance as a religious centre. This is emphasized by Herodotus's account (2.178), which centers on the various sanctuaries and the Hellenion. However, he also relates the procedure by which ships were forced to land at Naukratis (2.179). The sanctuaries can be regarded a secondary phenomenon, following the needs of traders and travelers alike. All the possible side effects of Naukratis—its religious importance or the better acquaintance with Egyptian culture—are overshadowed by its economic function as the place of external exchange in Egypt.

After considering Polanyi's concept of the port of trade, the status of Naukratis can certainly no longer be interpreted as "the fulcrum by which the enterprising Hellenic race brought the power of their arms and of their wits to bear on the most ancient and venerable empire in the world," but as the place where the quite powerful Saïte pharaohs granted the enterprising Greeks access to grain and much sought-after luxury items. By granting the Greeks a port of trade, the Egyptian pharaoh managed to integrate them into his system of external trade, turning them indeed into "Egyptian traders" (Bresson 1980, 322), while guaranteeing Egypt's passive trade.

NOTES

Versions of this paper were delivered at the Sixth International Karl Polanyi Conference in Montreal in 1996 and the 129th Annual Meeting of the American Philological Association in Chicago in 1997; on both occasions my participation was made possible by a travel grant from the *Deutsche Forschungsgemeinschaft.* I am most grateful to David Tandy for polishing my English style and for the discussion that clarified what became the nine aspects of the port of trade.

1. Cf. Max Weber 1988, 191. A clear introduction to Weber's thought can be found in Parkin 1982, esp. 28ff. on ideal types.

2. A full account of the results of my research can be read in Möller 2000.

3. We may compare such an ideal-type model with what Peter Burke describes as a polythetic group of entities: "A polythetic group...is a group in which membership does not depend on a single attribute. The group is defined in terms of a set of attributes such that each entity possesses most of the attributes and each attribute is shared by most of the entities" (Burke 1992, 32).

4. Polanyi 1957, 263; Polanyi 1977, 95; cf. the slightly different version according to a March 1951 manuscript edited by George Dalton in Sabloff and Lamberg-Karlofsky 1975, 133-54, esp. 152.

5. It is Figueira's assumption (1984), however, that every *emporion* was a port of trade, and so he claims that since this cannot be the case the whole concept is invalid for Greece. For the meaning of *emporion* see Bresson and Rouillard 1993; Rouillard 1995.

6. Bowden (1996, 28ff.) claims a separation between the *polis* Naukratis and the *emporion* of Naukratis: The sanctuaries of the northern part would belong to those who, according to Herodotus 2.178, did not want to settle there, and so the *temenos* of Aphrodite would belong to the settlers. However, on closer inspection, the *temenos* of Aphrodite seems to have been the sanctuary the Chians regarded as their prime focus of dedication. However, others like Teians and Mytilenians are also among the dedicants, but nothing confirms their status as settlers.

7. Jeremy Sabloff and David Freidel (1975) do not take the model of the port of trade in its strict sense but scrutinize more generally "trading centers" in their context. Kenn Hirth (1978, 35-45) takes the "gateway community" as oppositional to the "central place." Robert Hodges (1988, 42-52, 54) considers gateway communities an outcome of the mode of production of a developed tribal society. The solar central places that are found in tribal societies seem to function as centres of accumulative consumption (Hodges 1988, 55-59). Barry Cunliffe (1988, 5f, 200) fuses the port of trade and the gateway community into one concept (cf. Hodges 1978, 116 and n. 97f. for the *entrepôt*).

8. However, Coulson and Leonard (1981, 72) mention apparently early pottery in Kom Firin which was reported earlier (*Fasti Archaeologici 5* (1952):no. 61). Marjorie Venit (1985, 397) casts doubts on these early pottery finds, since she only knows of finds from the fourth century B.C.E.

9. Barry Kemp (1989, 232-60) examines the economic conditions in Egypt with consideration of Polanyi's concepts.

10. The latter assumption is maintained by Robin Osborne (1996).

11. See Arnold 1957, 166, for ritual practice in Whydah.

12. Petrie 1886, 21; Gardner 1888, 72: Chian amphora from the late seventh century, further Chian amphorae and black-glazed krater or amphora. The layers above can be dated roughly to around 600 B.C.E. and later. D.G. Hogarth (1898/99, 43) insisted that there were only Egyptian finds in the southern area.

13. Pace David Gill (1994, 107).

14. The most famous was Rhodopis, mentioned by Sappho (fr. 202 LP) as Doricha; the ancient sources are Herodotus 2.135, Strabo 17.1.33, and Athenaeus 13.596c.

15. Ursula Höckmann (Mainz) currently works on the statuettes from Naukratis and generously informed me about her preliminary results.

16. We may hope that one day there might be a find for Naukratis like the one from Elephantine: a papyrus palimpsest records the customs duties on all imports and exports on Ionian and Phoenician ships and the kind of goods carried during the sailing season of the year 475 B.C.E.; see Porten and Yardeni 1993, C3.7; Yardeni 1994.

17. Hodges 1988, 55-59. He emphasizes their function as political and religious centres subordinating their meaning as local market places.

BIBLIOGRAPHY

Arnold, Rosemary. 1957. A port of trade: Wydah on the Guinea coast. In Polanyi, Arensberg, and Pearson 1957, 154-76.

Austin, M.M. 1970. *Greece and Egypt in the archaic age*. Proceedings of the Cambridge Philological Society Suppl. 2. Cambridge: Cambridge Philological Society.

Boardman, John. 1980. *The Greeks Overseas*. 3rd ed. London: Thames and Hudson.

———. 1986. Archaic Chian pottery at Naukratis. In *Chios: A conference at the Homereion in Chios 1984*, edited by John Boardman and C.E. Vaphopoulou-Richardson, 251-58. Oxford: Clarendon Press.

Bowden, Hugh. 1996. The Greek settlement and sanctuaries at Naukratis: Herodotus and archaeology. In *More studies in the ancient Greek polis*, edited by Mogens Herman Hansen and Kurt Raaflaub, 17-37. *Historia Einzelschriften* 108. Stuttgart: Franz Steiner.

Bresson, Alain. 1980. Rhodes, l'Hellénion et le statut de Naucratis (VIᵉ–IVᴱ siècle a.C.). *Dialogues d'Histoire Ancienne* 6:291-349.

Bresson, Alain, and Pierre Rouillard, eds. 1993. *L'Emporion*. Paris: de Boccard.

Burke, Peter. 1992. *History and social theory*. Cambridge: Polity Press.

Chapman, Anne M. 1957. Port of trade enclaves in Aztec and Maya civilization. In Polanyi, Arensberg, and Pearson, 114-53.

Coulson, William D.E., and Albert Leonard, Jr. 1981. *Cities of the Delta I: Naukratis*. Malibu, Cal.: Undena.

Coulson, William D.E. et al. 1997. *Ancient Naukratis*. Vol. II, part 1, *The survey at Naukratis and environs.*, Oxford: Oxbow.

Cunliffe, Barry W. 1988. *Greeks, Romans and barbarians: Spheres of interaction*. New York: Methuen.

Dalton, George, ed. 1968. *Primitive, archaic, and modern economies: Essays of Karl Polanyi*. Garden City, N.Y.: Anchor Books.

Dalton, George. 1978. Comments on ports of trade in early medieval Europe, *Norwegian Archaeological Review* 11:102-8.

Feghali Gorton, Andree. 1996. *Egyptian and Egyptianizing scarabs: A typology of steatite, faience and paste scarabs from Punic and other Mediterranean sites*. Oxford: Oxbow.

Figueira, Thomas J. 1984. Karl Polanyi and ancient Greek trade: The port of trade. *Ancient World* 10:15-30.

Gardner, Ernest Arthur. 1988. *Naukratis II*. London: Trübner and Co.

Gardner, Percy. 1892. *New chapters in Greek history*. London: John Murray.

Geertz, Clifford. 1980. Ports of trade in nineteenth-century Bali. *Research in Economic Anthropology* 3:109-22.

Gill, David W.J. 1994. Positivism, pots and long-distance trade. In *Classical Greece: Ancient histories and modern archaeologies*, edited by Ian Morris, 99-107. Cambridge: Cambridge University Press.

Hirth, Kenneth G. 1978. Inter-regional trade and the formation of prehistoric gateway communities. *American Antiquity* 43:25-45.

Hodges, Robert. 1978. Ports of trade in early medieval Europe, *Norwegian Archaeological Review* 11:97-101, 114-17.

———. 1988. *Primitive and peasant markets.* Oxford: B. Blackwell.

Hogarth, D.G. 1898/99. Excavations at Naukratis. *Annual of the British School at Athens* 5:26-97.

Humphreys, S.C., 1978. History, economics, and anthropology: The work of Karl Polanyi. In her *Anthropology and the Greeks*, 31-75. London: Routledge. First published in *History and Theory* 8(1969):165-212.

Kemp, Barry J. 1989. *Ancient Egypt: Anatomy of a civilization.* London: Routledge.

Leeds, Anthony. 1961. The port of trade in pre-European India as an ecological and evolutionary type. *Proceedings of the Annual Spring Meeting of the American Ethnological Society* (Seattle), 26-48.

Lehmann-Hartleben, Karl. 1923. Die antiken Hafenanlagen des Mittelmeeres: Beiträge zur Geschichte des Stadtbaues im Altertum. *Klio Beiheft* 14. Leipzig: Dieterich. Reprinted Aalen: Scientia Verlag, 1963.

Lichtheim, Miriam. 1980. *Ancient Egyptian literature: A book of readings.* Vol. 3. Berkeley: University of California.

Möller, Astrid. 2000. *Naukratis: Trade in archaic Greece.* Oxford: Oxford University Press.

Osborne, Robin. 1996. Pots, trade and the archaic Greek economy. *Antiquity* 70:31-44.

Parkin, Frank. 1982. *Max Weber.* New York: Tavistock.

Petrie, W. Flinders. 1886. *Naukratis I.* London: Trübner and Co.

Pirenne, Henri. 1956. *Medieval cities: Their origins and the revival of trade.* Translated by Frank D. Halsey. Princeton: Princeton University Press.

Polanyi, Karl. 1957. The economy as instituted process. In Polanyi, Arensberg, and Pearson 1957, 243-70. Reprinted in Dalton 1968, 139-74.

———. 1963. Ports of trade in early societies. *Journal of Economic History* 23:30-45. Reprinted in Dalton 1968, 238-60.

———. 1977. *The livelihood of man.* Edited by Harry W. Pearson. New York: Academic Press.

Polanyi, Karl, Conrad Arensberg, and Harry W. Pearson, eds. 1957. *Trade and Market in the Early Empires.* Glencoe, Ill.: Free Press.

Porláksson, H. 1978. Comments on ports of trade in early medieval Europe. *Norwegian Archaeological Review* 11, 112-14.

Porten, Betsalel, and Ada Yardeni. 1993. *Textbook of Aramaic Documents from Ancient Egypt.* Vol. 3. Winona Lakes, Ind.: Eisenbrauns.

Posener, Georges. 1947. Les douanes de la Mediterranée dans l'Egypte Saïte. *Revue de Philologie* 21:121-31.

Rathje, William L. & Sabloff, Jeremy A. 1973. Ancient Maya commercial systems: A research design for the island of Cozumel, Mexico. *World Archaeology* 5:221-231.

Revere, Robert B. 1957. "No man's coast": Ports of trade in the eastern Mediterranean. In Polanyi, Arensberg, and Pearson 1957, 38-63.

Rouillard, Pierre. 1995. Les *emporia* dans la Méditerranée occidentale aux époques archaïque et classique. In *Les Grecs et l'occident*. Actes du colloque de la villa Kérylos (1991), 95-108. Rome: École Française de Rome.

Sabloff, Jeremy A., and David A. Freidel. 1975. A model of a pre-Columbian trading center. In Sabloff and Lamberg-Karlovsky 1975, 369-408.

Sabloff, Jeremy A. and C.C. Lamberg-Karlovsky, eds. 1975. *Ancient civilization and trade*. Albuquerque: University of New Mexico.

Torrence, Robin. 1978. Comments on ports of trade in early medieval Europe. *Norwegian Archaeological Review* 11, 108-11.

Tresson, Paul. 1931. Sur deux monuments inédits de l'époque d'Amasis et de Nectanébo Ier. *Kêmi* 4:126-44.

Venit, Marjorie Susan. 1985. Laconian Black Figure in Egypt. *American Journal of Archaeology* 89:391-98.

Weber, Max. 1988. Die "Objektivität" sozialwissenschaftlicher und sozialpolitischer Erkenntnis. In his *Gesammelte Aufsätze zur Wissenschaftslehre*, 7th ed., 146-214. Tübingen: Mohr.

Yardeni, Ada. 1994. Maritime trade and royal accountancy in an erased customs account from 475 B.C.E. on the Ahiqar scroll from Elephantine. *Bulletin of the American Schools of Oriental Research* 293:67-78.

Chapter Six

AGROSKOPIA: MATERIAL CENTRIPETALISM AND THE CONTINGENT NATURE OF EARLY GREEK ECONOMIC DEVELOPMENT

David W. Tandy

> Historically, the relation of the city to agriculture has in no way been
> unambiguous and simple.   —Max Weber (1921, 1217)

The Landscape

There were many players as the *polis* took shape in the course of the eighth
and seventh centuries B.C.E. There were also many who were not asked to
play, or perhaps who chose not to play, or who began to play but changed
their minds. One of the eventual non-players was Hesiod of Askra, who
farmed the land in Boiotia in central Greece in about 700 and left us two
poems about his world, the *Theogony* and *Works and Days*.[1] Hesiod
witnessed the rise of the earliest reported consumer-city in the West—Hesiod
himself is the reporter—and so he witnessed the relations between
town-dwellers and agrarian producers. In this paper I will apply
(incompletely) two different sets of models to Hesiod's world:
Consumer-city theory (as I am choosing to call it) on the one hand, which
focuses on the rise of the early city from the perspective of the town, and on

the other hand peasant theory, which is concerned with the same subject, but usually from the perspective of the fields. I will try to show that it is possible to identify a consumer-city in Hesiod's life, betrayed as it is by the centripetal force it generates, and also that Hesiod meets our expectation that his is a peasant's life, typical in its reluctant dependence on the city. I will then try to show that there is something wrong with this picture, and this may lead us to appreciate just how contingent economic (as well as social and political) development was in eighth-century central Boiotia and, presumably, in many other parts of the Aegean world, as what we call the West was just getting started.

City theory, and more specifically, consumer-city theory, has always ignored, discounted, or discarded the ancient Greco-Roman city from its field of vision. Gideon Sjoberg's *Preindustrial City* (Sjoberg 1960), one of the standard modern studies of the city in history, makes no use of antiquity; Lewis Mumford's classic study, *The City in History* (Mumford 1961), likewise shows little interest. There have been terrific recent advances in the study of urban Rome (see, e.g., the fine and diverse essays in Parkins 1997), and the Greek *polis* has received much fruitful and recent attention, especially from the institute in Copenhagen devoted to it and led by Mogens Hansen (see Hansen 1993; Hansen and Raaflaub 1995; 1996). And all students of Homer have benefitted from the work on the earliest *polis* by Stephen Scully (1990), Richard Seaford (1994), and others. But the economic history of the first Greek poleis is not a primary focus of any of these scholars; this specific material and economic history is only slowly being worked out by a relatively small number of classicists and ancient historians who are committed to an understanding that the literary and the material records are inseparable (among them Snodgrass 1980; 1994a; 1994b; Morris 1986; 1994a; 1994b; Rose 1992; Tandy 1997; Thalmann 1998; Donlan 1999; Pomeroy et al. 1999, chs. 2 and 3; Thomas and Conant 1999).

There are basically two reasons why, in the big-picture accounts, the premodern city, and especially its economic history, tends to begin with the Middle Ages. The first is quantitative: we don't have nearly the evidentiary materials to study that will be available later, beginning with Imperial Rome but not really rich until the Medieval period. The second is qualitative: the ancient city, especially on the Greek side and especially early on, had the disconcerting habit of not clearly distinguishing between town and fields. How can you have a consumer-city if you cannot separate it from the agricultural production sector? How profitable is it to pursue the theft of value from agricultural labor if you can't isolate the very productive sector? These difficulties notwithstanding, I think consumer-city theory can help us get a handle on central Boiotia specifically, and the incipient West generally. What follows is a quick overview of consumer-city theory. In each case, the theorist is identifying the division that is important between city consumers and country producers, a division that is important to both those who seek to explain the beginnings of cities and those who attempt to describe the continuing history of cities, as well as those who seek to explain the continuous struggle between capital and labor.

The focus in this brief paper on structures or ideal types grows from my agreement with Karl Polanyi, who insisted on focussing on institutions and on *how* goods move within the community at large, as opposed *why* individuals move goods.[2] We will be guided to some extent by Moses Finley, Polanyi's close young friend, back to Max Weber and farther back as well.

The Consumer-City

By consumer-city I mean an urban setting (i) which is inhabited by town-dwellers to whom come taxes and rents from beyond the "walls," and (ii) whose economy and power relations depend on the wealth generated by these rents and taxes. By this definition, there were consumer-cities in the second millennium in Mycenaean Greece. These Mycenaean cities are vanished from the landscape by about 1050 B.C.E. When cities reappear in the eighth century, the same arrangement appears to obtain. But it does not work out so cleanly as we would like, which is the main point of this paper. In fact, the not-so-cleanly part may prove to be a constructive way of talking about the beginning of the West.

The division between town and field is long-recognized.[3] First, Adam Smith in *Wealth of Nations*:

> The great commerce of every civilized society is that carried on between the inhabitants of the town and those of the country...The country supplies the town with the means of subsistence, and the materials of manufacture. The town repays this supply by sending back a part of the manufactures produce to the inhabitants of the country (Smith 1776, 3.1).

> Every town draws its whole subsistence, and all the materials of its industry from the country...The whole annual produce of the labour of the society is annually between these two different sets of people (Smith 1776, 1.10.c).[4]

Smith's influence on Marx was enormous, so it is no wonder that we find this same idea over and over in Marx's work, first, I believe, in the *German Ideology*, where we find Marx writing the following in 1845 or 1846:

> The division of labour inside a nation leads at first to the separation of industrial and commercial from agricultural labour, and hence to the separation of *town* (*Stadt*) and *country* (*Land*) and to the conflict of their interests (italics original).[5]

To this add Werner Sombart, from his *Vorkapitalistische Wirtschaft*:

> I call a consumer city the kind of city that pays for its livelihood (*Lebensunterhalt*)...not with its own products, as this is not at all necessary. It acquires, rather, its livelihood on the strength of some legal claim (taxes, rents, etc.) without having to give back value.[6]

Finally, Max Weber, who was not intimidated by antiquity:

> If we were to attempt a definition [of "city"] in purely economic terms, the city would be a settlement whose inhabitants live primarily from commerce and the trades rather than from agriculture... Economic diversity can be called forth in two ways: by the presence of a court, or by that of a market...A city is always a market center

(*Marktort*). It has a local market which forms the economic center (*ökonomische Mittelpunkt*) of the settlement and on which both the non-urban population and the townsmen satisfy their wants for crafts products or trade articles by means of exchange on the basis of an existing specialization in production. It was originally quite normal for a city, wherever it structurally differentiated from the countryside, to be both a seignorial or princely residence and a market place and thus to possess economic centers of both types, *oikos* and market (Weber 1921, 121).

I am sure there are other, more recent, observations that would supplement these venerable expositions of the phenomenon we are looking at; we will return to the consumer-city. For now I ask the reader to notice the regularly observed advantage that comes to the town, which I suggest we all choose to succinctly term *material centripetalism*. It is clear to me that the town that enjoys this advantage will have an easier time in its economic (and political and social) development than the town that does not. Put obversely, the town that does not capture this advantage will develop economically (and politically and socially) with greater difficulty than the town that does.

Peasants

Let us turn also briefly to the question of whether Hesiod is appropriately identified as a peasant and then, further, whether this would help us in any way understand what is happening in Boiotia.[7] Fifteen years ago Paul Millett's crystal-clear paper on Hesiod demonstrated that the Boiotian is certainly a peasant (Millett 1984), as opposed to an impoverished *aristos* ([pl. *aristoi*], the term the elite class gave to themselves) (Bravo 1977), a spin doctor for the *aristoi* (Mele 1977), a semi-*aristos*,[8] or an imposter *aristos*.[9]

Many of these following definitions are in Millett's article, and I repeat them here and add some as well.

Robert Redfield: The peasant is a rural native whose long established order of life take important account of the city (Redfield 1953, 31).[10]

Teodor Shanin: The peasantry consist of small producers on land who, with the help of simple equipment and the labour of their families, produce mainly for their own consumption, and for the fulfilment of their duties to the holders of political and economic power (Shanin 1966, 6).

Eric Wolf: It is only when a cultivator is integrated into a society with a state—that is, when the cultivator becomes subject to the demands and sanctions of power-holders outside his social culture—that we can appropriately speak of peasantry (Wolf 1967, 11).

Frank Ellis: [Peasants are] often thrust out of where they were by powerful world forces outside their previous experience (e.g., colonialism) and they are undergoing a continuous process of adaptation to the changing world around them (Ellis 1988, 5).

To these may be added the rich contributions of Rhoda Halperin, who importantly emphasizes that a peasant society will take on different characteristics and behaviors depending on the nature of the state with which it is in contact and on the nature of that contact (Halperin 1977, esp. 11-13). I refer the reader also to the excellent survey of the literature that is the first chapter of *Communities of Grain* by Victor Magagna, who argues for the advantage of speaking of peasants in terms of their awareness of community rather than in terms of their awareness of class (Magagna 1993).

What all these observers agree on is that the peasant has a *necessary* relationship with a political center ("city"), does not like it, and cannot avoid it. The peasant is *dependent*. There are two points I want to highlight here. First, that each of these definitions and statements echoes the division of town and fields that we saw in the consumer-city analyses and definitions earlier, and each also emphasizes the autarky to which both Hesiod and the ancient *polis* were committed. Second, and growing especially from the latter part of the first, that they all line up very well with Hesiod's description of the world around him, to which we will finally get very soon.

Some further qualifications before moving on. It is important to observe that defining Hesiod and his cohort as "peasants" is in fact an abstraction, and perhaps a distraction as well, for what we are trying to identify is the dependent position of Hesiod *vis-à-vis* the town. Put simply: whether peasant or not, Hesiod is dependent and unhappy about it.

Hesiod And His World (And, Again, Is He A Peasant?)

I urge the reader who wishes greater detail to go to the literature that is out there on Hesiod and his agricultural and social production (Millett 1984; Tandy and Neale 1996, 1-48; Tandy 1997, ch. 8; more citations in Nelson 1998, 175, n.10). Hesiod is an agrarian producer in Boiotia, who, lining up with Redfield's definition of peasant (Redfield 1956, 112), has a nearly sentimental attachment to the land (see further on this Nelson 1998). He grows grains and is the leader of an *oikos* of about ten to twelve persons (Tandy 1997, 211 and n. 93; Tandy and Neale 1996, 27-31). He has become engaged in an argument with his brother Perses over their inheritance, and it is clear that there are men from the city that dominates the region who are making decisions that are in some way potentially binding and that are going against Hesiod and his personal best interest. It is also the case that we can see that Hesiod's brother has lost his own *oikos*, through the accumulation of debts against his property, debts that have probably been incurred through his dealings with the town (Tandy 1997, 132-35). We can see, then, that Perses' loss of his *oikos* appears attributable to the simple advantage that the town has over the fields by providing juridical opportunities and by generating (perhaps subsequent to the courts) extra rents and debt services that ultimately lead to transfers of possessions, including real property, from those in the field to those in the town. All of this scenario lines up well with all the observations of the consumer-city theorizers.

To move back to the peasant question: Hesiod regularly grows crops and minds livestock with an eye toward the autarky of his *oikos*, and with apparently no regard at all for "market demand"; this is a typically peasant outlook. It is also typical, however, that while peasants produce according to traditional patterns, they nevertheless bring their production to the market center that is the very focus and even the very cause of their dissatisfaction, and this is where things begin to get interesting in Boiotia, for Hesiod does not bring his excess production to town. We will see that he takes it elsewhere.

Karl Polanyi's most important contribution to the study of antiquity was not the set of studies of various problems that he undertook over the years but the tools he left for us (Tandy and Neale 1994). Not only in his *Great Transformation* (Polanyi 1944) but also in his magisterial *Trade and Market* (Polanyi, Arensberg, and Pearson 1957), Polanyi, and in the latter volume also his students and colleagues in the Interdisciplinary Project at Columbia University, argued that there are any number of mechanisms or institutions that can be perceived in preindustrial societies that serve to integrate economic activities into the fabrics of societies. Many of the papers in this volume are seeking applications of these forms of integration onto archaeological and literary materials. One such form, redistribution, is a centralizing economic formation that accounts for much of the movement of goods in slightly stratified, or rank, societies. Goods move in and out from the periphery to the center and back out again. These movements take place along fairly clearly articulated spokes. We can see how a natural advantage for the center might develop. Redistribution routinely has a particular character and there are expectations about it, expectations that are shared by center and periphery; there are rules that people can count on. When a redistributive arrangement collapses, which is what I think is happening in Hesiod's world, all the rules change. Elsewhere Polanyi and I have articulated just what a redistributive formation entails[11]; I have at length articulated what happens when a redistributive formation collapses, as in the case of Hesiod's world (Tandy 1997, ch. 5).

Peasants ordinarily participate, albeit reluctantly, in a redistributive formation. All participants are not necessarily thrilled with the formation, and often it may be said that the center (the town) *dominates* the periphery (the fields). Theoretically, redistribution works best (for the center, for everyone) when it is generally agreed that the center is *good,* for the myth of redistribution, that the center is good, is what allows and abets the maintenance of economic (and political and cultural) *hegemony* over participants in the formation. When the movement of goods and services is two-way and generally speaking mutually beneficial to both center and periphery, then the structure provides not only political and cultural hegemony to the center, but also the center—the city—accrues the incremental material advantage noted by Smith and all the others: this incremental material advantage is a result of the economic formation that Polanyi called redistribution.

When this centripetal movement is interrupted, when it is less easy to accomplish, when it is encumbered by indefensible taxes and other costs such as unreasonable rents and debts (and the service of debts), then the economic formation collapses and—poof!—the centripetal advantage is gone as well. The importance of the centripetal advantage is perhaps routinely underestimated or misperceived (like the surplus that does not exist until it is named[12]) until it is gone. Here is where the state becomes the State.

Bringing in the Focus: The Questions *Noch Einmal*

Are we able to say that we are not defining Hesiod's world for him by imposing theory on his text? I am especially concerned with the entire notion of the consumer-city as what we have at Thespiai. Let us ratchet up our inquiry by trying to see what it is we are trying to find, and in what kind of evidence. First, is there a consumer-city in Hesiod's world both in the broader picture (as we have seen) and in the details (not checked yet)? Second, what, exactly, would the answer "Yes" mean?

I answer the first question with Yes. I see a consumer-city in *Works and Days.* I see a centripetal power drawing into the *polis* the goods, services, and controls over the means of production that were formerly (at least partially) controlled by the periphery. There is a net ingo from outside of precisely the sort that Adam Smith observed about incremental advantage to the town:

Whatever regulations, therefore, tend to increase those wages and profits beyond what they otherwise would be, tend to enable the town to purchase, with a smaller quantity of its labour, the produce of a greater quantity of labour of the country...By means of those regulations a greater share of [the annual produce] is given to the inhabitants of the town than would otherwise fall to them; and a less to those of the country (Smith 1776, 1.10.c.19).

In Hesiod's world this ingo is comprised at least partly of *chrea* (debts). These *chrea*—together with hunger the great fear of the periphery—are the (apparently) solitary means by which land holdings are alienated, as happened to Perses, Hesiod's brother.[13]

Hesiod addresses *Works and Days* to his brother Perses, who appears to have lost his *oikos*. There are inconsistencies in the depiction of Perses' situation, but we are able to be sure of this much: Perses has lost his land because he accumulated too many debts. Perses appears to have encumbered his own holding (*kleros*) with *chrea* until he lost it.[14]

If we turn to Weber, we can see how well Hesiod lines up with him. Weber asserted that the consumer-city has an advantage because of the presence either of a princely court (or princely *oikos*) or of a market, whereby the advantage is achieved. According to Weber, there ought to be a princely class. In both of Hesiod's poems we can see located in the *agora* Weber's princely class:

All the people watch [the *basileus*] as he decides law cases with straight judgments; and he, speaking surely, would put a stop to even a great wrangling. For therefore there are *basilees* with wise hearts, for when the people are being misled in the *agora*, they easily settle cases that might bring harm, moving them with soothing words. When he goes through the assembly, they greet him as a god, and he is conspicuous among those gathered (*Theogony* 84-92).

Do not let the evil-rejoicing Strife hold your spirit back from work while you closely watch wranglings and play the listener in the *agora*.

There is little interest in wranglings and *agora*-activities for the man whose seasonal sustenance does not lie stored up in abundance indoors, what the earth bears, Demeter's grain. When you have collected your fill of sustenance, then you might support wranglings and contention over the possessions of others. You will never have a second chance to do these things: right here let us settle our wrangling with straight judgments, which are from Zeus and best. For we had already distributed the holding, but you snatched and carried off many other things, energetically feeding the pride of gift-eating *basilees*, who are willing to propose a judgment in this case (*Works and Days* 28ff.).

I don't think that it is very hard to see Weber's city in these descriptions, for the princely *basilees* are striding through the *agora*, where the market of the town must also be located (every Greek city had an *agora* and the market was always located in it). There are two reasons that Hesiod is not happy that he depends on the *agora*. One is the legal rulings that work against him and his fellow peasants; the other is (presumably) a market for his production that is there, a market for which he has no fondness. There is no question that the *agora* is the *locus* where the advantage (both in theory and in Hesiod's text) is being exercised, is being worked out.

What the princely class seems to be generating especially is judgments. It is unclear to what extent Hesiod and his fellow fringers are required to deal with these judgment-giving arrangements in the town. The judgment centers clearly exist, more clearly in fact than any markets. The *basilees* about whom Hesiod is complaining in fact may be entrepreneurial dispute-settlers who are coming out of Thespiai trying to set up practices in the fields, in Askra and elsewhere. It appears that the leaders in the town are trying to gain influence in the hinterland by offering their judicial services to those who would voluntarily approach them. In Hesiod's brother's case, it appears that Perses became involved and also harmed. On one hand, this can be analyzed as evidence of *domination*. On another, it can be perceived as a mechanism by which the incremental material centripetality is being enhanced. This entrepreneurial spirit may find its explanation in the answer to our second question.

Question #2: What does it mean to identify a consumer-city in Hesiod's world? It means that we able to adopt certain further expectations, and here now we are arrived at what is wrong with this picture: Here is Hesiod's advice on what to do with one's surplus production (or extra anything):

> You yourself wait for sailing time, until it comes; then drag your swift ship to the sea and furnish on board a fitting cargo in order to make a gain and bring it to the *oikos*…Praise a little ship but put your cargo in a big one; the greater the cargo, the greater will be the gain on top of gain, if the winds hold back the evil blasts (*Works and Days* 630-32; 643-45)

We can see that Hesiod explicitly advises that his listener take his goods to sea and *not to town*. We will address the possible destination(s) soon, but for now let us observe that the surplus is *not* going to the market that we lead ourselves reasonably to expect this consumer-city to be providing.

In fact, Hesiod's production is undertaken without regard for the centripetal force that is bringing in rents and other payments from the edges. This fact is a source of the friction. That is, Hesiod and his fellow peasant are not producing specific goods in response to any single or specific market (what many might suspect, especially those who do not believe Hesiod to be a peasant); rather, they are producing what tradition has encouraged them to produce and then they are bringing it to the market that offers a good if not the best return, apparently never to the market at Thespiai and perhaps to a market controlled by a different *polis*.

Put another way, and in more Polanyian terms, the town—"we have/want a surplus"—comes into hard conflict with the embedded economy on the periphery, which itself remains unhegemonized on account, partly, of its very embeddedness. The resulting uncertainty is a great threat to economic success in the town.

Where Is Hesiod Sending His Surplus?

As Polanyi and his colleagues showed long ago,[15] it is clear that the ports of trade of the ancient Mediterranean almost always functioned to allow interaction between outside groups and the home territories. In this way the home territory insulated itself from outside influences. Thomas Tartaron and Astrid Möller, in their papers in this collection, show how the port of trade worked. This often took the form also of a gateway community, as David Rupp argues in this volume for Iron Age Cyprus.

We can imagine cases where one-time markets might arise without state involvement, but these would be very small-scale and probably equally short-lived, for Smith, Marx, and Weber are right about the built-in advantage of controlling the market: the material that accrues incrementally to the market will lead to the town and then the state (if different) moving into and taking over regular independent ports of trade, in order to extract value from the exchanges there.

Thus we can surmise for many developing states in the Aegean this additional source of capital—not only the regular market at home but also the border market or port of trade. Thespiai, as well as any other non-hegemonic *polis*, gets its come-uppance by failing to provide an attractive market for its agrarian producers. Thus Thespiai not only loses (some portion of) its incremental advantage from (some portion of) its hinterland; this loss is in fact the gain of a port of trade elsewhere, *theoretically under the control of another state.*

From what we know about ancient ports of trade and long-distance trading arrangements and tendencies,[16] I am confident that Hesiod took his goods to a market that either had fixed prices or provided such high returns that the only risk Hesiod faced was in transportation. These would be ports of trade or places, easily identified[17] on a seasonal basis, which were suffering from the regional famines that regularly afflicted micro-environments in Greece due mostly to variability in interannual rainfall.[18] Hesiod's actions would be a predictable response not so much to famine away from Boiotia as to a good year's production at home. When famine came to Askra, as it must have occasionally, outsiders brought their goods into Hesiod's area. Thus we could observe how wise Hesiod was, that he took advantage of these opportunities; I would add, however, that this behavior also indicates on a more macro-scale that there is a powerful tension between town and fields in Hesiod's world, for although there is a market in the town, Hesiod takes his extra goods elsewhere. When Hesiod has a surplus, he takes it to sea—this is remarkable.

In good years, Thespiai would not have immediate need for Hesiod's extra grains, for it would have all it needed, presumably. In bad years, Hesiod would have nothing to offer. In critical junctures of development and with a self-awareness of its surplus and the importance of it for a successful future, however, Thespiai needs to *store* and it needs to make regular, incremental centripetal gains from market activity. Not all centripetal gains come through the market, of course, but the inability to accomplish those market gains presents a formidable obstacle to the city-state's economic and political development.

It is very clear that Hesiod is living near an arrangement that is not easily going to develop into the classical *polis*, the *Stadtstaat* that enjoyed its myth of *isotes* ("equality") and its own rules of exclusion. Hesiod's pattern of production and bringing-to-market clearly indicates the precariousness of Thespiai's ability to achieve autarky, the goal as much of the *polis* as of the peasant. The reason it is important to observe that Hesiod fits the paradigm of peasant is that it makes it easier to see that the fields are dominated, not hegemonized, by the town (Thespiai). This failure to hegemonize the hinterland is, at the end of the day, my point. Without hegemony development is certainly imperiled, and perhaps nearly impossible. For what Hesiod and his fellow producers fail to provide, Thespiai must turn to outside producers to generate a substitution for the market increment that under "normal" circumstances Thespiai could have "counted on" from its own hinterland, which included Hesiod's community of Askra. Here lies the nub of the precariousness of one *polis*'s development.

Unlike Marx, Hesiod had no consumer-city theory to guide his decisions. Hesiod had no Adam Smith on his bookshelf to point out the incremental advantage that accrued to the town over time. But Hesiod didn't need Adam Smith: he saw hunger and he saw losses to the town. He concluded, certainly, that the losses were occurring through the semi-institutionalized medium of the *agora* and, perhaps further, that his bringing goods to market there would accelerate or exaggerate the advantage that the town enjoyed. From the standpoint of economic history, where Hesiod did *not* bring his goods is a much richer story than where he *did*, even if we could determine that.

The lesson here is perhaps as simple as this: in pre-industrial societies, state hegemony is nearly necessary for successful development. This observation makes even more remarkable the eventual success of many city-states in the beginning if the West. It would be an interesting inquiry—and different from this one—to determine which poleis of the Archaic Period embraced the largest portion of their peripheral populations into their political mainstreams and see to what extent we can correlate these poleis with those poleis that enjoyed economic success.[19]

NOTES

Portions of this piece appeared in different papers delivered at the annual meeting of the American Philological Association in San Diego, December 1995, and at the Sixth International Polanyi Conference, November 1996, in Montreal. My thanks for discussions there, especially to Francis Dunn and Anthony Edwards. *Agroskopia* would have been Hesiod's word, had he used it, for "view from the field."

1. For an overview of Hesiod and his world, see Tandy and Neale 1996, 1-48. The poems are not terribly long, each about the length of a book of the *Iliad. Works and Days* is conveniently translated in Tandy and Neale 1996 and Nelson 1998; both poems are contained in West 1988.

2. See Tandy and Neale 1994.

3. Many classicists will recognize that much (not all) of what follows is distilled from Moses Finley's occasional work on the ancient city as ideal type (e.g., Finley 1976/77; 1985, 88-103). Smith and Sombart I owe to Finley 1976/77; so, also, his wake-up call to Weber. I urge readers to pursue Finley's work there. I use it here as a starting point, and I supplement it in order to set a specific foundation on which to build an argument that is quite apart from anything Finley was even interested

in: forms of resistance and the roles they had to play in the economic development of the earliest Greek city-states.

4. Cf. 2.1.28: "This is the real exchange that is annually made between these two orders of people." Cf. also generally 1.1: "The annual labour of every nation is the fund which originally supplies it with all the necessities and conveniences of life which it annually consumes, and which consists always, either in the immediate produce of that labour, or in what is purchased with the produce from other nations."

5. 1845/46, 38: "Die Teilung der Arbeit innerhalb einer Nation führt zunächst die Trennung der industriellen und kommerziellen von der ackerbauenden Arbeit und damit die Trennung von *Stadt* und *Land* und den Gegensatz der Interessen Beider herbei (*Werke*, Band 3, S. 22).

6. Eine Konsumtionsstadt nenne ich diejenige Stadt, die ihren Lebensunterhalt . . . nicht mit eigenen Produkten bezahlt, weil sie es nicht nötig hat. Sie bezieht vielmehr diesen Lebensunterhalt auf Grund irgendeines Rechtstitels (Steuern, Rente oder dergleichen) ohne Gegenwerte leisten zu müssen (Sombart 1916, 1.142).

7. I have discussed this subject in Tandy 1997, ch. 8, and hope to develop further the idea of Hesiod *qua* peasant in the future. Anthony Edwards disagrees with me.

8. Whatever Chester Starr may have meant by this: Starr 1977, 125-27; 1982, 432-33, 434; 1986, 93-94.

9. Wilamowitz 1928, 76. I am not sure what to do with R.M. Cook's admitted speculation that "Hesiod's father married an heiress, the only child of a fairly prosperous farmer (Cook 1989, 170). This is not a good place to address whether Hesiod is more persona than person (Nagy 1979, 296-97, 303-308; 1982, 49-52; Martin 1992; Rosen 1990), on which see Tandy and Neale 1996, 7-8; Tandy 1997, 205-208. On one hand, whether Hesiod is persona or person may have no bearing on the testimony he provides about his relationship to the town; on another, Hesiod as persona may be more reliable than an actual Hesiod because ideological trappings are thus nearly impossible to hide and the testimony thus bears the imprimatur of a larger group or class.

10. See further 31-40. Redfield elsewhere emphasized other attributes that are readily recognized in peasant societies, but are not relevant to this study: "I seemed to find a cluster of three closely related attitudes or values: an intimate and reverent attitude toward the land; the idea that agricultural work is good and commerce not so good; and an emphasis on productive industry as a prime virtue" (1956, 112).

11. On the nature of redistribution as a form of integration see Polanyi 1944, 48-53; 1957, 253-54; Tandy 1997, 101-106.

12. Here I refer to the fundamental demonstration of the embeddedness of the economy. A fully embedded economy has no surplus; see Pearson 1957.

13. The mechanisms for alienations, and the forms alienations could take, are discussed more fully in Tandy and Neale 1996, 39-42, and Tandy 1997, ch. 5.

14. "I command you to consider discharge of *chrea* and avoidance of hunger. First of all [get yourself] an *oikos* and a woman and a plower ox...Whenever you turn your witless spirit to trade and wish to evade *chrea* and delightless hunger, I will point out to you the rules of the much-roaring sea..."(404-405, 646ff.)

15. On ports of trade generally, see Polanyi 1963; also Arnold 1957; Revere 1957. On Babylonian and Dahomeyan ports of trade see Belshaw 1965, 85-94; on medieval Norway, see Hodges 1978.

16. We have already seen Polanyi's hand in the development of our understanding of the port of trade (see n. 15). For Polanyi and long-distance trade, see especially Dalton 1975, and further Polanyi 1975 (= 1977, 81-96); Zaccagnini 1987; Tandy 1997, chs. 3 and 5.

17. Actually, of course, Hesiod could care less. From what he tells us, he simply takes his surplus to the sea. Where it goes from there is not his concern. His concerns are different: don't bring too much to port, be sure to put your cargo on a big ship, not a small one. We cannot tell even what Hesiod received for his delivery, but we can be fairly certain that he didn't care where his stuff was bound:

"At that time (early August) the breezes are well-defined and the open sea is without disaster. Then without anxiety entrust your swift ship to the winds, drag it into the open sea and put all your cargo in it. Then hurry as quickly as you can to get back to your *oikos.*" (*Works and Days* 670ff.)

See further Tandy and Neale 1996; Tandy 1997, chs. 5 and 8.

18. See Garnsey 1988, 8-16; Garnsey and Morris 1989; Halstead 1989, esp. 72-75; Halstead and O'Shea 1989b, esp. 3-6. On the variability of interannual rainfall see Sallares 1991, 390-95.

19. We might further divide economically successful poleis into two meaningful groups: those that were *closed* and successful and those that were expansionist. The states that were expansionist may not have been wealthy through hegemony but rather forced (like Thespiai?) to find the lost portion of increment elsewhere. Thus, the expansionist states, the argument may prove to be, were less hegemonic in their territories and so had to develop outside capital flows. This is for later study.

BIBLIOGRAPHY

Arnold, Rosemary. 1957. A port of trade: Whydah on the Guinea coast. In Polanyi, Arensberg, and Pearson 1957, 154-76.

Belshaw, Cyril S. 1965. *Traditional exchange and modern markets.* Englewood Cliffs, N.J.: Prentice-Hall.

Bravo, Benedetto. 1977. Remarques sur les assises sociales, les formes d'organisation et la terminologie du commerce maritime grec à l'époque archaique. *Dialogues d'Histoire Ancienne* 3:1-59.

Cook, R.M. 1989. Hesiod's father. *Journal of Hellenic Studies* 109:170-71.

Dalton, George. 1975. Karl Polanyi's analysis of long-distance trade and his wider paradigm. In Sabloff and Lamberg-Karlovsky 1975, 63-132.

Donlan, Walter. 1999. *The* Aristocratic Ideal *and selected papers.* Wauconda, Ill.: Bolchazy-Carducci.

Duncan, Colin A.M., and David W. Tandy, eds. 1994. *From political economy to anthropology: Situating economic life in past societies.* Montreal: Black Rose Books.

Ellis, Frank. 1988. *Peasant economies: Farm households and agrarian development.* Cambridge: Cambridge University Press.

Finley, Moses I. 1976/77. The ancient city: From Fustel de Coulanges to Max Weber and beyond. *Comparative Studies in Society and History* 19:305-27.

———. 1985. *Ancient history: Evidence and models.* London: and Windus.

Garnsey, Peter. 1988. *Famine and food supply in the Greco-Roman world: Responses to risk and crisis.* Cambridge: Cambridge University Press.

Garnsey, Peter, and Ian Morris. 1989. Risk and the *polis*: The evolution of institutionalised responses to food supply problems in the ancient Greek state. In Halstead and O'Shea 1989a, 98-105.

Halperin, Rhoda H. 1977. Introduction: The substantive economy in peasant societies. In *Peasant livelihood: Studies in economic anthropology and cultural ecology,* edited by Rhoda Halperin and James Dow, 1-16. New York: St. Martin's.

Halstead, Paul, and John O'Shea, eds. 1989a. *Bad year economics: Cultural responses to risk and uncertainty.* Cambridge: Cambridge University Press.

Halstead, Paul, and John O'Shea. 1989b. Introduction: Cultural responses to risk and uncertainty. In Halstead and O'Shea 1989a, 1-7.

Hansen, Mogens Herman, ed. 1993. *The ancient Greek city-state.* Acts of the Copenhagen *Polis* Centre 1. Copenhagen: Munksgaard.

Hansen, Mogens Herman, and Kurt Raaflaub, eds. 1995. *Studies in the ancient Greek polis.* Historia Einzelschriften 95. Stuttgart: Franz Steiner Verlag.

———. 1996. *More studies in the ancient Greek Polis.* Papers from the Copenhagen *Polis* Centre 3. Historia Einzelschriften 108. Stuttgart: Franz Steiner Verlag.

Hodges, Robert. 1978. Ports of trade in early medieval Europe. *Norwegian Archaeological Review* 11:97-101, 114-17.

Magagna, Victor V. 1991. *Communities of grain: Rural rebellion in comparative perspective.* Ithaca, N.Y.: Cornell University Press.

Martin, Richard P. 1992. Hesiod's metanastic poetics. *Ramus* 2.1:11-33.

Marx, Karl. 1945/46. *The German ideology.* Moscow: Progress Publishers, 1976.

Marx, Karl, and Friedrich Engels. 1973. *Werke.* Band 3. Berlin: Dietz Verlag.

Mele, Alfonso. 1977. *Il commercio greco arcaico: Prexis ed emporie.* Cahiers du Centre Jean Bérard, no. 4. Naples: Institut Français de Naples.

Millett, Paul. 1984. Hesiod and his world. *Proceedings of the Cambridge Philological Society* 210:84-115.

Morris, Ian. 1986. Gift and commodity in archaic Greece. *Man* 21:1-17.

———. 1994a. The Athenian economy twenty years after *The Ancient Economy.* *Classical Philology* 89:351-66.

———. 1994b. The community against the market in classical Athens. In Duncan and Tandy 1994, 52-79.

Mumford, Lewis. 1961. *The city in history: Its origins, its transformations, and its prospects.* New York: Harcourt, Brace, and World.

Nagy, Gregory. 1979. *The best of the Achaeans: Concepts of the hero in archaic Greek poetry.* Baltimore: Johns Hopkins University Press.

———. 1982. . In *Ancient writers: Greece and Rome,* edited by T. James Luce, 1:43-73. New York: Charles Scribner's Sons

Nelson, Stephanie A. 1998. *God and the land: The metaphysics of farming in Hesoid and Vergil*. New York: Oxford University Press.

Parkins, Helen, ed. 1997. *Roman urbanism: Beyond the consumer city*. London: Routledge.

Pearson, Harry W. 1957. The economy has no surplus: Critique of a theory of development. In Polanyi, Arensberg, and Pearson 1957, 320-41.

Polanyi, Karl. 1944. *The great transformation: The political and economic origins of our time*. New York: Holt Rinehart.

———. 1957. The economy as instituted process. In Polanyi, Arensberg, and Pearson 1957, 243-70.

———. 1963, Ports of trade in early societies. *Journal of Economic History*. 23:30-45.

———. 1975. Traders and trade. In Sabloff and Lamberg-Karlovsky 1975, 133-54.

———. 1977. *The livelihood of man*. Edited by Harry W. Pearson. New York: Academic Press.

Polanyi, Karl, Conrad M. Arensberg, and Harry W. Pearson, eds. 1957. *Trade and market in the early empires*. Glencoe, Ill: Free Press.

Pomeroy, Sarah, Stanley M. Burstein, Walter Donlan, and Jennifer Tolbert Roberts. 1999. *Ancient Greece: A political, social, and cultural history*. Oxford: Oxford University Press.

Redfield, Robert. 1953. *The primitive world and its transformation*. Ithaca, N.Y.: Cornell University Press.

———. 1956. *Peasant society and culture*. Chicago: University of Chicago Press.

Revere, Robert B. 1957. "No man's coast": Ports of trade in the eastern Mediterranean. In Polanyi, Arensberg, and Pearson 1957, 38-63.

Rose, Peter W. 1992. *Sons of the gods, children of earth: Ideology and literary form in ancient Greece*. Ithaca: Cornell University Press.

Rosen, Ralph M. 1990. Poetry and sailing in Hesiod's *Works and Days*. *Classical Antiquity* 9:99-113.

Sallares, Robert. 1991. *The ecology of the ancient Greek world*. Ithaca: Cornell University Press.

Scully, Stephen. 1990. *Homer and the sacred city*. Ithaca: Cornell University Press.

Seaford, Richard. 1994. *Reciprocity and ritual: Homer and tragedy in the developing city-state*. Oxford: Clarendon Press.

Shanin, Teodor. 1966. The peasantry as political factor. *Sociological Review* 14:5-27.

Sjoberg, Gideon. 1960. *The preindustrial city, past and present*. Glencoe, Ill.: Free Press.

Snodgrass, Anthony. 1980. *Archaic Greece: The age of experiment*. Berkeley: University of California Press.

———. 1994a. The Euboeans in Macedonia: A new precedent for western expansion. *Annali dell'Istituto Universitario Prientale di Napoli (archeol.)* 16:88-93.

————. 1994b. The growth and standing of the early western colonies. In *The archaeology of Greek colonization: Essays dedicated to Sir John Boardman*, edited by Gocha R. Tsetskhladze and Franco De Angelis, 1-10. Oxford University Committee for Archaeology Monograph 40. Oxford: Oxford University Press.

Sombart, Werner. 1916. *Der moderne Kapitalismus. Vol. 1. Die vorkapitalistische Wirtschaft*. 2d ed. Munich and Leipzig: von Duncker und Holmbolt.

Starr, Chester G. 1977. *The economic and social growth of early Greece: 800-500 b.c.* New York: Oxford University Press.

————. 1982. Economic and social conditions in the Greek world. In *The Cambridge ancient history*, vol. 3, pt. 3, 417-41. 2d ed. Cambridge: Cambridge University Press.

————. 1986. *Individual and community: The rise of the polis, 800-500 b.c.* New York: Oxford University Press.

Tandy, David W. 1997. *Warriors into traders: The power of the market in early Greece*. Berkeley: University of California Press.

Tandy, David W., and Walter C. Neale. 1994. Karl Polanyi's distinctive approach to social analysis and the case of ancient Greece: Ideas, criticisms, consequences. In Duncan and Tandy 1994, 9-33.

————. 1996. *Hesiod's Works and Days: Introduction and commentary for the social sciences*. Berkeley: University of California Press.

Thalmann, William G. 1998. *The swineherd and the bow: Representations of class in the* Odyssey. Ithaca: Cornell University Press.

Thomas, Carol G., and Craig Conant. 1999. *Citadel to city-state: The transformation of Greece, 1200-700 BC*. Bloomington: Indiana University Press.

Weber, Max. 1921. *Economy and society*. 5th ed. Berkeley: University of California Press, 1978.

West, M.L., tr. 1988. *Hesiod,* Theogony *and* Works and Days. Oxford: Oxford University Press.

Wilamowitz-Moellendorff, Ulrich von, ed. 1928. *Hesiodos Erga*. Berlin: Weidmann.

Wolf, Eric. R. 1967. *Peasants*. Englewood Cliffs, N.J.: Prentice-Hall.

Zaccagnini, Carlo. 1987. Aspects of ceremonial exchange in the Near East during the late second millennium B.C. In *Centre and periphery in the ancient world*, edited by Michael J. Rowlands, Mogens Larsen, and Kristian Kristiansen, 57-65. Cambridge: Cambridge University Press.

Chapter Seven

TRADE, TRADERS, AND THE ECONOMY OF ATHENS IN THE FOURTH CENTURY B.C.E.

Darel Tai Engen

The nature of the ancient Greek economy has been at the center of one of the great debates of historical scholarship. Despite more than a century's worth of contributions from a variety of eminent scholars, however, the debate remains unresolved. Among the contributors to the debate was Karl Polanyi.[1] Although he too failed to resolve the debate, his work did provide a new approach, some elements of which may yet aid in the resolution of the problem if applied properly. I will attempt to apply Polanyi's approach to a reexamination of the nature of the ancient Athenian economy.

Throughout its long history the debate about the ancient Greek economy has been plagued by oversimplification. Those involved in the debate have taken a synthetic approach and sought to characterize the economy as a whole in general and static terms, often on the basis of assumptions about its various constituent parts that are sorely in need of reexamination. This paper will offer a fresh look at those responsible for overseas trade in fourth-century B.C.E. Athens. It will be evident that Athenian overseas trade in the late classical period was too complex to fit neatly into broad characterizations of the economy as a whole and that we need to take an analytic, rather than a synthetic, approach towards understanding the ancient Greek economy.

As is well known, the debate about the ancient Greek economy was initiated by Bücher and Meyer, whose opposing views gained followings that characterized the economy as either "primitive" or "modern."[2] The "primitivists" characterized ancient Greece as having a "household economy," in which production within the household and exchange of goods between households existed on only a small scale and primarily for the purpose of household consumption. In short, the economy was driven and organized in accordance with a consumptive mentality.

Even when in time it became possible for some households to produce greater amounts of goods, deeply-rooted social values prohibited the rise of "capitalistic" behavior in which individuals engage in production and exchange not for the purpose of consumption, but in order to make a "profit." According to the primitivist view, then, ancient Greek households sought to grow only enough grain to feed themselves, i.e., to be self-sufficient. They did not seek to go beyond their own immediate needs and to produce surpluses for the purpose of selling it to others for a profit.

Consequently, there were no regular markets in which goods were bought and sold as commodities and long-distance trade was limited to luxury goods. What markets did exist, were merely gathering places in which small farmers would dispose of their unplanned surpluses of goods and foreign traders would sell exotic imports from abroad.

The so-called "modernists," on the other hand, believed that the ancient Greek economy was similar to modern western ones. Production and exchange occurred on a large scale; there was a significant volume of long-distance trade; and it was common for individuals to engage in production and exchange of goods for the purpose of making a profit, without any intention of consuming the goods themselves. In short, there was a productive mentality among ancient Greeks that inspired them to produce and exchange for profit and this, in turn, allowed the economy to develop and grow into an early version of our own modern western economy.

However, the primitivist and modernist models suffer, in my opinion, from three major flaws. First, they erroneously presuppose that economies must follow some sort of linear evolutionary path from primitive to modern (with the model of modernity being, of course, our own market economy). Second, even in spite of the first flaw, the primitivist and modernist models are completely static. They fail to account for any change in the nature of the ancient Greek economy over a period from the seventh through the fourth centuries and seem to hold that throughout these three hundred years, the economy could be characterized simply as either primitive or modern. Third, they characterize the ancient Greek economy as a whole in rather all-encompassing terms that do not account for evidence concerning the various individual sectors that together comprise the economy.

Unfortunately, having begun in such a fashion, the debate about the ancient Greek economy was held in a virtual straight-jacket, as subsequent scholars tended to fall into either the primitivist or modernist camps. A case in point concerns the work of the famous sociologist Max Weber, who tried to understand the ancient Greek economy not in terms of its primitivism or modernism, but rather in terms of its place within Greek society. Weber argued that citizens in ancient Greek city-states were *homines politici*, not *homines oeconomici* (Weber 1921, 1339-72, esp. 1354). They were citizens by virtue of their birth from citizen parents and adult males were expected to exercise their citizenship by taking an active part in the public life of the community. In his Funeral Oration, Pericles said, "we do not say that a man who takes no interest in politics is a man who minds his own business; we say that he has no business here at all" (Thucydides 2.40, tr. Warner).

In order to live up to this citizen ideal, a man had to be a farmer, preferably one who owned a few slaves, so that he could be present in the city and have the leisure time to participate actively in politics. Therefore, only the poorer citizens who could not afford to live such a life and resident non-citizens who were not allowed to own land and participate in politics engaged in such economic activities as manufacturing of crafts, money changing, and overseas trade. These activities did not allow a person adequate leisure and, in the case of overseas trade, required a person to be away from the city for long periods of time.

Weber largely succeeded in illustrating the place of various economic activities in Greek society. But instead of using Weber's work to shift the focus of the debate away from the primitivist-modernist alternatives, historians merely tried to adapt his work to either of the two broad alternatives. Hasebroek basically used Weber's approach to argue that trade and, thus, the economy as a whole in ancient Greece was primitive (Hasebroek 1933, esp. 30-43). The political movers of Greek city-states were landowners who aimed at self-sufficiency and were not at all interested in the concerns of professional traders who were largely poor citizens or non-citizens. Such an attitude among those in power in Greek cities prohibited the ancient Greek economy from becoming "modern" until well into the Hellenistic period.

Despite this stranglehold that the primitivist and modernist models held on the debate for over half a century, their inadequacy prompted others to seek more sophisticated conceptual tools. In the mid-twentieth century Polanyi tried to shift the focus of the debate by offering the terms "embedded" or "disembedded" as a means of characterizing economies (see in particular Polanyi 1957b). For Polanyi, an economy is disembedded when it encompasses a discrete sphere of activities, governed by impersonal mechanisms, such as supply and demand, that function independently of non-economic social relations. Conversely, an economy is embedded when what we would call "economic" activities are governed by the personal mechanisms that govern non-economic social relations, such as religious strictures, kinship obligations, or political concerns.

For example, if exchanges of goods in an economy are predominantly organized as mutual gift-giving based on a social tradition of good-neighborliness, rather than as sales at prices determined by supply and demand, such an economy is embedded in non-economic social relations. On the other hand, in an economy in which exchanges are characterized by prices determined by the impersonal market forces of supply and demand, regardless of the personal relationship of the parties involved in the exchange, then we have an economy that is disembedded from non-economic social relations.

Polanyi, however, applied his more sophisticated terms in much the same way as his predecessors had applied theirs. He believed that the ancient Greek economy as a whole in the classical period was still embedded in non-economic social relations. Polanyi based his belief in part on the notion that Greek states commonly fixed prices on the basis of prevailing social values and political needs, rather than allowing them to be determined by the economic forces of supply and demand.[3]

It is true that Athens, for example, often fixed retail prices; but there is no evidence to suggest that it ever compelled wholesale importers to sell their goods at fixed prices. In fact, Athens set the retail price of grain in relation to a wholesale price on imports that was determined by the impersonal market mechanisms of supply and demand. When Aristotle describes the functions of various Athenian magistrates, he states that it is the responsibility of the grain police (*hoi sitophylakes*) to make sure that millers sell meal in accordance with the price that they paid for barley and that bread makers sell bread in accordance with the price that they paid for wheat. There is no mention of any regulations concerning the wholesale price of imported barley or wheat or of any magistrates who would enforce such regulations.[4]

In the absence of any regulation by Athenian law, the wholesale price of imported grain was determined freely and as a rule in accordance with the impersonal market mechanisms of supply and demand. Although there is very little, if any, evidence for the influence of demand on prices in fourth-century Athens, there is abundant evidence for the influence of supply on prices, particularly with regard to imports of grain from abroad. For example, in a speech attributed to Demosthenes ([Dem.] 56.7.9) the speaker describes the schemes of Cleomenes, Alexander the Great's governor of Egypt. This man bought up Egyptian grain and fixed its price for resale. His agents in Athens then informed him of the prevailing price there. If grain were dear in the Athenian market, he would ship more grain there. But if the price fell in Athens, he would ship the grain elsewhere. The speaker says that this practice was the chief reason why the price of grain rose in Athens and goes on to associate the arrival of ships from Sicily (that they were loaded with grain is implied) with a decrease in the price of grain in Athens.[5] Polanyi, therefore, made the same mistake as his predecessors in the debate; he failed to distinguish between specific sectors of the economy (in this case, retail exchanges and wholesale trade) in an attempt to characterize the economy as a whole.

More recently, Humphreys has applied the terms of the sociologists Parsons and Smelser to characterize the economy as either "undifferentiated" or "differentiated," rather than "embedded" or "disembedded." More important than refining the terms, which essentially convey the same meaning as those of Polanyi, is her *application* of them. In her 1970 article, "Economy and Society in Classical Athens," she examines several sectors of the economy, such as slavery, land ownership, division of labor, banking, and maritime trade, and adeptly demonstrates that they were becoming differentiated from non-economic social relations (Humphreys 1970).

In seeing the Athenian economy as complex and dynamic, comprised of many sectors that were undergoing significant organizational change in the fourth century, Humphreys is on the right track. Yet her ultimate aim is still conditioned by the debate's focus on general characterizations of the economy. She concludes that the Athenian economy as a whole was becoming a differentiated sphere of social activity during the fourth century just as several of its various sectors were (Humphreys 1970, 4f., 25, and passim; cf. Similar conclusions in Burke 1992, 200-201, and passim).

Although both synthetic and analytic approaches to the study of institutions can be useful, their relative value depends on the nature of the institution in question and its historical context. The failure of scholars to resolve the debate about the ancient Greek economy is a clear indication that the subject requires an analytic approach that emphasizes the complexity and dynamism of its constituent parts, rather than a synthetic one that tends to obscure them. The various sectors of the ancient Greek economy have not been sufficiently examined or understood and are in any case too complex to fit neatly into simple generalizations about the economy as a whole.[6] This can be illustrated by an examination of those who were responsible for overseas trade in fourth-century Athens.

An Analytic Approach to the Fourth-century Grain Trade

The literary evidence

Ever since the work of Hasebroek, the prevailing view has been that trade in ancient Greece, even in fourth-century Athens, was left to unesteemed foreign professional traders who had little capital of their own. Trade "was a clearly defined and distinct form of economic activity, carried on by a class of whole-time professional traders," who were "entirely...metics" and, "if we may judge from those of them who appear in the private speeches of the Athenian orators, were invariably without any capital worth mentioning of their own" and, therefore, "had to depend entirely upon borrowed funds for carrying on their business" (Hasebroek 1933, 4, 7, 10, 22).

Within the last twenty five years, Eberhard Erxleben (1974) and Paul Millett (1983; 1991) have provided further arguments in support of Hasebroek's view. Despite their differing methods, both rely on literary evidence. Erxleben combs the private speeches of the Attic orators to compile statistics showing that the majority of professional traders fit Hasebroek's paradigm. Millett argues that the frequency with which maritime loans appear in the trading ventures described by the Attic orators proves that traders were impoverished and relied on borrowed money for their enterprises (Millett 1983, 41f.; 1991, 191, 230).

Although there have been attempts by Signe Isager and Mogens Herman Hansen (1975, 66f., 72f.), Marianne Hansen (1984), and Edward Cohen (1992, 134f., 140f., 152f.) to revise the prevailing view, their efforts have had little effect. Doubtless, their limited impact stems from the fact that they have simply provided alternative interpretations of the same evidence that had been used to support the prevailing view, namely the literary sources. Isager, Hansen, and Hansen compile statistics from the private speeches of the Attic orators, but on the basis of criteria that differ from Erxleben's. Their statistics reveal that larger numbers of traders had sufficient wealth to provide capital for their own ventures than Erxleben holds. Cohen argues that the common presence of maritime loans in the trading ventures described by the orators is not an indication of the poverty of traders, as Millett argues, but of their wealth, since traders had to put up capital in order to secure such loans.

The fact that it is possible to argue plausibly for either the prevailing view that trade was carried out by foreign professional traders of modest means or the view of revisionists, who hold that greater numbers of wealthy men took an active part in trade, shows that the literary evidence is inadequate. Moreover, such evidence attests to only one form of trade that existed in fourth-century Athens. Since the literary evidence consists primarily of forensic speeches delivered in trials involving trading ventures, it tells us only about trading ventures that could lead to disputes, almost always over maritime loans. But was all or even the majority of trade in fourth-century Athens conducted by professionals who took out loans? The literary sources alone cannot answer this question.

The epigraphic evidence

Fortunately, however, there exists another source of evidence about those who were responsible for trade in fourth-century Athens: inscriptions of honorary decrees for those who had performed trade-related services for the city. These inscriptions have yet to be fully appreciated. It may be objected that they, too, provide a somewhat one-sided picture of trade. Those who merited honors from Athens for trade-related services had to perform outstanding services often entailing a great deal of power, or wealth, or both. Thus, the literary and epigraphic sources represent two extremes. Traders who neither entangled themselves in lawsuits nor provided noteworthy services for Athens are absent from such evidence. Nevertheless, when combined with the literary evidence, the inscriptions at least help to provide some balance to our picture of trade in fourth-century Athens.[6] They show that, contrary to the prevailing view, a much more diverse assortment of agents was responsible for initiating and carrying out trade than is attested in the private speeches of the Attic orators.

Archaeological evidence, on the other hand, can tell us what was traded and when, but little about who traded and how they did so. Nor can archaeology tell us what policies, if any, a city such as Athens had concerning trade. Despite extensive use of archaeological evidence in his great work on the social and economic history of the Hellenistic world, Michael Rostovtzeff (1941), who was incidentally a modernist of the first order (Reinhold 1946), was no more successful than anyone else in resolving the debate about the ancient Greek economy.[7]

More recent works, such as those by Peter Garnsey (1985; 1988), Richard Sallares (1991), and Thomas Gallant (1991), have attempted to revise earlier estimates (principally Jardé 1925) of the grain yield of Athenian agriculture with clear implications for the import needs of the city. But, as Michael Whitby (1998) has more recently argued, such studies give a false impression of certainty in their mathematical calculations, which are based on a host of dubious assumptions. Even if it could be shown that Athens had a minimal need to import grain, one would still have to account for the host of Athenian institutions that dealt with the grain trade and the significant number of references to it in both the literary and epigraphic sources.

Even more dubious is the recent trend toward treating historical sources merely as cultural "representations" that can tell us nothing about the ancient economy on account of our inability to see them independently of our own cultural biases.[8] True enough, the literary sources, in particular the forensic speeches, are laced with representations that obscure the "facts" about the ancient economy in an attempt to manipulate their audiences. Inscriptions of Athenian honorary decrees obviously also contain representations fostered by the people of Athens. Therefore, such representations certainly demand our attention and are a worthy subject of study in their own right.

But they should not be seen as the *only* subject worthy of our research. Represented or not, the production, distribution, and exchange of goods did take place in ancient Greece and demand our attention just as much as the

Greek representations of them. And if it be asserted that attempts to penetrate such representations involve modern cultural biases that result in overly subjective interpretations of the ancient Greek economy, then we must abandon the study of ancient history altogether, including that of ancient representations, since it too entails the same dangers of subjectivity as does the study of the ancient Greek economy.

The question of who was responsible for trade in fourth-century Athens is worth asking and can be answered. However, the answer must necessarily rely on a combination of the literary and epigraphic evidence. A careful consideration of such evidence shows that a much more diverse assortment of agents was responsible for initiating and carrying out trade than is currently held by the prevailing view.

Before examining the epigraphic evidence, however, we must make it clear that it is necessary to understand "trade" in its broadest sense: "a relatively peaceful method of acquiring goods which are not available on the spot." Polanyi provided such a broad, "substantivist," definition of "trade" in order to free us from the modernizing tendency to assume that trade must be organized according to market principles, which is typically the case in the modern western world.[9] If we were to limit ourselves to considering only market trade in classical Athens, we would be excluding so-called "non-modern" forms of trade, such as gift exchange, and seeing the ancient world through modern blinders. Ironically, by relying solely on the literary evidence, those who hold the prevailing view, i.e., that trade was carried out primarily by foreign professional traders of modest means, have made precisely such a mistake. They have obtained a distorted understanding of the ancient Greek economy by considering only the "modern" forms of trade that predominate in the literary sources.

An analysis of the epigraphic evidence reveals a much broader picture. Some Athenian decrees honor men for the trade-related service of simply transporting grain to Athens during a shortage and selling it at the going, market, price: for example, see inscriptions 1-3 in the appendix. These decrees use words derived from *agô* and *komizô*, which essentially mean "to bring" or "to convey," to describe the manner in which the honorands shipped grain to Athens. Such words show that they personally sailed to Athens with their cargoes and, thus, were almost certainly professional traders, i.e., those who actively engaged in trade on a regular basis for the purpose of making their livelihood.

It is true that some men who sailed the seas to transport goods for trade in fourth-century Greece did so on only an occasional basis and should not be classified as professionals. Such a man was the son of Sopaios of the Bosporos, who is the speaker of Isocrates' *Trapezitikos* (17). But the vast majority of traders must have been experienced professionals. Overseas trade in ancient times was a risky business. Those who depended on trade for their livelihood could not afford the kind of mishaps that befell the son of Sopaios, who alleges in the speech that he was defrauded by the Athenian banker, Pasion. Successful traders required a great deal of expertise concerning sea travel, maritime weather conditions, navigation, the favorite haunts of pirates, and so on.[10] Even if a trader did not own the ship on which he transported his goods, in order to be successful he would still need to know where and how to purchase goods at the best price, which were the best ports with the most favorable laws and markets, and who were the most trustworthy people with whom to engage in business. Knowledge of this sort came from years of active and regular involvement in overseas trade.

It is also fairly certain that the traders who were honored in the aforementioned inscriptions sold their grain at the going price, which was determined by the market. When those honored by Athens for trade-related services sold their goods below the going rate or gave their goods as a gift free of charge, the decrees are explicit. Since there is no indication that these men could afford to give away their goods or to sell them at a discount, we will assume that they were like many of the traders who appear in the private speeches of the Attic orators, namely professionals of modest means.

But other Athenian decrees exist that honor professional traders, who, having personally transported grain to Athens, sold it at a discounted price or gave it as a gift. Inscription 4 again employs a word derived from *agô* to describe how the honorand personally shipped grain into Athens from Egypt. Once again this shows that he was a professional trader. The decree also states, however, that he sold his goods at a discounted price, *euônoterôn*. In addition, he paid a ransom from his own funds to obtain the release of some captive Athenian citizens and even gave Athens the large sum of a talent for other purposes.[11]

Another honorand, named in inscription 5, one Herakleides of Cyprian Salamis, was also a professional trader, since the decree states that he was the first of the *emporoi* ("traders") to sail into Athens with a cargo of grain during a shortage. But he too sold his grain below the going price. The decree states that he sold 3,000 *medimnoi* of wheat at five *drachmai* per *medimnos*.[12] In the year 330/29, when this Herakleides performed his service, wheat sold for as much as 16 and even 32 *drachmai* per *medimnos*.[13]

Herakleides had probably obtained his grain at a price close to five *drachmai* per *medimnos*, since the normal price of grain in Athens appears to have been five to six drachmai per medimnos in the last half of the fourth century.[14] Being a Cypriot, Herakleides probably obtained his grain in Egypt. There was frequent traffic on the trading route between Greece and Egypt at this time and Cyprus was a common stopping point along that route, which also touched on Rhodes.[15] The well-known series of grain crises in the early 320s apparently affected the whole of Greece and perhaps other areas of the eastern Mediterranean.[16] Egypt, however, seems to have avoided the worst of whatever conditions gave rise to these crises. It was during this time that Cleomenes was able to capitalize on Greece's shortage of grain by buying up Egyptian grain and shipping it to wherever in Greece he could obtain the highest price. For Cleomenes to have profited from this scheme, the price of grain in Egypt had to have been lower than that in Greece and probably not that far from the normal, non-crisis, price in Athens. It is likely, therefore, that Herakleides did not lose money because of his discount.

Nevertheless, Herakleides did voluntarily give up from 33,000 to 84,000 *drachmai* of potential profits. Moreover, the decree also states that he gave Athens 3,000 *drachmai* for a purchase of grain. Clearly, the honorands of inscriptions 5 and 6 were not only professional traders, but were wealthy enough to be able to forgo significant amounts of monetary profit in their sales of goods and even to give Athens large sums of money outright.

To these cases may be added two others from literary sources, which those who hold the prevailing view would otherwise have dismissed as rare exceptions to the rule. The first case comes from Pseudo-Demosthenes' speech, *Against Phormion*. The speaker and his partner were clearly professional traders; he employs a word derived from *agô* to tell the jury that they have "continually brought grain (*sitêgountes*) to your [Athens'] market" ([Demosthenes] 34.38). In addition, the two men performed services for Athens during three separate crises that required a significant amount of wealth. On one occasion, they gave Athens a talent in cash. On another, they brought in (*eisagagontes*) more than 10,000 *medimnoi* of wheat and sold it for five *drachmai* per *medimnos*, although the going price at that time was sixteen *drachmai* per *medimnos*. Finally, the two traders also gave Athens a talent for the express purpose of buying grain for the people during a shortage (34.38-39).

Not only does this literary source provide us with another example of wealthy professional traders, but it also provides a first-hand account of the motives for their beneficence. The speaker states that he and his partner performed such services in order to win a good reputation among the people of Athens (34.40). Given that ancient Greece was a "shame culture," it is not surprising that a good reputation could be worth such a large monetary expenditure to the two traders. Note, however, that their desire for a good reputation had more tangible benefits as well. The speaker repeatedly makes reference to this good reputation on the assumption that it will win over the jury. It is reasonable to believe that similar motives drove the wealthy professional traders who are attested as having given up large sums of money in the epigraphic sources.

The second example of wealthy professional traders from a literary source comes from Athenaeus's *Deipnosophistai* (3.119f-120a). He quotes a passage from a comic play by Alexis that tells how a man named Chairephilos obtained Athenian citizenship for having imported salted fish. Again, since a word derived from *agô* is used to describe Chairephilos's activity, he almost certainly was a professional trader. Chairephilos must also have been wealthy. His sons are recorded as having performed trierarchic service in Athens shortly after his naturalization. In order to be eligible for trierarchic service, one had to be among the wealthiest Athenian citizens.[17]

In addition to the aforementioned common and wealthy professional traders, Athenian honorary decrees show that foreign potentates, who were not professional traders at all, were also responsible for a significant proportion of Athenian trade. In such cases, although the potentates did not sail the seas to transport goods themselves, it was they who initiated the trading exchange. The professional traders who undoubtedly carried out the actual transport of goods on behalf of the potentates served as hired labor, not as entrepreneurs.

Inscription 6 is an Athenian honorary decree for Spartokos II and Pairisades I, co-rulers of the kingdom of the Bosporos in Crimea. The decree praises the two kings for continuing to provide Athens with the same "gifts" as their predecessors, Leukon and Satyros, who earlier had also received honors and privileges from Athens. Demosthenes' speech, *Against Leptines* (20.29-32), states that Leukon allowed traders bound for Athens to have priority of loading and a reduction of the taxes levied on exports from Bosporan ports. Moreover, the same source indicates that Leukon himself once gave Athens grain as a gift during a shortage, so much so that the city was able to feed its population and still have enough grain left to be able to sell it for 15 talents (to whom is unknown).

No doubt the Bosporan kings desired to receive the same kind of good reputation or honor from Athens in return for their trade-related services as did wealthy professional traders. In addition, however, they too hoped for and received more tangible benefits. Inscription 6, at lines 59-65, states that the kings shall receive the military ships' petty officers (*hupêresiai*) that they had requested from Athens. Just as the wealthy professional traders of [Dem.] 34 exploited their hard won (and expensive) reputation to gain the goodwill of the Athenian jury, the Bosporan kings did so to win the kind of diplomatic goodwill that could secure military aid from Athens. In fact, Dem. 20 is a speech against a proposed law that would have revoked the Bosporan kings' honors and privileges. Demosthenes was well aware that such honors and privileges were necessary to encourage men to perform trade-related services for Athens.

Nor is the case of the Bosporan kings an isolated one. Inscription 7, a decree honoring Dionysios, the ruler of Pontic Heraklea, states that he had previously promised to give 3,000 *medimnoi* of grain to Athens during a shortage, the gift of which probably led to the extant honorary decree. Yet another case can be found in number 8, which is an inscription recording several gifts of grain, including 100,000 *medimnoi* for Athens, from the city of Kyrene. In a recent article Bonnie Kingsley identifies this gift with one known to have been given by Harpalos, Alexander the Great's treasurer (Kingsley 1986). According to a fragment from a comic play of Python that is preserved by Athenaios, Harpalos received Athenian citizenship in recognition of his large gift of grain to the city (Athenaeus 13.586d, 595e-596b). But even if Kyrene's gift of grain to Athens cannot be attributed to the actions of Harpalos, it is still clear that such a gift is not an example of a professional trader of modest means supplying Athens with grain through market trade.

Such diversity in the types of trading agents attests to the complex organization of fourth-century Athenian trade. Each group of trading agents had different trading interests and methods. Common professional traders sought primarily to obtain monetary profit through impersonal exchanges, in which prices were set by the market. Wealthy professional traders sought to obtain not only monetary profit, but also honors and privileges from Athens through sales of goods at discounted prices and through outright gifts of goods. Foreign potentates participated in gift exchanges with the Athenian state, in which they provided grain or trading privileges in return for lavish honors, privileges, and, most importantly, diplomatic goodwill. Trade was organized not only according to the "modern," "disembedded," and "differentiated" principles of the market that existed among common professional traders, but also according to the more "primitive," "embedded," and "undifferentiated" principles, such as gift exchange, that we see between foreign potentates and the Athenian state. To complicate matters even further, the activities and interests of wealthy professional traders seem to occupy a place that oscillates between these extremes of economic organization.

Such complexity in the organization of Athenian trade in the fourth century was underappreciated by Polanyi, who identified overly schematic categories of traders. Although he allowed for some combination of status and profit as motives for traders, he believed it was more important to draw a sharp distinction between them. The consequence was that he identified only two distinct types of traders: the "factor," who traded from motivations of status, and the "mercator," who did so for profit. He believed that "factors" predominated in Greece before the sixth century, when traders, hoping to obtain status, merely carried out trade that was initiated by chiefs or kings. Subsequently, trade in Greece was dominated by mercators, lower-class men who initiated trading ventures in search of profit (Polanyi 1975, 136-42). Despite his many qualifying statements that warn against oversimplification, the net result of Polanyi's analysis again leads us away from appreciating the complexity of Athenian trade.

During the fourth century, antithetical organizing principles co-existed in the Athenian economy. For this reason, a synthetic approach, which employs general terms to characterize the economy as a whole, will never bring the debate about the ancient Greek economy to a resolution. It is necessary instead to emphasize the complexity and dynamism of the ancient Greek economy by taking an analytic approach that reexamines the constituent parts of the economy and considers all the evidence.[18]

NOTES

This paper was initially presented at the 1996 meeting of the American Philological Association, and some portions of it have appeared in my doctoral dissertation, *Athenian Trade Policy, 415-307 B.C.: Honors and Privileges for Trade-Related*

Services (UCLA 1996). I would like to thank M.H. Chambers, E.M. Harris, W.V. Harris, D. Hood, and F. Frost for their helpful comments and criticisms of earlier versions. Of course, I bear sole responsibility for all ideas and, unfortunately, errors herein.

1. Among Polanyi's works that directly address the nature of the ancient Greek economy are "Aristotle Discovers the Economy" (1957a), "On the Comparative Treatment of Economic Institutions in Antiquity with Illustrations from Athens, Mycenae, and Alalakh" (1960), and "Ports of Trade in Early Societies" (1963).

2. The relevant works of Bücher and Meyer have been conveniently collected in Finley 1979. Excellent critical surveys of the debate can be found in Will 1954; Pearson 1957; Austin and Vidal-Naquet 1977, 1-5; Cartledge 1983; Tandy 1997, 84-88.

3. Polanyi 1957, 87; 1968, 312-18. Other notable scholars, such as Finley (1965, 26f., 33; 1985, 22, 77f.), have also held this view.

4. Aristotle, *Ath. Pol.* 51.3. Lysias's speech *Against the Grain Dealers* (22.12) seems to refer to the same law regulating retail prices of grain in relation to wholesale prices of imported grain. But again, there is no mention of any regulations on the wholesale price of imported grain anywhere in the speech.

5. See also Lysias 22.14-15, Demosthenes 50.6, and Xenophon *Poroi* 4.7-10, for similar examples that tie the price of a good in Athens to its supply. For further arguments against Polanyi's view and for the existence of price-making markets in the grain trade of fourth-century Athens, see de Ste. Croix 1959/60, 510-11; J.A.O. Larsen 1960; Humphreys 1969, 186f. Even Finley (1985,178) acknowledges, despite n. 3 above, that "prices fluctuated considerably and rapidly, with an almost instantaneous response to changes in supply." Finley's and Humphreys's arguments that prices did not serve to *integrate* various markets is irrelevant to my point.

6. Cartledge 1998, 5, 8-9, prudently notes the tendency of scholars to oversimplify the ancient Greek economy, pointing out that the economy of Athens was clearly different from, say, that of Sparta. Furthermore, unlike most Greek cities, it may well have been that a "commercial" or "market" mentality existed in classical Athens and in the Piraeus in particular. Nevertheless, Cartledge chooses to emphasize that Athens was exceptional and its economy was not truly representative of that of the typical city-state. Although that may be the case, since Athens is the best documented city-state and the focus of most modern studies of ancient Greece, it seems unwise to downplay it in the debate about the nature of the ancient Greek economy.

7. See also Morris 1994, 361-64, and Cartledge 1998, 7-9, for other views concerning the usefulness of archaeological evidence for the study of the ancient Greek economy.

8. See von Reden 1995, 1-9 and *passim*; Morris 1994, 351-52, 355-60; Cartledge 1998, 5-7.

9. Polanyi 1957b, 257. See also Polanyi 1975, 133 for similar sentiments.

10. See Andocides 1.137f., Demosthenes 4.34, 8.25, 12.5, 50.21, [Demosthenes] 17.19-20, 33.4, 34.8, 35.11, 13, and 36, Isocrates 17.36, Lycurgus 1.14-15 and 18, and [Aristotle], *Oikonomika* 2.1346 b 29.) In fact, it is because of the high risks of sea travel that the so-called "maritime loans" had such high rates of interest or

"yield." See Xenophon, *Poroi* 3.9-10, Demosthenes 50.17, and [Demosthenes] 34.23 and 25; also Cohen 1992, 44-46 , 52-58.

11. One talent (*talanton*) = 60 minai (*mna*); 1 mina = 100 drachmai.; 1 drachma = 6 obols. The highest pay for a skilled artisan in the Eleusinian building accounts of 377/6 was two and half *drachmai* per day, or 650 *drachmai* per year, assuming a five-day work week, 52 weeks a year (IG ii^2 1672 and 1673).

12. One *medimnos* = 6 *hekteis*; 1 *hekteus* = 8 *choinikes*. One choinix was the typical day's rations of grain for one man, approximately 1/4 liter. Thus, one *medimnos* was equivalent to approximately twelve liters.

13. For these prices, see [Demosthenes] 34.39, Demosthenes 42.20, and [Aristotle], *Oikonomika* 2.1352b19.

14. See Böckh 1857, 130, and Isager and Hansen 1975, 200, who determine the normal price of grain on the basis of IG ii^2 1672.283 and 287 and [Demosthenes] 34.39.

15. Gernet 1909, 307; Isager and Hansen 1975, 23-25.

16. For evidence and discussions concerning this grain crisis, see Isager and Hansen 1975, 200-206; Camp 1982; Garnsey 1988, 150-62.

17. See Michell 1957, 378-81, concerning requirements for the trierarchy. A trierarch was responsible for maintaining trireme and serving as its captain in the state's navy.

18. This paper has attempted only the beginnings of such an approach by examining the complexity of just one sector of the Greek economy in the fourth century B.C.E. It has not considered its dynamism, i.e., how it changed over time. There is no doubt, however, that the Greek economy was undergoing rapid and significant change from about the time of the Peloponnesian War down through the fourth century and onward. I addressed this issue in my doctoral dissertation on trade in fourth-century Athens and hope to offer the results of my researches in future publications. In this endeavor the work of Karl Polanyi will no doubt continue to have a fundamental impact.

BIBLIOGRAPHY

Austin, M.M. and P. Vidal-Naquet. 1977. *Economic and social history of ancient Greece: An introduction.* Translated by M.M. Austin. Berkeley and Los Angeles: University of California Press.

Böckh, August. 1857. *The public economy of the Athenians.* Translated from the 2d ed. by Anthony Lamb. Boston: Little, Brown.

Burke, Edmund M. 1992. The economy of Athens in the classical era: Some adjustments to the primitivist model. *Transactions of the American Philological Association* 122:199-226

Camp, John McK., II. 1982. Drought and famine in the 4th century B.C. *Hesperia,* Suppl. 20:9-17.

Cartledge, Paul. 1983. "Trade and politics" revisited: Archaic Greece. In Garnsey, Hopkins, and Whittaker 1983, 1-15.

Cohen, Edward E. 1992. *Athenian economy and society: A banking perspective.* Princeton: Princeton University Press.

Erxleben, Eberhard. 1974. Die Rolle der Bevölkerungsklassen im Aussenhandel Athens im 4. Jahrhundert v.u.Z. In *Hellenische Poleis: Krise, Wandlung, Wirkung*, vol. 1, edited by Elisabeth Charlotte Welskopf, 460-520. Berlin: Akademie-Verlag.

Finley, Moses I. 1962. Classical Greece. In *Trade and politics in the ancient world*. Deuxième Conférence Internationale d'Histoire Économique, Aix-en-Province, 1962, vol. 1, edited by Moses I. Finley, 11-35. Paris: Mouton, 1965.

———. 1979. *The Bücher-Meyer controversy*. New York: Arno.

———. 1985. *The ancient economy*. 2d ed. Berkeley and Los Angeles: University of California Press.

Gallant, Thomas W. 1991. *Risk and Survival in ancient Greece: Reconstructing the rural domestic economy*. Stanford: Stanford University Press.

Garnsey, Peter. 1985. Grain for Athens. In *Crux: Essays in Greek history presented to G.E.M. de Ste. Croix on his 75th birthday*, edited by Paul Cartledge and F.D. Harvey, 62-75. Exeter: Imprint Academic.

———. 1988. *Famine and food supply in the Greco-Roman world*. Cambridge: Cambridge University Press.

Garnsey, Peter, Keith Hopkins, and C.R. Whittaker, eds. 1983. *Trade in the ancient economy*. Berkeley and Los Angeles: University of California Press.

Gernet, Louis. 1909. L'approvisionement d'Athènes en blé au V\u1d49 et au IV\u1d31 siècle. Bibl. Fac. Lett. 25. *Mélanges d'histoire ancienne*. Paris: Université de Paris.

Hansen, Marianne V. 1984. Athenian maritime trade in the 4th century B.C.: Operation and finance. *Classica et Mediaevalia* 35:71-92.

Hasebroek, Johannes. 1923. Die Betriebsformen des griechischen Handels im IV. Jahrh. *Hermes* 58:393-425.

———. 1933. *Trade and politics in ancient Greece*. Translated by L.M. Fraser and D.C. MacGregor. London: G. Bell and Sons.

Humphreys, S.C. 1969. History, economics, and anthropology: the work of Karl Polanyi. *History and Theory* 8:165-212.

———. 1970. Economy and society in classical Athens. *Annali della Scuola Normale Superiore di Pisa* 39:1-26.

Isager, Signe and Mogens Herman Hansen. 1975. *Aspects of Athenian society in the fourth century B.C.* Translated by Judith Hsiang Rosenmeier. Odense: Odense Universitetsforlag.

Jardé, Auguste. 1925. *Les cereales dans l'antiquité qrecque*. Paris: de Boccard. Reprinted 1979, Paris: de Boccard.

Kingsley, B.M. 1986. Harpalos in the Megarid (333-331 B.C.) and the grain shipments from Cyrene. *Zeitschrift für Papyrologie und Epigraphik* 66:165-77.

Kraeling, Carl H., and Robert M. Adams, eds. 1960. *City invincible: A symposium on urbanization and cultural development in the ancient Near East*. Chicago: University of Chicago.

Larson, J.A.O. 1960. Response to Polanyi. In Kraeling and Adams 1960, 216-18.

Michell, Humfrey. 1957. *The economics of ancient Greece*, 2d ed. Cambridge: W. Heffer and Sons.

Millett, Paul. 1983. Maritime loans and the structure of credit in fourth-century Athens. In Garnsey, Whittaker, and Hopkins 1983, 36-52.

————. 1991. *Lending and borrowing in ancient Athens.* Cambridge: Cambridge University Press.

Pearson, Harry W. 1957. The secular debate on economic primitivism. In Polanyi, Arensberg, and Pearson 1957, 3-11.

Morris, Ian. 1994. The Athenian economy twenty years after *The Ancient Economy. Classical Philology* 89:351-66.

Polanyi, Karl. 1957a. Aristotle discovers the economy. In Polanyi, Arensberg, and Pearson 1957, 64-94.

————. 1957b. The economy as instituted process, In Polanyi, Arensberg, and Pearson 1957, 242-70.

————. 1960. On the comparative treatment of economic institutions in antiquity with illustrations from Athens, Mycenae, and Alalakh. In Kraeling and Adams 1960, 329-50. Reprinted in and cited from Polanyi 1968, 306-27.

————. 1963. Ports of trade in early societies. *Journal of Economic History* 23:03-45. Reprinted in Polanyi 1968, 238-60.

————. 1968. *Primitive, archaic, and modern economies: Essays of Karl Polanyi,* edited by George Dalton. Garden City, N.Y.: Anchor Books.

————. 1975. Traders and trade. In Sabloff and Lamberg-Karlovsky 1975, 133-54. A different but very similar version may be found in Polanyi 1977, 81-96.

————. 1977. *The livelihood of man.* Edited by Harry W. Pearson. New York: Academic Press.

Polanyi, Karl, Conrad Arensberg, and Harry W. Pearson, eds. 1957. *Trade and market in the early empires.* Glencoe, Ill.: Free Press.

Reden, Sitta von. 1995. *Exchange in ancient Greece.* London: Duckworth.

Reinhold, Meyer. 1946. Historian of the classical world: Critique of Rostovtzeff. *Science and Society* 10:361-91.

Rostovtzeff, Michael. 1941. *The social and economic history of the Hellenistic world.* Vol. 1. Oxford: Oxford University Press.

Sabloff, Jeremy A., and C.C. Lamberg-Karlovsky, e's. 1975. *Ancient civilization and trade.* Albuquerque: University of New Mexico.

Ste. Croix, G.E.M de. 1959/60. Review of Polanyi, Arensberg, and Pearson 1957. *Economic History Review* 12:510-11.

Sallares, Richard. 1991. *The ecology of the ancient Greek world.* Ithaca, N.Y.: Cornel University Press.

Tandy, David W. 1997. *Warriors into traders: The power of the market in early Greece.* Berkeley and Los Angeles: University of California Press.

Warner, Rex, tr. 1954. *Thucydides, History of the Peloponnesian war.* Harmondsworth: Penguin.

Weber, Max. 1921. *Economy and society.* 5th ed. Berkeley and Los Angeles: University of California Press, 1978.

Whitby, Michael. 1998. The grain trade of Athens in the fourth century. In *Trade, traders and the ancient city,* edited by Helen Parkins and Christopher Smith, 102-28. London: Routledge.

Will, Edouard. 1954. Trois quarts de siècle de recherches sur l'économie grecque antique. *Annales, Économies, Sociétés, Civilisations* 9:6-22.

APPENDIX:
THE EPIGRAPHIC EVIDENCE

1. *IG* ii² 342+Stroud, *Hesperia* (1971) no. 29; after Walbank, *ZPE* (1985)
107-111, c. 350-320

     [........κ]εκόμικ[εν............]

4   [........]ν ἦ ὃ ἐξ Ἰτ[α]λίας καθίστ[ησι]-

     [ν καὶ εἰς τ]ὸν λοιπὸν χρόνον ἐπαγ[γέλ]-

     [λετ]α[ι] σιτ[ηγήσει]ν Ἀθήναζε

     ....he has conveyed............

     ....n or which he brings back from Italy

     and in the future he pro-

     mises to bring grain to Athens

2. Schweigert, *Hesperia* (1940) no. 39, c. 330

            τὸ

     [ν σῖτον ἀπῆγε τῶι δήμ]ωι. ὅ τε πα-

     [τὴρ.......καὶ αὐτὸ]ς σιτηγῶ-

8   [ν εἰς τὸ ἐμπόριον τὸ Ἀ]θηναίων

     [καὶ τῆς τοῦ σίτου πομπ]ῆς

     he brought back the grain to the people. Both his fa-

     ther, ..., and he, who brings grain

     to the emporium of the Athenians,

     and of the escort of grain

3. Camp, *Hesperia* (1974) no. 3, c. 331-324

   π[ρ]άττων ὅπως ἂν ὡς ἀ[φ]-

10 [θο]νώτα[τ]ος ᾿Αθήναζε κομίζη-
   ται σῖτ[ο]ς

   acting in order that as

   plentiful as possible grain is conveyed

   to Athens

4. *IG* ii² 283, before 336/5

2 [..........ἐσιτ]ήγησεν ἐξ Αἰγύπτου τ...

   ....υλλων εὐωνοτέρων

   ....he brought grain from Egypt t...

   ....ullon at a lower price

8 [πολλοὺς τῶν πολιτῶν] λυτρωσάμενος ἐξ Σικ-
   [ελίας ἀπέστειλε ᾿Αθ]ήναζε τοῖς αὐτοῦ ἀναλ-
   [ώμασιν]

   many of the citizens, after he ransomed them, he

   sent back to Athens from Sicily at his own ex-

   pense

12   [κ]αὶ νῦν εἰς τὴν φυλακὴν
   [ἐπέδωκε τάλαντον] ἀργυρίου

            and now for the protection

   he has given a talent of silver

5. *IG* ii² 360, 325/4

8 καὶ πρότερόν τε ἐπέδωκεν ἐν τῆι σ-
   πανοσιτίαι : XXX : μεδίμνους πυρῶν : Π : δράχμου-
   ς πρῶτος τῶν καταπλευσάντων ἐμπόρων· καὶ πάλιν
   ὅτε αἱ ἐπιδόσεις ἦσαν ἐπέδωκε : XXX : δραχμὰς εἰ-
   ς σιτωνίαν

            and earlier he both gave in the

   shortage of grain 3,000 medimnoi of wheat at five drachma-

   i, the first of the *emporoi* who sailed in, and again

when there were the *epidoseis*, he gave 3,000 drachmai for
a purchase of grain

6. *IG* ii² 212, 347-6

    ἐπ[αγ]-
γέλλονται τῶι δήμωι [τ]ῶι ᾿Α[θ]ην[α]ίων ἐπιμε[λ]-
ήσεσθαι τῆς ἐκ[π]ομπῆς τοῦ [σ]ίτου καθάπερ ὁ
16 πατὴρ αὐτῶν ἐπεμελεῖτο

   they pro-
mise to the people of Athens to take
care of the sending out of the grain just as their
father used to do

20 [ἐπ]ε[ι]δὴ δὲ [τὰ]ς δω[ρει]ὰς διδόασι-
ν ᾿Αθηναίοι[ς ἄσ]περ Σ[άτ]υ[ρ]ος καὶ Λεύκων ἔδο-
σαν, εἶναι [Σπαρτ]ό[κ]ωι [κ]αὶ Παιρισάδει τὰς δ-
ωρειάς, ἃς [ὁ δῆμ]ος ἔδωκε Σατύρωι καὶ Λεύκω-
24 νι

   whereas they give the gifts
to the Athenians, the very ones which Satyros and Leukon gave,
there shall be for Spartokos and Pairisades the
gifts which the people gave to Satyros and Leukon

60 δοῦναι δ[ὲ τὰ]ς ὑπη[ρεσί]-
[α]ς, ἃς αἰτοῦσι Σπάρτοκος καὶ Παιρισ[άδης, τ]-
[οὺ]ς δὲ πρ[έ]σβεις ἀπογράψαι τὰ ὀνόματ[α τῶν]
[ὑπ]ηρ[εσι]ῶν, ὧν ἂν λάβωσιν τῶι γραμμα[τεῖ τῆ]-
[ς β]ουλῆς· οὓς δ᾿ ἂν ἀπογράψωσιν, εἶνα[ι ἐν τῶι]
τ[ε]ταγμένωι ποιοῦντας ἀγαθὸν ὅ τι [ἂν δύνω]-
νται τοὺς παῖδας τοὺς Λεύκωνος.

  the people shall give the petty officers,
which Spartokos and Pairisades seek,
but the ambassadors shall register the names of the
petty officers, which they should take to the
Boulé: but those whom they should register, they shall be

on record as doing what good they could
for the children of Leukon.

7. *IG* ii² 363, c. 335/4-326/5

8   [ἐπει]δὴ Διον[ύσ]-
[ιος πρό]τερόν τε [ἐπηγγείλ]ατο τῶι [δή]-
[μωι ἐπι]δώσειν τ[ρισχιλίου]ς μεδίμν-
[ους ἔτ]ι δὲ οἱ π.............κεν ἐν
[τῆι προ]τέρ[αι σπανοσιτίαι...]

         whereas Diony-
sios earlier both promised to the people to give three thousand medimnoi, but further the p.............ken in
the earlier shortage of grain...

8. Tod 2.196, c. 332-326

[Π]όσοις σῖτον ἔδωκε ἁ πόλις,
ὄκα ἁ σιτοδεία ἐγένετο

4   ἐν τᾶι Ἑλλάδι·
Ἀθαναίοις δέκα μυριάδας

To the following people the city gave grain,
When there was a famine
In Greece:
To the Athenians one hundred thousand (medimnoi)

FROM POLITICAL ECONOMY TO ANTHROPOLOGY

Situating Economic Life in Past Societies

Colin M. Duncan, David W. Tandy, editors

The life and work of Karl Polanyi (1886-1964) touched themes in philosophy and social theory that led to collaboration with scholars in many disciplines. The most recent group of scholars affected by Polanyi's ideas came together to present talks at various international conferences, and from those conferences arose this collection which represents a move toward a better understanding of the ancient people's attempts at situating economic life within particular societies.

Some of the topics covered include a social and economical analysis of ancient, pre-State Greece, Athens in particular; of the classical Maya; the Maori women and slaves; of rural India; rural Kentucky; and of pre-industrial Japan.

> Makes good on its promise to display "the breath of Polanyi's influence and the importance of the tools that he has left us." Displays a good balance between interpretation and description. I recommend the book to anyone interested in the place of the economy in society.
>
> —*Journal of Economic Issues*

Contributors include: Colin M. Duncan, David W. Tandy, Walter Donlan, Ian Morris, John Adams, Vernon L. Scarborough, William C. Schaniel, Walter C. Neale, Makoto Maruyama, and Rhoda Halperin.

About the editors

COLIN M. DUNCAN is adjunct assistant professor of history at Queen's University in Kingston, where he specializes in the environmental history of British agriculture.

DAVID W. TANDY is associate professor of classics at the University of Tennessee in Knoxville; his speciality is early Greece.

192 pages, index

Paperback ISBN: 1-895431-88-3 $19.99

Hardcover ISBN: 1-895431-89-1 $38.99

ISSN: 1195-1869

CRITICAL PERSPECTIVES ON HISTORIC ISSUES

This series, from the work of the Karl Polanyi Institute of Political Economy at Concordia University in Montréal, is intended to present important research by leading international scholars and critics. Black Rose Books has published the following volumes:

Artful Practices, *Henri Lustiger-Thaler, Daniel Salée, editors*
Culture and Social Change, *Colin Leys, Marguerite Mendell, editors*
Europe: Central and East, *Marguerite Mendell, Klaus Nielsen, editors*
From Political Economy to Anthropology, *Colin M. Duncan, David W. Tandy, editors*
Humanity, Society and Commitment, *Kenneth McRobbie, editor*
Karl Polanyi in Vienna, *Kenneth McRobbie, Kari Polanyi Levitt, editor*
Life and Work of Karl Polanyi, *Kari Polanyi Levitt, editor*
Milano Papers, *Michele Cangiani, editor*
Social Economy, *Eric Shragge, Jean-Marc Fontan, editors*

 has published the following books of related interest

Essays on Marx's Theory of Value, *by Isaak Illich Rubin*
Political Economy of International Labour Migration, *by Hassan Gardezi*
Political Economy of the State, *by Dimitri Roussopoulos, editor*
Toward a Humanist Political Economy, *by Phillip Hansen and Harold Chorney*

send for a free catalogue of all our titles
BLACK ROSE BOOKS
C.P. 1258, Succ. Place du Parc
Montréal, Québec
H3W 2R3 Canada
or visit our web site at: http://www.web.net/blackrosebooks

To order books in North America:
(phone) 1-800-565-9523 (fax) 1-800-221-9985
In the UK & Europe: (phone) 44(0)20 8986-4854 (fax) 44(0)20 8533-5821

Printed by the workers of
MARC VEILLEUX IMPRIMEUR INC.
Boucherville, Québec
for Black Rose Books Ltd.